SHORT LIVES

SHORT LIVES

*Portraits in Creativity
and Self-Destruction*

KATINKA MATSON

William Morrow and Company, Inc.
New York   *1980*

Library of Congress Cataloging in Publication Data

Matson, Katinka.
  Short lives.

  "Morrow quill paperbacks."

  1. Artists—Biography.   2. Authors—Biography.
3. Arts.   I. Title.
NX90.M3   1980b   700'.92'2 [B]   79-27796
ISBN 0-688-03614-7
ISBN 0-688-08614-4 pbk.

Printed in the United States of America

First Morrow Quill Paperback Edition
1   2   3   4   5   6   7   8   9   10

Book Design by Bernard Schleifer

Grateful acknowledgment is made for permission to reprint the following previously published material:

An excerpt from Susan Sontag's Introduction to *Selected Writings* by Antonin Artaud. Copyright © 1973, 1976 by Susan Sontag. Reprinted by permission of Farrar, Straus and Giroux, Inc.

From *Antonin Artaud: Selected Writings,* translated from the French by Helen Weaver. Translation Copyright © 1976 by Farrar, Straus and Giroux, Inc. Translated from the French Oeuvres Complètes © Éditions Gallimard 1956, 1961, 1964, 1966, 1967, 1969, 1970, 1971, 1974. Reprinted by permission of Farrar, Straus and Giroux, Inc.

Lines by Hart Crane from *The Complete Poems and Selected Letters and Prose of Hart Crane,* edited by Brom Weber. Copyright 1933, © 1958, 1966 by Liveright Publishing Corp. Reprinted by permission of Liveright Publishing Corp.

From *The Letters of Hart Crane (1916–1932),* edited by Brom Weber. Copyright 1952 by Brom Weber. Reprinted by permission of the University of California Press.

For John Brockman

CONTENTS

INTRODUCTION

IN 1962, as a freshman at college, I met Thomas "Tyler" Bootman, a young poet. I was eighteen. He was twenty-two. We would spend the next thirteen years together. Early in our relationship, Tom told me: "I'll be dead by the time I'm forty." He would burn out, he said, but his life would be intense. Tom was ultrasensitive, and his idea that he would have a short life made him a romantic and sympathetic figure.

Tom's prediction was tragically prophetic. At the age of thirty-six, he died in a small town in Mexico. Although his death was not a suicide in the literal sense, no one who knew him was surprised by the news. How could it have been an accident? I wondered, knowing the way he had lived the last four years of his life, and remembering the meticulously ordered shelf of his favorite books. The names on the bindings were Artaud, Byron, Crane, Keats, Kerouac, Lowry, Plath, Poe, Rimbaud, Sexton, Shelley, Thomas, Van Gogh. Poets, writers, and artists who had lived short lives were his models and heroes. Tom's ambition: to have his own books placed with theirs on the bookshelf.

Short Lives came into being as I finally understood that Tom Bootman was pursuing his own death. I realized that the way he lived was eerily similar to the lives of the people whose works he so admired. This book is thus a presentation of such lives and, in the Epilogue, the short life of Tom Bootman.

ANTONIN ARTAUD
1896-1948

If I commit suicide, it will not be to destroy myself but to put myself back together again. Suicide
will be for me only one means of violently recon-
quering myself, of brutally invading my being,
of anticipating the unpredictable approaches of
God. By suicide, I reintroduce my design in
nature, I shall for the first time give things the
shape of my will.[1]

ANTONIN ARTAUD. French actor, director, dramatist, essayist, poet. A seminal figure in contemporary culture, he is best known for his creation of the "Theater of Cruelty" and his volume *The Theater and Its Double* (1938), considered one of the most influential and revolutionary texts of our time.

The influence of Artaud's theories is most obvious in the work of the avant-garde figures of the 1950s and 1960s: in the theatrical productions of Peter Brook, Judith Malina and Julian Beck, Jerzy Grotowski, Joseph Chaikin, Richard Schechner; in the plays of Beckett, Genet, Ionesco; in the Happenings and mixed-media works of Gerd Stern and Kenneth Dewey; in La Monte Young's Theater of Eternal Music.

Artaud was a madman and prophet whose ideas were ahead of his time. Judged insane by the society in which he lived, he was locked away for the last nine years of his life.

> Susan Sontag:
>   In Artaud, the artist as seer crystallizes, for the first time, into the figure of the artist as pure victim of his consciousness. What is prefigured in Baudelaire's prose poetry of spleen and

Rimbaud's record of a season in hell becomes Artaud's statement of his unremitting, agonizing awareness of the inadequacy of his own consciousness to itself—the torments of a sensibility that judges itself to be irreparably estranged from thought. Thinking and using language become a perpetual calvary.[2]

Antonin Artaud was born on September 4, 1896, in Marseilles, France. His father, Antoine-Roi Artaud, was a prosperous shipfitter who had married Euphrasie Nalpas, a first cousin. The couple's firstborn of nine children, Artaud was one of three who survived infancy. A frail child, he contacted meningitis at the age of five. For the rest of his life he suffered from a nervous disorder marked by severe headpains, stuttering, and horrible contractions of his facial nerves and tongue, complicated by corresponding "psychic problems." The torments of his body and mind would be his obsessive subject matter.

> The little lost poet
> Leaves his celestial place
> With an idea from beyond the earth
> Pressed to his long-haired heart.[3]

Artaud was overprotected by his mother; his father, whose interest was in business, misunderstood his son who, by the age of fourteen, had begun to write poems and short stories. In school, Artaud founded a literary magazine in which he published his own writing under a pseudonym, "Louis des Attides." He read the symbolist poets, Poe and Baudelaire. At the age of eighteen, suffering from depression, he destroyed all his manuscripts and gave away his books. His parents sent him to a nursing home where he spent nearly a year. Again, in 1919, after nine months in the army, he displayed signs of mental instability and was sent to Au Chanet, a mental hospital in Switzerland.

> I suffer because the Mind is not in life and life is not the Mind. I suffer from the Mind as organ, the Mind as interpreter, the Mind as intimidator of things to force them to enter the Mind.[4]

In March, 1920, Artaud was deemed well enough to leave Au Chanet and go to Paris where he lived under the care of Dr. Edouard Toulouse, a psychiatrist with literary interests. Dr. Toulouse encouraged Artaud's creativity and put him to work on his literary review, *Demain*, to which Artaud contributed articles and poems. In Dr. Toulouse's home, Artaud met many of the key literary and theatrical figures of Paris in the twenties. He began to develop an interest in acting and theater. Early in 1921, he met avant-garde director Lugné-Poe, who gave him his first role in a play, *Sganarelle's Scruples* by Henri de Regnier. Artaud went on to study and perform with Charles Dullin's Théâtre de l'Atelier and was significantly influenced by the director's unconventional training methods. Artaud, however, did not readily fit into the troupe. Highly individualistic, he had a tendency to carry his interpretations too far: playing the part of Emperor Charlemagne, he would crawl to his throne on his hands and knees. Eventually he and Dullin parted ways, Artaud too unconventional even for Dullin.

> Jean-Louis Barrault (French actor and mimist):
> He had an extraordinary forehead that he always thrust in front of him as if to light his path. From this magnificent brow sheaves of hair sprouted. His piercing blue eyes sank into their sockets as if in that way they could scrutinize further. The eyes of a rapacious bird—an eagle. His thin pinched nose quivered incessantly. His mouth, like the whole of Artaud, preyed upon itself. His spine was bent like a bow. His lean arms with their long hands, like two twisted forked trunks, seemed to be trying to plough up his belly.[5]

While at the Théâtre de l'Atelier, Artaud met Génica Athanasiou, a young Romanian actress and member of the group, with whom he fell in love. Their relationship, which lasted for seven years, was passionate and stormy, marked by jealousies and intolerance on both sides. She would be the only woman with whom Artaud sustained a relationship for any length of time. By now, he was using opium regularly to treat his "nervous disease," a treatment he had begun at the age of nineteen.

To Génica Athanasiou:

You are always talking about my life, about being cured someday, but you must understand that *the idea of suffering is stronger than the idea of healing, the idea of life.*[6]

The acting profession soon lost its fascination for Artaud. He grew tired of its repetitiousness. On May 4, 1922, his first book of poems *Tric Trac du Ciel* was published by Henry Kahnweiler, an art dealer. That year Artaud published two issues of a literary review, *Bilboquet*, and began corresponding with Jacques Rivière, editor of *La Nouvelle Revue Française*, a prestigious and highly esteemed literary review, to which Artaud had submitted eight poems.

To Jacques Rivière:

I suffer from a horrible sickness of the mind. My thought abandons me at every level. From the simple fact of thought to the external fact of its materialization in words. Words, shapes of sentences, internal directions of thought, simple reactions of the mind—I am in constant pursuit of my intellectual being. Thus as soon as *I can grasp a form*, however imperfect, I pin it down, for fear of losing the whole thought, I lower myself, I know, and I suffer from it, but I consent to it for fear of dying altogether.[7]

Artaud, twenty-seven years old, was now on his own, living a transient life, moving from hotel room to hotel room. Without his family's financial support, he was having difficulty making a living in the theater: the roles he got were minor. He was too tortured, too eccentric, too intense. His mental and physical state continued to torment and obsess him. He was his own most interesting subject matter.

a sharp burning sensation in the limbs,

muscles twisted, as if flayed, the sense of being made of glass and breakable, a fear, a recoiling from movement and noise. An unconscious confusion in walking, gestures, movements. A will that is perpetually strained to make the simplest gestures,

renunciation of the simple gesture,
a staggering and central fatigue, a kind of gasping
fatigue.[8]

In April, 1924, while still employed in the theater, Artaud got his first part in a film, *Fait Divers*, directed by Claude Autant-Lara. Henceforth, he would seek to make his living in films, which proved to be somewhat more lucrative than the theater. His father had died that year, and apparently the estate was small since his mother, who subsequently moved to Paris, lived in modest circumstances. Any chance of financial support from home had ended for Artaud.

In the autumn Artaud's correspondence with Jacques Rivière was published in the *Nouvelle Revue Française*. As a result he was brought to the attention of a group of artists who called themselves Surrealists. Their leader was former Dadaist André Breton. Soon after, Artaud had joined the movement.

> André Breton:
> SURREALISM, *n.* Psychic automatism in its pure state, by which one proposes to express—verbally, by means of the written word, or in any other manner—the actual functioning of thought. Dictated by thought, in the absence of any control exercised by reason, exempt from any aesthetic or moral concern.[9]

The group included Philippe Soupault, Roger Vitrac, Paul Eluard, Robert Desnos, and Louis Aragon among others. Artaud was considered one of their leading figures and was soon made editor of their review, *La Révolution surréaliste*. His two most surrealistic works were published in 1925: *L'Ombilic des Limbes* and *Le Pèse-Nerfs*, prose poems.

> ALL WRITING IS GARBAGE.
> People who come out of nowhere to try to put into words any part of what goes on in their minds are pigs.
> The whole literary scene is a pigpen, especially today. . . .
> Those for whom certain words have meaning, and certain modes of being, those who are so precise, those for whom emo-

tions can be classified and who quibble over some point of
their hilarious classifications, those who still believe in "terms,"
those who discuss the ranking ideologies of the age, those
whom women discuss so intelligently and the women themselves who speak so well and who discuss the currents of the
age, those who still believe in an orientation of the mind,
those who follow paths, who drop names, who recommend
books,
    —these are the worst pigs of all.[10]

Artaud's affiliation with the Surrealists was short-lived. He was
too surrealistic for them. Also he had incurred their disfavor as a
result of his friendship with Roger Vitrac, a playwright, who had
been expelled from the group in 1924. Artaud and Vitrac had been
discussing plans for the creation of an avant-garde theater. This kind
of enterprise conflicted with the goals of the Surrealists who were
becoming more politically oriented. Artaud, however, was concerned
with literature not Communism. In November, 1926, he was for-
mally expelled from the group. The official document of expulsion
characterized Artaud as being "mentally defective, impotent, and
cowardly."

> I have too much contempt for life to think that any sort
> of change that might develop in the realm of appearances
> could in any way change my detestable condition. What
> divides me from the Surrealists is that they love life as much
> as I despise it.[11]

The same month, *La Nouvelle Revue Française* published his
"First Manifesto of the Theater Alfred Jarry." Alfred Jarry (d. 1909)
was one of the precursors of Dada and Surrealism. He had become
famous in 1896 with the production of his play *Ubu Roi*, a wild,
humorous, and unconventional parody of middle-class life and culture. Its hero is a fat and greedy father whose head is shaped like
a turnip. Artaud identified with Jarry's use of the bizarre and the
irrational to shock his audience—which Artaud took a step further
in his own work. In Artaud's "Manifesto" can be found the seeds of
his Theater of Cruelty.

We ask of our audience an intimate and profound involvement. Discretion is not our concern. With each spectacle we put on, we are playing a serious game. Unless we are determined to follow our principles wherever they may lead us, we do not feel the game is worth playing. The spectator who comes to our theater will know that he is about to undergo a real operation in which not only his mind but his senses and his flesh are at stake. If we were not convinced that we could reach him as deeply as possible, we would consider ourselves inadequate to our most absolute duty. He must be totally convinced that we are capable of making him scream.[12]

With a financial contribution from Dr. René Allendy, a psychiatrist with whom he attempted a cure for his drug addiction, Artaud, Roger Vitrac, and Robert Aron, essayist, mounted their first Alfred Jarry production on June 1 and 2, 1927, at the Théâtre de Crenelle. A debt of 7,000 francs was the only tangible result of this first endeavor. The reaction of critics and audience was generally unfavorable, and uninterested. Artaud persisted, however.

In 1927, he had better success with his film career, appearing in two now-famous roles: as Marat in Abel Gance's *Napoléon*, and as the monk, Massieu, in Carl Dreyer's *La Passion de Jeanne d'Arc*.

The Alfred Jarry Theater mounted three more productions in 1928, each offering a measure of shock and meeting with a certain amount of scandal. But the press and public were unsympathetic, and the Surrealists were openly hostile, so by 1929 the Alfred Jarry Theater was defunct. Continuing to support himself through work in films, Artaud pursued his dream of having his own theater. His quest for a "metaphysic of speech, gesture, and expression" was realized in July, 1931, when he witnessed the performance of a group of Balinese actors at the Colonial Exhibition in the Bois de Vincennes. In their preverbal performance—dancing, singing, music, and pantomime—Artaud discovered theater reduced to its purest level.

Anaïs Nin:
Artaud. Lean, taut. A gaunt face, with visionary eyes. A sardonic manner. Now weary, now fiery and malicious.

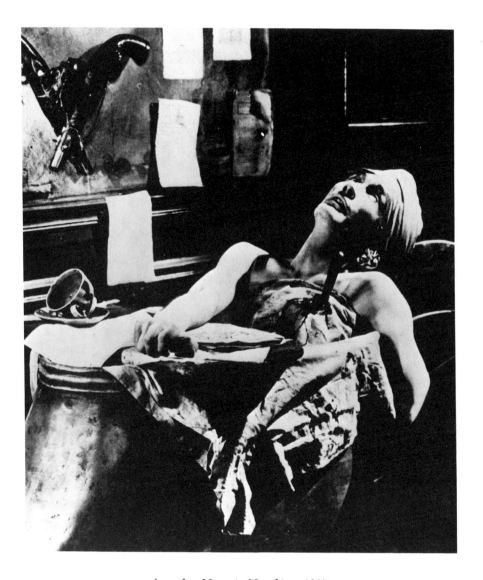

Artaud as Marat in Napoléon, *1927*

The theater, for him, is a place to shout pain, anger, hatred, to enact the violence in us. The most violent life can burst from terror and death. . . .

Artaud is the surrealist whom the Surrealists disavowed, the lean, ghostly figure who haunts the cafés but who is never seen at the counter, drinking or sitting among people, laughing. He is the drugged, contracted being who walks always alone, who is seeking to produce plays which are like scenes of torture.

His eyes are blue with languor, black with pain. He is all nerves.[13]

Artaud now began to write essays and lectures, beginning with "Sur Le Théâtre Balinais," which would eventually make up the collection he entitled *The Theater and Its Double*. In October, 1932, the *Nouvelle Revue Française* published the "First Manifesto of the Theater of Cruelty." Artaud hoped that his "practical and objective manifesto" would inspire investors to contribute to the realization of his theories.

The theater that Artaud proposed would offer the spectator an experience of an elemental, even magical, nature. Through the use of the violent physical images of the spectacle, the spectator would be freed to experience the repressed, dark side of his being—his erotic obsessions, his savagery, his criminal desires, his hypocrisy, even his cannibalism. In essence he would experience his unconscious, his evil side, and in doing so be purged and cleansed of it. Artaud compares the action of his theater to the plague, in that it would, like the plague, force the spectator to drop his mask and see himself as he really is.

In 1933 and 1934 he gave recitals and lectures to raise money. Although aided and encouraged by his publishers, Robert DeNoël and Bernard Steele, he was unsuccessful in raising the necessary funds. During this period Artaud, who had broken off with Génica some time before, met novelist Anaïs Nin, with whom he became infatuated. He invited her to a lecture he gave at the Sorbonne on "The Theater and the Plague," and she watched the audience begin to laugh and hiss and finally walk out as Artaud, onstage, enacted "his own death, his own execution."

I want to give them the experience itself, the plague itself, so they will be terrified, and awaken. I want to awaken them. They do not realize *they are dead.* Their death is total, like deafness, blindness.[14]

In 1935, the Theater of Cruelty produced a single play, *Les Cenci*, Artaud's adaptation of Shelley's play. Artaud both directed and starred in the production, which closed after seventeen performances. This was his last attempt to realize his revolutionary theater. He was broke and had alienated himself from Paris theater. Although Jean-Louis Barrault approached him about working together, Artaud had finished with collaborations, the theater, and the "bankrupt" European civilization.

Anaïs Nin:
I loved his madness. I looked at his mouth, with the edges darkened by laudanum, a mouth I did not want to kiss. To be kissed by Artaud was to be drawn toward death, toward insanity.[15]

With money borrowed from friends and with the token endorsement of the French Ministry of Education, Artaud sailed for Mexico in January, 1936, "to look for a new idea of man." In Mexico City he lectured at the University and wrote articles for *El Nacional Revolucionario*, a daily newspaper. In August, with financial aid from the University, he made a grueling journey by horseback into the mountains of northern Mexico to study a tribe of Indians, the Tarahumaras. While among them he was allowed to participate in their peyote rite. He was, at this time, addicted to heroin. When he returned to Paris in November he was in urgent need of rest and recovery from his physically debilitating trip and the ravages of his drug addiction.

Back in Paris, Artaud resumed seeing Cécile Schramme, a young Belgian woman he had met before leaving for Mexico. He intended to marry her. To this end, in the spring of 1937, he hospitalized himself twice in an attempt to cure his drug addiction but with no success. Since Mexico his mental and emotional state had become dangerously unbalanced. In May, while lecturing at the Brussels

Maison de l'Arte, Artaud began raving. His performance scandalized Cécile Schramme's parents, who were in the audience, and their engagement was terminated.

> To André Breton:
> I agree to go on living only because I think and believe that this World with which Life insults me and insults You will die before I do.[16]

Artaud's derangement worsened. In August, 1937, under the delusion that he was "obeying the orders of Jesus Christ," he journeyed to Ireland. In Dublin, he sought refuge in a Jesuit institution but was refused admittance. He became violent and began shouting. He was arrested for disturbing the peace and sent back to France by ship. When the ship docked at Le Havre on September 30, Artaud, who had been placed in irons while on board, was taken to an asylum at Sotte Villes-les-Rouen. His mother did not discover her son's whereabouts until December. When she did and visited him, Artaud did not recognize her.

> There is in every lunatic a misunderstood genius whose idea, shining in his head, frightened people, and for whom delirium was the only solution to the strangulation that life had prepared for him.[17]

Artaud, who had been labeled incurable, was moved to Ville-Evrard where, for the next five years, he was locked up in a ward for drug addicts. The miserable conditions at the public asylum were made more so by the war and the German occupation. The toll on Artaud's health was severe. As a result of the efforts of his friend Roger Desnos, in January, 1943, Artaud, malnourished, skeletal, and looking much older than his years, was transferred to a hospital at Rodez. He was put under the care of Dr. Gaston Ferdière, a psychiatrist who took a personal interest in his patient. While encouraging Artaud to write and draw, Ferdière also subjected him to electric-shock therapy which caused him extreme anguish.

> I myself spent nine years in an insane asylum and I never

had the obsession of suicide, but I know that each conversation with a psychiatrist, every morning at the time of his visit, made me want to hang myself, realizing that I would not be able to cut his throat.[18]

Artaud was released from Rodez on March 19, 1946. He spent the last two years of his life at Ivry, a private clinic at the edge of Paris where he was cared for but could come and go as he pleased. For the first time his finances were secure, the result of a highly successful auction of his manuscripts and drawings. Artaud reentered the social and creative life of Paris. He continued to write—poetry and letters as well as numerous texts.

In January, 1947, an evening was organized in Artaud's honor at the Théâtre du Vieux-Colombier. In front of an audience of friends and admirers like André Gide, Albert Camus, André Breton, and Jean Paulhan, Artaud read and improvised, shouted and cursed in a passionate and wild performance that went on until he had exhausted himself. The spectators were stunned.

In February, 1947, after visiting an exhibition of Van Gogh's paintings, he wrote *Van Gogh le suicidé de la société*. The book received the Prix Sainte-Beuve, the only literary prize ever awarded Artaud.

Artaud's health rapidly declined. He suffered from severe abdominal pain which he eased with strong doses of opium and laudanum. In February, 1948, a physical examination revealed that he was suffering from a terminal ailment, cancer of the rectum. Nothing could be done but allow him enough drugs to relieve the pain. Antonin Artaud died in his bed at Ivry on March 4, 1948. He was fifty-two years old.

And what is an authentic madman?

It is a man who preferred to become mad, in the socially accepted sense of the word, rather than forfeit a certain superior idea of human honor.

So society has strangled in its asylums all those it wanted to get rid of or protect itself from, because they refused to become its accomplices in certain great nastinesses.

For a madman is also a man whom society did not want to

hear and whom it wanted to prevent from uttering certain intolerable truths.[19]

Notes

1 Artaud, *Artaud Anthology*, p. 56.
2 Susan Sontag, Introduction to *Selected Writings*, p. xx.
3 Artaud, "Cry," *Selected Writings*, p. 38.
4 Artaud, "The Umbilicus of Limbo," *Selected Writings*, p. 59.
5 Hayman, *Artaud and After*, p. 82.
6 Artaud, *Selected Writings*, p. 22.
7 Ibid., p. 31.
8 Artaud, "The Umbilicus of Limbo," *Selected Writings*, p. 64.
9 André Breton, *The Manifestoes of Surrealism*, translated by Richard Seaver and Helen R. Lane. Ann Arbor: University of Michigan Press, 1969, p. 26.
10 Artaud, "The Nerve Meter," *Selected Writings*, p. 85.
11 Artaud, "In Total Darkness," *Selected Writings*, p. 141.
12 Artaud, "On the Alfred Jarry Theater," *Selected Writings*, p. 158.
13 Anaïs Nin, *The Diaries of Anaïs Nin, 1931–1934*, p. 187.
14 Ibid., p. 192.
15 Ibid., p. 229.
16 Artaud, *Selected Writings*, p. 400.
17 Ibid., pp. 492–93.
18 Artaud, "Van Gogh, The Man Suicided by Society," *Selected Writings*, pp. 496–97.
19 Ibid., p. 485.

Sources

Artaud, Antonin. *Artaud Anthology*. Edited by Jack Hirschman. San Francisco: City Lights Books, 1965.
———. *The Theater and Its Double*, translated by Mary Caroline Richards. New York: Grove Press, 1958.
———. *Selected Writings*. Edited by Susan Sontag, translated by Helen Weaver. New York: Farrar Straus & Giroux, 1976.
Esslin, Martin. *Antonin Artaud*. New York: Penguin Books, 1977.
Green, Naomi. *Poet Without Words*. New York: Simon & Schuster, 1970.

Hayman, Ronald. *Artaud and After*. Oxford: Oxford University Press, 1977.

Knapp, Bettina L. *Antonin Artaud: Man of Vision*. New York: David Lewis, 1969.

Nin, Anaïs. *The Diaries of Anaïs Nin, 1931–1934*. Edited by Gunther Stuhlmann. New York: Harcourt Brace & World, 1966.

LENNY BRUCE
1925-1966

There is only what *is*. The what-*should*-be never
did exist, but people keep trying to live *up* to it.
There is only what *is*.[1]

LENNY BRUCE. American comedian and satirist. He was a popular and controversial entertainer who was elevated to shaman/prophet of the counterculture in the early 1960s because of the antiestablishment content of his material. Bruce's uninhibited routines, liberally sprinkled with four-letter words, took on everything sacred to middle-class America from religion to marriage and motherhood to sex and race. Anything and anyone was fair game: the Lone Ranger, Jesus Christ, Rin Tin Tin, the President, and the Pope, as well as Bruce himself. He was called the "most radically relevant of all contemporary social satirists" and compared to Jonathan Swift, Rabelais, and Mark Twain.

The establishment he was attacking, however, counterattacked. It found him "sick" and "patently offensive," his humor "obscene," and his possession of certain hard drugs illegal. Bruce was thus drawn into the law courts, time and again, on a painful odyssey that led to his exile and martyrdom.

> Jonathan Miller (English comedian):
> Underneath all that hipster cool, it is to be remembered that Bruce was . . . so keen to be accepted and admired by educated people that he was sometimes deceived by the over-

complicated program which certain missionary intellectuals read into his act . . . he began to take seriously all that stuff about being the prophet of the new morality and would replace a lot of his regular material with sententious sermons . . . he sometimes failed to realize how much he was being used as a dispensible stalking horse for middle-class liberal dares.[2]

Lenny Bruce was born Leonard Alfred Schneider on October 13, 1925, on Long Island, New York. He was the only child of Mickey Schneider, a hard-working shoe clerk from Kent, England, and Sadie Kitchenberg, an amateur dancer and comedienne. Her dreams of the stage and stardom would be passed on to her son. The marriage ended in divorce when Bruce was eight years old. Sadie opened a dancing school on Long Island; Mickey Schneider remarried in 1936 and bought a house in Lawrence, Long Island, where Bruce lived until the age of seventeen. In October, 1942, unhappy at home, Bruce enlisted in the Navy. He served for two years aboard the U.S.S. *Brooklyn* and saw action in the Mediterranean. In the fall of 1945, he got himself dishonorably discharged by claiming homosexual urges.

So everything worked out all right, except they took away my WAVE's uniform. It bugged me because I wanted to have it as sort of a keepsake of the War. I wouldn't ever wear it, naturally—except maybe on Halloween.[3]

Interested in a stage or movie career, Bruce went to Hollywood and attended the Geller Dramatic Workshop. When nothing materialized in the way of acting jobs, he returned to New York where his mother put him in touch with a booking agent. Bruce did amateur shows and he appeared on the "Major Bowes Hour." The general opinion was that he was a sweet boy but "nothing special."

Bruce and his mother shared a New York apartment. They also shared an agent who arranged Bruce's bookings over the next two years. He was doing impressions, but he was not especially funny. In 1948, appearing on the "Arthur Godfrey Talent Scouts" (his mother was his "scout"), he did impressions of James Cagney, Humphrey Bogart, and Edward G. Robinson. He won the contest and as a result appeared at the Strand Theater on Broadway for several unsuccessful weeks.

Bruce performed wherever he could get work. In his free time he spent hours with other fledgling comics at Hanson's Drug Store on West Fifty-first Street in New York City, where Milton Berle, Jerry Lewis, and Jackie Gleason had once hung out, and occasionally made surprise visits.

> My first laugh.
> It was like the flash that I have heard morphine addicts describe, a warm sensual blanket that comes after a cold, sick rejection.
> I was hooked.[4]

In 1950, twenty-five-year-old Bruce, in Baltimore on a club date, met Honey Harlow (born Harriet Jolliff in Manila, Arkansas), a stripper, twice divorced, once jailed. She was tall with long red hair and a fair complexion. Discouraged by his lack of success as a comedian, Bruce had signed up to ship out on a merchant ship after his engagement in Baltimore. However, he returned months later to track Honey Harlow down and marry her.

In 1953, after two lean years in New York working clubs up and down the East Coast from Miami to the Mountains, Lenny and Honey moved to Los Angeles to try their luck. He worked the clubs along the Strip, while she worked the burlesque houses. Sometimes they worked together. During this period, Bruce first began to throw dirty words into his material to get laughs. In the seedy clubs, he discovered how far he could go: one night after the conclusion of a long strip act, Bruce, as M. C., walked out onstage stark naked. The story became the first Lenny Bruce legend.

Lenny and Honey both became heroin users in Los Angeles. The elixir of club entertainers and jazz musicians began to play the part of a third member in their marriage.

> Look, you only have sixty-five years to live. Before you're twenty, you can't enjoy anything because you don't know what's going on. After you're fifty, you can't enjoy it either,

because you don't have the physical energies. So you only have around twenty-five years to swing. In those twenty-five years, *I'm going to swing!* [5]

Honey Bruce gave birth to a daughter, Kitty, in 1955, and the Bruces held together as a family for a while. Honey stayed home while Lenny organized a show for Duffys, a new club opening in Los Angeles. Soon, however, they were back into drugs and their marriage began to fall apart. Bruce left Honey in 1956 and filed for divorce, which was granted in January, 1957. He got custody of Kitty because Honey had been sentenced to two years in prison for possession of marijuana. A live-in baby-sitter was hired to care for the child.

Bruce received his first major break in January, 1958, when he played Ann's 440, a risqué nightclub in San Francisco. He was well-paid for a change, and he received his first important publicity when he was written up by jazz critic Ralph J. Gleason, and *San Francisco Chronicle* columnist Herb Caen. Bruce had finally made the transition from warm-up comic for stripteasers to feature act. As word got out, he drew an enthusiastic crowd of hip people to his shows. At the Club 440 he developed his style. Many of his now-famous routines came out of this period of experimentation with ad-libs, improvisations, and monologues.

> Benjamin DeMott (writer, *Saturday Review*):
> The major marvel was Bruce's way of erupting into voices—his sudden jagged furious casting off from himself into multiple personae. How many languages this man knew from inside! With that ferocity, agility, and swiftness he darted among them, snapping, searing, a wild mimetic wire—"early American demagogue," "hick," "old Jewish man," "impersonal commentator," "MCA shill," "senile moron," "delinquent kid," "tough gunman," "Britisher," "German agent," "religious leader," dozens more. Time and time over the laughter welled from an image of furious incomprehension—somebody stunned to blankness by accents that hadn't been heard before. [6]

While in San Francisco, Bruce was signed by Fantasy Records, a jazz label, for whom he recorded two albums, the second exclusively devoted to Bruce material. Both records were successful and earned him substantial royalties until just before his death when his reputation turned against him.

Bruce's career and his earning power accelerated. He became a client of MCA, a large talent agency, and began working steadily. In September, 1958, he appeared for a month at The Cloister, a new club in Chicago. He returned to San Francisco to appear at Fack's No. 2; later he staged a musical skit, "A Wonderful Sick Evening with Lenny Bruce," at the Attic Theater in Los Angeles. His appearance in New York was a crucial test of his drawing power as a name performer. There he played a new club, the Den in the Duane. Because the owners did not want to pay his price, he agreed to work for scale wages plus a percentage of the proceeds. As a result of Bruce's popularity, they wound up paying him $1,000 per night. He went on to the Hungry i in San Francisco. Everywhere he appeared, he was packing them in.

> Herb Caen (columnist, *San Francisco Chronicle*):
> They call Lenny Bruce a sick comic—and sick he is. Sick of the pretentious phoniness of a generation that makes his vicious humor meaningful. He is a rebel, but not without a cause, for there are shirts that need unstuffing, egos that need deflating, and precious few to do the sticky job with talent and style.[7]

While Bruce's reputation attracted an audience far and wide, his brand of entertainment also ensured that he would never be fare for the mass-media exposure of television. Lenny Bruce was dangerous.

> Rin Tin Tin is a junkie. Didn't you notice?[8]

In the spring of 1960, Bruce was riding high. He had just bought a $50,000 house on a hill on Hollywood Boulevard. Honey was back in his life, although not permanently. His records were earning royalties. His drug habits were under control. Not yet thirty-five, Bruce was becoming famous.

That year he encountered the first resistance to his humor. His free-form stream of consciousness, "saying what is," outraged both audience and critics at his opening night at the Blue Angel, a conservative and expensive New York nightclub. The following night a policeman, armed with a tape recorder, was sitting in the audience. Bruce had been forewarned and censored himself. In the meantime, he had earned the label of "America's No. 1 Vomic," bestowed on him by Walter Winchell. *Time* magazine proclaimed him "the most successful of the newer sickniks." He was "the sickest of the sick!"

> Alright, I'm going to do something you never thought I'd do onstage. . . . I'm going to tell you the dirtiest word you've ever heard onstage. It is just *disgusting!*
>
> I'm not going to look at you when I say it, 'cause this way we won't know who said it . . . It's a four-letter word, starts with an "s" and ends with a "t" . . . and . . . just don't take me off the stage, just . . . don't embarrass my mom. I'll go quietly.
>
> The word is—Oh, I'm going to *say* it and just get it *done* with. I'm tired of walking the streets.
>
> (Whispers) "Snot!" [9]

Bruce went on the road in the fall of 1960, appearing in clubs in Baltimore, Philadelphia, Boston, and winding up at Carnegie Hall in February, 1961. Despite a raging blizzard, the concert was sold out. Shortly thereafter, Bruce became seriously ill with a drug-related infection. He landed in the intensive care unit of a Miami hospital for nearly a month. When he had recovered sufficiently to be moved, his mother, who had been by his side throughout his illness, took him home to Los Angeles for recuperation and rest. Bruce's life on the road, his indulgence in drugs of several varieties, and his illness had altered his appearance. The once handsome, virile man now had a grayish tinge to his complexion, and his face was puffy.

Bruce's long odyssey into self-exile soon began. In September, 1961, he was arrested for possession of narcotics while appearing at the Red Hill Inn, a jazz club in Philadelphia. Although he had two doctors testify in his behalf that the numerous drugs and needles found in his possession were medically prescribed, Bruce was slated to return for a trial.

Only a few days after the incident in Philadelphia, Bruce was arrested for obscenity, for saying "cocksucker," in a performance at the Jazz Workshop in San Francisco. At his trial, held without benefit of jury, Bruce was found guilty. His lawyer appealed and he was granted a new trial to be held in March, 1962. The next time, with Ralph Gleason among his witnesses, Bruce was acquitted. In the meantime, he had to return to Philadelphia for trial on the narcotics possession charge. He believed he had been set up, and attacked the Philadelphia judicial system in the press, labeling it corrupt. The charges against him were eventually dropped.

> (To be accompanied by cymbals and drums)
> *Toooooooo*
>   is a preposition
> To is a preposition
> *Commmmmmmme*
>   is a verb!
> To is a preposition,
> Come is a verb.
> To is a preposition,
> Come is a verb the verb intransitive.
> To
> Come
> To come.[10]

Bruce went to London in the spring of 1962 where he appeared at the Establishment, a private Soho nightclub, in the black Nehru jacket which had become his regular costume. His show caused heated controversy among critics like Kenneth Tynan, a devoted fan, and others more conservative who were shocked and outraged by Bruce's message. The anti-Bruce contingency ultimately won. Although he tried to return several times, Bruce was never allowed to enter England again. He was considered an "undesirable alien."

Kenneth Tynan:
    Constant, abrasive irritation produces the pearl: it is a

disease of the oyster. Similarly—according to Gustave Flaubert —the artist is a disease of society. By the same token, Lenny Bruce is a disease of America. The very existence of comedy like his is evidence of unease in the body politic. Class chafes against class, ignorance against intelligence, puritanism against pleasure, majority against minority, easy hypocrisy against hard sincerity . . . suspicion against trust, death against life— and out of all these collisions and contradictions there emerges the troubled voice of Lenny Bruce, a nightclub Cassandra bringing news of impending chaos, a tightrope walker between morality and nihilism, a pearl miscast before swine.[11]

In October, 1962, Bruce happened to be present when the police decided to raid a hobby store in Los Angeles that had been under surveillance as a drug connection. He was charged with possession of heroin, although none was found on his person. At his arraignment, Bruce attacked a news cameraman and was served with a $100,000 assault suit. Two weeks later, he was arrested while appearing at the Troubadour in Los Angeles and charged with giving an obscene performance. The following night the police arrested him again, bringing him to the precinct house and charging him with the same "obscene performance."

> Touch it once, touch it once.
> What's "it?" That's what I got busted for. "It."
> "It" is Clara Bow.[12]

His arrests, hearings, and trials continued. On December 6, 1962, at the Gate of Horn in Chicago, Bruce was arrested while onstage. Two months later, in February, 1963, he was tried for obscenity in Beverly Hills. When the jury deadlocked, the judge declared a mistrial and set a date for retrial: six months later the case was dismissed. The same month he was tried for obscenity in Chicago. This time, he was his own counsel. He jumped bail, flew home to Los Angeles, and was immediately arrested for possession of narcotics, which earned him four days in jail. While sitting in the Los Angeles jail, Bruce was found guilty of the obscenity charges in Chicago in absentia and sentenced to a year in jail and a $1,000 fine. This sentence was later reversed on appeal.

> I want you to know another thing, too. That I've never been in jail. I've never been arrested. . . . What it is, see, I got a publicity agent that's dynamite. And we have nine phoney cops that work for Pinkerton, and we go from town to town, the same bullshit, you know. I get busted, I write the column the next day, and that's where it's at, man.[13]

In May, 1963, Bruce's October, 1962, arrest for possession of narcotics resulted in a guilty verdict. He was sentenced in June to treatment at the State Rehabilitation Center for narcotics addiction. Through an appeal Bruce avoided serving the sentence. He was, however, placed on parole and had to report to a parole board once a month.

In April, 1964, at the Café Au Go Go in Greenwich Village, Bruce was arrested twice for obscenity. A group of artists, poets, and performers, led by Allen Ginsberg, drew up a petition protesting the entertainer's latest arrest. The witnesses at his trial included Dorothy Kilgallen, Nat Hentoff, Richard Gilman, and others; nevertheless, Bruce was found guilty. He fired his lawyers after the verdict was in and unsuccessfully sought to reopen the case. He was sentenced to four months in prison, which he began to appeal.

> The police are here, so be careful you don't spill the heroin out of its paper. The first thing, I come in, the waitress hit on me, *"They're here!* There's five of them here!" How do you like that? There's five guys who never kissed any ladies or choked children![14]

Bruce was no longer the good-looking, sexy, daring young comedian who made his liberal fans laugh and applaud. At thirty-nine, he had become an overweight, puffy-faced, ill man caught up in a legal scenario he described as "Kafka." Slowly he had become persona non grata at the clubs where he had once been welcomed. Even his records were boycotted. Heavily in debt as the result of extensive

Lenny Bruce on stage

legal fees and because he was not earning any money, Bruce filed for bankruptcy and was officially declared a pauper. Fueled by amphetamines, he spent the last eighteen months of his life lost in a private labyrinth of legal books, petitions, and briefs. His obsession had become a three-year-old narcotics conviction for which he had yet to receive sentencing.

> The New Yorker, "Talk of the Town":
> As a public figure who could seldom work in public, he became obsessed with the purity of the law, focusing his prodigious energies on a Talmudic poring over of texts and lawbooks to prove that he was not Joseph K.—that he could win the ultimate trial which would release him to return to the skewering of hypocrisy and pietism that he did so well.[15]

In April, 1966, Bruce appeared at the Los Angeles Municipal Court for sentencing. His lawyer requested a new trial and was denied. Bruce asked to be allowed to speak. He read from a sheaf of papers he had prepared. The judge stopped him, stating that what Bruce was saying was irrelevant, and expressed the opinion that he felt Bruce's conflict was with himself and not with society. He pronounced sentence: two years' probation and a small fine.

> Burt Kleiner (friend):
> I was a great fan of his and would go to San Francisco just to hear him. I met him and spent time with him in the last years of his life when he was into his lawsuit and his tapes and he was a bore! He taped everything. He taped the tapes taping the tapes. He was totally into legal stuff. It was just boring.[16]

Lenny Bruce died on August 3, 1966. He was discovered on the floor in the bathroom of his house, a needle in his arm and his pants around his knees. He was forty years old.

There is nothing sadder than an old hipster.[17]

Notes

1 Bruce, *How to Talk Dirty*, p. 235.
2 Benjamin DeMott, "Lenny Bruce: Case Continued," *Saturday Review*, March 25, 1976, p. 50.
3 Bruce, op. cit., p. 32.
4 Ibid., p. 39.
5 Goldman, *Ladies and Gentlemen: Lenny Bruce!*, p. 199.
6 DeMott, op. cit., p. 46.
7 Goldman, op. cit., p. 299.
8 Cohen, *The Essential Lenny Bruce*, p. 130.
9 Ibid., p. 224.
10 Ibid., pp. 250–51.
11 Kenneth Tynan, Foreword to *How To Talk Dirty*, p. vi.
12 Cohen, op. cit., p. 239.
13 Ibid., p. 131.
14 Ibid., p. 263.
15 *New Yorker*, "Talk of the Town," August 20, 1966.
16 Burt Kleiner, conversation with author, July 17, 1979.
17 Bruce, op. cit., p. 46.

Sources

Bruce, Lenny. *How To Talk Dirty and Influence People*. Chicago: Playboy Press, 1972.
Cohen, John, ed. *The Essential Lenny Bruce*. New York: Ballantine Books, 1967.
Goldman, Albert. *Ladies and Gentlemen: Lenny Bruce!* New York: Ballantine Books, 1974.

THOMAS CHATTERTON
1752-1770

Oh Chatterton! how very sad thy fate!
  Dear child of sorrow—son of misery!
  How soon the film of death obscur'd that eye,
Whence Genius wildly flash'd, and high debate.
How soon that voice, majestic and elate,
  Melted in dying numbers! Oh! How nigh
  Was night to thy fair morning. Thou didst die
A half-blown flow'ret which cold blasts amate.[1]

THOMAS CHATTERTON. English poet, author of the Thomas Rowley poems, brilliant forgeries of fifteenth-century verse that were the subject of heated controversy and debate after his death. Chatterton, who poisoned himself to death before he was eighteen, became a symbolic hero as well as literary influence to the Romantic poets of the nineteenth century: Keats and Shelley, Wordsworth and Coleridge. His poetic genius and his early, miserable death elevated him to the status of cult figure, "the most extraordinary man that ever appeared in this country," according to poet Robert Southey. To Wordsworth he was "The marvellous boy,/The sleepless soul that perished in his pride." Chatterton was, in fact, the first Romantic poet of the English language.

> Paint me an angel, with wings and a trumpet,
> *to trumpet my name over the world.*[2]

Thomas Chatterton was born in the crowded, industrial city of Bristol, England, on November 20, 1752. His father, a schoolmaster, died two months before his birth. To feed her daughter and infant son, Chatterton's mother took in sewing and taught sewing classes. At the age of five, Chatterton was sent to the Pyle Street School where his father had taught. The school authorities considered the boy to be a dunce and unteachable. He was sent home. At six, Chatterton became fascinated with the illuminated capitals of an old French manuscript and began to learn to read. He progressed to an ancient black-letter Bible. A moody, fitful child, he would hide away to read all day in a tower or in the cemetery among the gravestones of the nearby Church of St. Mary Redcliffe, one of the most famous parish churches in England. It became Chatterton's haunt as well as his source of inspiration.

> Sir Herbert Croft (biographer):
> Chatterton when a boy hardly ever touched meat, and drank only water: when a child he would often refuse to take anything but bread and water even if it did happen that his mother had a hot meal, "because he had work in hand, and he must not make himself more stupid than God had made him." [3]

In August, 1760, eight-year-old Chatterton entered Colston's Hospital, a charity school that trained its students for business apprenticeships. His head shaved like a monk's, dressed in a blue uniform, Chatterton's every hour at Colston's was strictly regulated. The curriculum was dull and practical and there were few books to be found. Chatterton disliked Colston's. At home, if his mother gave him a bit of pocket money, he spent it at the library on borrowed books. He hungrily read everything from heraldry, his favorite subject, to religion, history, music, and antiquities. At ten years of age he began to write poetry, religious and satirical verse. At eleven he wrote the poem *Apostate Will.*

> Robert Southey (poet):
> Chatterton had one ruling passion which governed his whole conduct and that was the desire of literary fame; this passion intruded itself on every occasion and absorbed his whole attention. [4]

Chatterton discovered a trunk in his home which his father had removed from the muniments room of St. Mary's Church. The trunk contained old records and parchments which his father, believing worthless, had used to cover schoolbooks and Bibles. On holiday from Colston's Chatterton secretly began to make use of the old parchments. Secluded in the lumber room with his equipment—a piece of ochre, charcoal dust, and black-lead powder, and the yellowed parchments—he began to fashion "medieval" poems. When Chatterton presented himself for tea, his face would be covered with black and yellow stains, much to his family's alarm.

Chatterton presented his first forgery to a poet-teacher at Colston's who was successfully duped, believing the poem on the crumbling and singed parchment to be medieval. Soon after, Chatterton began to create the poems of an imaginary fifteenth-century secular monk whom he named Sir Thomas Rowley.

> There was a stateliness and a manly bearing in Chatterton, beyond what might have been expected for his years. "He had a proud air," says one who knew him well, and according to the general evidence he was as remarkable for the prematurity of his person as he was for that of his intellect and imagination. His mien and manner were exceedingly prepossessing; his eyes were grey, but piercingly brilliant; and when he was animated in conversation or excited by any passing event, the fire flashed and rolled in the lower part of the orbs in a wonderful and almost fearful way.[5]

In 1767, nearly fifteen years old, Chatterton left Colston's school, indentured for seven years to John Lambert, a Bristol attorney. At Lambert's, Chatterton's job was legal copying which occupied about two hours of his twelve-hour day. The rest of the time he had to himself, although he was stuck in the office, and Lambert sent spies to make sure he was there.

Chatterton obeyed the rules. He ate with the servants and slept with the footboy. The only sign of how he felt about his lowly station was revealed in his demeanor which was "sullen, uncommunicative, contemptuous." Lambert was unsympathetic and insulted the boy. If he caught him writing poems he ripped them up. Yet, during this time, it is believed that he was working on his Rowley poems.

To William Barrett:

It is my Pride, my damn'd, native, unconquerable Pride that plunges me into Distraction. You must know that 19/20th of my Composition is Pride—I must either live a Slave, a Servant; to have no will of my own, no Sentiments of my own which I may freely declare as such; —or Die—Perplexing Alternative! [6]

Chatterton's first published forgery appeared in 1768 in *Farley's Bristol Journal*, a weekly newspaper. The opening of a new bridge in Bristol had just been celebrated. Chatterton's forgery was an account by a "T. Rowley" of the opening ceremonies of the old bridge some two hundred years ago."taken from an old manuscript." He submitted the "ancient" account to the journal under a pseudonym but young Chatterton was soon discovered as the possessor of this work. He explained that the manuscript was but one of many that he had discovered in a large trunk of parchments that his father had removed from Redcliffe Church. Several gullible people were taken in by the forgeries including one businessman to whom he sold his masterpiece, *Aella*. William Barrett, a surgeon who was writing a history of Bristol, paid Chatterton for some of his "ancient" documents which he later included in his published history. Chatterton seemed to enjoy hoodwinking the citizens of Bristol. Ironically when he once confessed that he was the true author of the poems, he was laughed at and told he was not smart enough to have written them.

Poor superstitious Mortals! Wreak your Hate
Upon my cold remains. [7]

Chatterton's aim was to get his Thomas Rowley poems published and to do so he felt he needed a patron. In the spring of 1769 he wrote to Horace Walpole, himself the author of a famous forgery, *The Castle of Otranto*. His letter was accompanied by a sampling of the verse of Sir Thomas Rowley, poet-monk. Walpole was initially taken in by the artful forgeries. He replied: "Give me leave to ask you where Rowley's poems are to be found. I should not be sorry to print them." Chatterton sent Walpole further samples of the Rowley poems as well as an explanation of his personal situation in life, "hinting a wish," says Walpole, "that I would assist him with my interest in emerging out of so dull a profession, by procuring for him some place in which he could pursue his natural bent."

This letter aroused Walpole's suspicions and he sent the Rowley poems to poet Thomas Gray, who proclaimed them forgeries. When Walpole wrote back to Chatterton expressing doubts as to the authenticity of the poems, Chatterton asked for their return. It took three months for Walpole to return the poems and when he did so no note was enclosed. Walpole would later suffer from his unsympathetic treatment of young Chatterton as his actions implicated him in bringing about the young man's suicide.

> *Walpole,* I thought not I should ever see
> So mean a heart as thine has prov'd to be.
> Thou, who, in luxury nurst, beholdst with scorn
> The boy, who friendless, penniless, forlorn,
> Asks thy high favor—thou mayst call me cheat.
> Say, didst thou never practice such deceit?
> Who wrote *Otranto?* But I will not chide:
> Scorn I'll repay with scorn, pride with pride.[8]

Bent on fame, frustrated in his Rowley ruse, and suffering the daily humiliations of his position at Lambert's, Chatterton looked to London. He wrote to the London press and was soon supplying magazines, newspapers, and periodicals with a wide range of material: satires, poetry, essays, songs, squibs. To succeed as a professional writer he would have to be in London. But first, he had to end his indentured status. Chatterton accomplished this by treating Lambert to two carelessly placed personal documents, one of which was his last will and testament declaring his intention to commit suicide before eight o'clock of the following evening.

> This is the last Will and Testament of one Thomas Chatterton of the City of Bristol being sound in Body or it is the fault of my last Surgeon. The Soundness of my Mind the Coroner and Jury are to be the judges of—desiring them to take notice

that the most perfect Masters of Human Nature in Bristol, distinguish me by the Title of the Mad Genius therefore if I do a mad action it is conformable to every Action of my Life which all savoured of Insanity.[9]

Lambert wanted nothing to do with a suicidal apprentice and granted Chatterton's release. In April, 1770, aided by the contributions of friends, Chatterton went to London. He moved in with cousins living in Shoreditch and began to make the rounds of editors. At first, he found plentiful employment writing for magazines and newspapers and was able to survive on the meager payments. But as summer wore on, the work slackened. London shut down in August and most editors left the hot city. Chatterton moved from his cousins' to a cheaper room in Holborn, a seedy run-down section of the city. Although he wrote cheerful letters to his mother and sister describing his success as a writer, and sent them gifts with the little bit of money he made, Chatterton was destitute. He may also have been suffering from a venereal disease.

> Since we can die but once what matters it
> If Rope or Garter Poison Pistol Sword
> Slow wasting Sickness or the sudden burst
> Of Valve Arterial in the noble Parts
> Curtail the Miseries of human life?
> Tho' varied is the Cause the Effect's the same
> All to one common Dissolution tends.[10]

It was evident to his Holborn landlord, Mrs. Angel, that her young boarder was hungry. Yet, ruled by his overweening and youthful pride, he refused her offers of food, nor would he admit his miserable situation to anyone.

On the evening of August 24, 1770, Chatterton locked himself in his room and drank a dose of arsenic mixed in water. His body was discovered the following day, the floor of his room littered with the torn-up pieces of his manuscripts. The coroner's ruling: a suicidal death as the result of insanity. Chatterton, seventeen years and nine months old, was buried among paupers in the cemetery of the Shore Lane workhouse.

The Rowley poems were published in 1777 and the "Rowley Controversy" continued until the end of the century. By then, however, most people were convinced that the poems were the brilliant work of Thomas Chatterton. Seen as a symbol of society's neglect of the artist, he was elevated to the status of hero and martyr by the Romantics.

> Farewell, Bristolia's dingy piles of brick,
> Lovers of Mammon, worshippers of Trick!
> Ye spurn'd the boy who gave you antique lays,
> And paid for learning with your empty praise.
> Farewell, ye guzzling aldermanic fools,
> By nature fitted for Corruption's tools!
> I go to where celestial anthems swell;
> But you, when you depart, will sink to Hell.
> Farewell, my Mother! Cease, my anguish'd soul,
> Nor let Distraction's billows o'er me roll!
> Have mercy, Heaven! when here I cease to live,
> And this last act of wretchedness forgive.[11]
>
> T.C.
> August 24, 1770

Notes

1 John Keats, "To Chatterton," *John Keats: The Complete Poems*, New York: Penguin Books, 1977, p. 40.
2 Chatterton, *The Poetical Works of Thomas Chatterton*, p. xxi.
3 Meyerstein, *A Life of Thomas Chatterton*, p. 33.
4 Southey, *The Works of Thomas Chatterton*, vol. 1, p. lxxx.
5 Chatterton, op. cit., p. cxlii.
6 Taylor, *The Complete Works of Thomas Chatterton*, p. 502.
7 Ibid., p. 503.
8 Lindop, *Thomas Chatterton*, p. 26.
9 Taylor, op. cit., p. 448.
10 Ibid., p. 446.
11 Lindop, op. cit., p. 94.

Sources

Chatterton, Thomas. *The Poetical Works of Thomas Chatterton.* Cambridge: W. P. Grant, 1842.

Kelly, Linda. *The Marvellous Boy: The Life and Myth of Thomas Chatterton.* London: Weidenfeld & Nicolson, 1971.

Lindop, Grevel, ed. *Thomas Chatterton.* Oxford: Fyfield Books, 1972.

Meyerstein, E. H. *A Life of Thomas Chatterton.* London: Ingpen and Grant, 1930.

Southey, Robert, ed. *The Works of Thomas Chatterton,* vol. 1. London: T. N. Longmans and O. Rees, 1803.

Taylor, Donald S., ed. *The Complete Works of Thomas Chatterton,* vol. 1. Oxford: Clarendon Press, 1971.

MONTGOMERY CLIFT
1920-1966

I'm trying to be an actor. Not a movie star—just
an actor.[1]

MONTGOMERY CLIFT. American stage and film actor. He appeared in sixteen plays and seventeen movies during his thirty-three-year career. He was nominated for an Academy Award for best performance three times, but never won an Oscar. When the names of film stars are mentioned, it is often overlooked that Clift preceded Marlon Brando, James Dean, Al Pacino. In a sense his work paved the way for their recognition and created a context for their art.

Montgomery Clift was a twin. He was bisexual. He was an alcoholic. Clift was an outsider, loner, stranger, victim, a part he played in his films again and again to eerie perfection.

> One tries his best to become a part of what one has to do. If you fail, you fail.[2]

Edward Montgomery Clift was born on October 17, 1920, in Omaha, Nebraska, arriving a few hours after his twin sister, Roberta. He was the third and last child of William Clift and Ethel Fogg; his older brother, Brooks, was a year and a half. His father, a quiet man, was Vice-President of the Omaha National Bank. His mother, the orphan of Southern aristocrats, was an ambitious and domineering woman, determined to raise her children as members of the privileged class.

Much of Clift's early life was spent abroad in Switzerland and France. There, he, Brooks, and Roberta were privately tutored, and taken to art galleries and museums, concerts and the theater under his mother's careful supervision. William Clift remained in the United States, working as an investment banker for a Wall Street firm to finance his children's expensive education. The Crash of 1929 and the Depression forced an end to their life abroad and, in 1931, Ethel Clift returned with her children to the States, and settled in Sarasota, Florida. William Clift remained in New York City.

> My childhood was hobgoblin—my parents traveled a lot. . . .
> That's *all* I can remember.[3]

Clift's career as an actor began in Florida in 1933 in an amateur theatrical production for which his mother served as stage manager. At thirteen, he was an extraordinarily beautiful child—slender, with dark brown hair, and a finely chiseled face. He liked acting and was poised and comfortable onstage. When the family moved to New York that year, Brooks and Roberta went to private schools, while Clift took music lessons, dancing lessons, elocution lessons, and was tutored privately. His mother took him the rounds for modeling jobs, and escorted him to auditions.

> Geraldine Kay (child actress):
> Mrs. Clift was a small, slender, rather unobtrusive little lady. But you always knew she was there. You felt her presence and her influence on Monty, because when she was not there he seemed to blossom and be himself, and the moment she appeared he would withdraw.[4]

He made his Broadway debut in 1935 at the age of fifteen in *Fly Away Home*. By 1938, Clift already had five Broadway plays to his credit and his name was in lights on the marquee of the Booth Theater. He was starring in a comedy, *Dame Nature*: his portrayal of a naive young man who gets his girl friend pregnant won him important critical praise as well as agent Leland Hayward.

Richard Watts (critic, *New York Herald Tribune*):

As the boy, young Mr. Clift has an enormously difficult characterization to manage, and on the whole handles it excellently, although there are times when he makes the youthful father too neurotic for comfort.[5]

In 1939, nineteen-year-old Clift traveled to Mexico with Lehman Engel, a musical conductor who had become a friend and mentor. They sailed on the S.S. *Orizaba*, the ship from which Hart Crane had jumped to his death seven years before. While in Mexico, Clift contracted amoebic dysentery. He never fully recovered from the effects of this illness, and was frequently plagued by painful cramps. It prevented him from serving in the armed forces during World War II.

Ned Smith (friend):

We all went into the front lines and some of us got shot and killed. Monty couldn't go into the war. Instead, he stayed in the theater. And he got shot and killed.[6]

Clift appeared on Broadway with Alfred Lunt and Lynn Fontanne in *There Shall Be No Night* by Robert Sherwood in April, 1940, and went on tour with the play for a year and a half. Working with Alfred Lunt was an important learning experience for Clift. Lunt was both a tremendous influence on the young actor as well as a source of great encouragement.

Privately, Clift was leading a double sexual life: he dated young actresses, he also had affairs with men. Although his homosexuality was not strictly a secret—his parents knew, and his close friends knew—he was not open about it. It would have been very damaging to his career.

Several key people entered Clift's life in 1942. All were involved in an experimental production of *Mexican Mural*, a play directed by Robert Lewis, one of the founders of the Group Theater: actor Kevin McCarthy and his wife Augusta Dabney became Clift's very close friends; Libby Holman, the former torch singer who had inherited a fortune upon her husband's suicide, became his confidante—she was thirteen years older than Monty; Mira Rostova, a

Russian émigrée and actress, five years his senior, became his acting coach and advisor.

> Mira Rostova:
> We found we both loved the process of working on a role, discovering what a part was really all about, making the right choices. Monty and I were the same: we could work endlessly studying parts . . . it was this preliminary probing that Monty really loved; performing on stage frightened him.[7]

Clift appeared in a succession of Broadway plays from 1942 through 1945: *The Skin of Our Teeth*, with Tallulah Bankhead and Fredric March, directed by Elia Kazan; a revival of *Our Town* at the City Center; Lillian Hellman's *The Searching Wind*; Guthrie McClintic's staging of Tennessee Williams's *You Touched Me!*; and Elsa Shelley's *Foxhole in the Parlor*. His performances were always singled out for praise.

> Howard Barnes (critic, *New York Herald Tribune*):
> Certainly whatever Miss Shelley had in mind is brilliantly illuminated by Clift. This young actor has given several outstanding performances in the past. He has never given so fine a one against such staggering odds. On more than one occasion he picks up a situation, as it were, by the bootstraps, making it ring with eloquence which is not there in the writing. His portrayal of a fighter discharged from an Army hospital for mental cases is something to witness.[8]

Clift had moved out of his family's apartment on Park Avenue and was living on his own for the first time in an apartment on East Fifty-fifth Street. He was deluged with screen plays and playscripts, which he read and considered, often advised by Mira Rostova or the McCarthys. Hollywood was interested in him and several producers had attempted to get him to sign a seven-year contract, something Clift would never consent to: he wanted to work picture by picture and pick and choose his parts very carefully.

I don't have a big urge to act. I can't play something I'm not interested in. And if I'm not interested, how can I expect the audience to be?[9]

In 1946, Howard Hawks offered Clift a part in *Red River*, a Western, in which he would play Matt Garth, the foster son of John Wayne. He accepted; his salary was $60,000.

Soon after the shooting of *Red River* was completed, Clift went on to do *The Search*, playing an American G.I. who befriends a lost Czech boy, and directed by Fred Zinnemann. Mira Rostova was with Clift on location in Zurich; she discussed dialogue and scenes with him, coached him, and helped him rewrite much of the script. Her presence was the cause of friction between Clift and Zinnemann. Rostova would accompany him again for other films.

The Search opened on March 26, 1948. Overnight, Montgomery Clift became a star, the new romantic hero to postwar America, a symbol of the sensitive, honest, disillusioned young man. His performance earned him an Academy Award nomination as well as the power to pick and choose the films he wanted to do. *Red River* opened soon after. Praise for Clift was unanimous. His picture appeared on the cover of *Life* magazine; *Look* called him the "hottest actor since Valentino." Most important, the public fell in love with him. He was Hollywood's most eligible bachelor; his fans recognized him wherever he went.

Caryl Rivers (writer):
"All the girls in the eighth grade fell in love with Montgomery Clift in *Red River*. His face had the perfection of a fragile porcelain vase; his beauty was so sensual, and at the same time so vulnerable, it was almost blinding. I think every girl who saw him in the quiet dark of a movie theater of a Saturday afternoon fell in love with Montgomery Clift, his dark eyes like the deep water of a cavern pool, holding promise of worlds of tenderness; the straight perfect blade of a nose that should have been the work of some sculptor the equal of Michelangelo.[10]

Clift made two more pictures in quick succession: *The Big Lift*, directed by George Seaton, which was a box office failure, and *A Place in the Sun*, directed by George Stevens, in which he starred opposite seventeen-year-old starlet Elizabeth Taylor. He won his second Academy Award nomination for his portrayal of George Eastman, the tortured young killer. And he and Elizabeth Taylor began a close friendship that continued until his death.

Although he failed, once more, to win the Oscar, Clift's career was at its peak and he was avidly pursued by directors who wanted him for their next picture. Montgomery Clift, the private man, however, was in trouble. He had developed a drinking problem and, when it got out of control, he was forced to seek help. He began to see a psychiatrist on a regular basis and would do so for the rest of his life, although he did not seem to make any headway with his drinking problem. In fact, it got worse.

> Then there is the problem, which is not to do with acting. It is being that word—a star! You become public property. I remember the way it happened. I had held off long enough. I was on the stage for eleven years, and all that time there were offers of contracts from Hollywood, always with these clauses. And if you sign up and go to Hollywood too young, they own you, and you never develop. . . . What I wanted was that when I did go, I should rise or fall by my own choice. And, if I had four hits or flops in a row, at least I would say it was because of me, that I was bad or good in that movie.[11]

His next important film was *From Here to Eternity*, directed by Fred Zinnemann. Clift, for the first time, was drinking heavily while working on a film. Nevertheless, his portrayal of Robert E. Lee Prewitt, the lonely soldier who avenges the death of his friend and gets himself killed, is one of the finest of his career. The picture was a huge financial success. Once again, Clift was nominated for an Academy Award. This time he was sure he would win. Once again, however, he lost.

> To Ned Smith:
> Failure and its accompanying misery is for the artist his

most vital source of creative energy. I mean inner failure—
failure to achieve what one strives for— Outward success has
little or nothing to do with this. Perhaps [success] deludes
people long enough so you yourself can try again.[12]

From this point on, Clift's life began to take on the qualities
that prompted Robert Lewis to describe it as "the slowest suicide in
show business." In 1954, Clift was involved in a Broadway production of The Seagull, with Kevin McCarthy and Mira Rostova,
that was both an artistic and critical disaster. It was his last stage
performance.

Clift signed to do Raintree County, based on Ross Lockridge's
novel, and costarring Elizabeth Taylor, in 1956. By now his drinking
problem had become so pronounced that MGM took out a life insur-
ance policy on him. On May 12 (with only half the film completed),
while driving home after a dinner party at Taylor's house, Clift
smashed his car into a telephone pole. His car was destroyed; so was
his face. Clift was unable to return to work for nine weeks. When he
did, his once-beautiful appearance had been dramatically altered,
and he was in continual pain from his injuries.

> Patricia Bosworth (biographer):
> He knew the worst part of his disfigurement was his
> upper lip. It had been ripped in half during the car crash.
> Sewn together, the flesh seemed pulled, almost curled back
> and blotted like a repaired hairlip. He'd never had plastic
> surgery; instead the doctors tried to preserve his appearance,
> so his features were not changed as much as thickened. The
> once-perfect nose and mouth seemed slightly off kilter.[13]

Raintree County was completed using only long shots of Clift.
The process was further complicated by the fact that the left side
of his face was paralyzed and only his right profile could be shown.
When the film was released, the difference in shooting techniques
was obvious. Many moviegoers became more interested in picking
out "before" and "after" shots of Clift than in the movie itself.

The accident had accelerated Clift's downward slide. To help endure the pain of his injured face and chronic sleeplessness he became more dependent on alcohol and drugs.

"Look! Look! If you look really hard at things you'll forget you're going to die." [14]

Clift considered his portrayal of Noah Ackerman, the Jew, in *The Young Lions*, which was completed in the fall of 1957, to be one of his best performances. He felt that his future career rode on its critical success. The reviews were mixed, however, and there was no Academy Award nomination for him. He continued to work: *Miss Lonelyhearts, Suddenly Last Summer,* and *Wild River* came and went without any indication that he might one day climb back up to the top. During the filming of *The Misfits*, he and Marilyn Monroe became friendly: they shared the torment of insomnia.

W. W. Weatherby (journalist):
Montgomery Clift arrived at last as if he was walking on air, a fixed grin turning this way and that . . . a small, thin man with a shy lope, his face, once as delicate and striking as a pretty girl's, now hurt looking. . . . He always gave me the impression of someone who wanted to cry but had decided to try to laugh it off. . . . He mumbled something that might have been in a foreign language for all the sense it made to me. I asked him to repeat it. He did so, much louder, grinning all the time, but still it made no sense. I realized then that he was so drunk, he was incoherent.[15]

In April, 1961, Clift had a small role in Stanley Kramer's *Judgment at Nuremberg*, portraying a retarded Jew who had been sterilized by the Nazis. He had been offered $100,000 to do the part, which he refused because it was a single scene and only required one day's work. Ironically, this small affecting part won Clift an Academy Award nomination for Best Supporting Actor.

His last major film was *Freud* in which he played the lead. The production was fraught with conflict between director John Huston and Clift, who was having difficulty memorizing his lines and trouble with his vision. He was drinking steadily, afraid he was going blind. When the picture was finally completed, weeks late and way over budget, Universal Pictures sued Clift for the delays, while Clift was hospitalized for cataract operations on both eyes.

As a direct result of the Universal lawsuit, no studio in Hollywood wanted to have anything to do with Montgomery Clift. He had been branded unreliable and a troublemaker, and he was no longer insurable. He did not work for four years, and remained secluded in his brownstone in New York. In 1966, he acted in his last movie, *The Defector*, a low-budget spy movie, directed by Raoul Levy. He did his own stunt work, although he was weak and in pain, still suffering from the injuries of his car accident.

> Macha Meril (costar in *The Defector*):
> He gives so much it is almost painful. Do you know, it reminds me a little of watching Marilyn Monroe. I feel one hardly has the right to be there. His acting is all . . . torn . . . from inside. Almost as though he were acting to destroy himself.[16]

When Clift returned to New York, he was planning to work with Elizabeth Taylor in *Reflections in a Golden Eye*. She had overcome Seven Arts' refusal to hire Clift by agreeing to insure him herself. John Huston was set to direct, with shooting to begin in August. In the meantime, Clift retreated to his brownstone and the care of his secretary/companion, Lorenzo James.

Several weeks later, on the morning of July 23, 1966, Montgomery Clift was found lying dead across his bed. The autopsy stated cause of death as "occlusive coronary artery disease." He was forty-four years old.

> To Ned Smith:
> If you have a goal—and you're busy growing—you're safe.
> It's only when you believe of yourself what the general public believes that you start losing the courage to risk outward failure. That is the biggest pitfall.
> *Look out!*[17]

Clift as Petersen in Judgment at Nuremberg, *1961*

Notes

1 "Montgomery Clift, The Movie Maverick," *New York Post*, July 25, 1966, p. 61.
2 "Montgomery Clift Dead at 45," *New York Times*, July 24, 1966, p. 79.
3 Bosworth, *Montgomery Clift*, p. 41.
4 LaGuardia, *Monty*, p. 13.
5 Bosworth, op. cit., pp. 66–67.
6 LaGuardia, op. cit., p. 38.
7 Ibid., p. 55.
8 Ibid., p. 51.
9 *New York Times*, July 24, 1966, p. 79.
10 Caryl Rivers, *Aphrodite at Mid Century*, Garden City: Doubleday & Co., 1973, p. 99.
11 Anthony Haden-Guest, "Montgomery Clift's Last Interview," *New York World Journal Tribune*, November 26, 1966, p. 26.
12 Bosworth, op. cit., p. 147.
13 Ibid., p. 310.
14 Bosworth, op. cit., p. 405.
15 W. W. Weatherby, *Conversations with Marilyn*, New York: Ballantine Books, 1976, p. 30.
16 Haden-Guest, op. cit., p. 28.
17 Bosworth, op. cit., p. 147.

Sources

Bosworth, Patricia. *Montgomery Clift*. New York: Harcourt Brace Jovanovich, 1978.
LaGuardia, Robert. *Monty*. New York: Avon Books, 1978.

HART CRANE
1899-1932

O brilliant kids, frisk with your dog,
Fondle your shells and sticks, bleached
By time and the elements; but there is a line
You must not cross nor ever trust beyond it
Spry cordage of your bodies to caresses
Too lichen-faithful from too wide a breast.
The bottom of the sea is cruel.[1]

HART CRANE. American poet. He stands as one of the most important voices in American poetry, although he published just two volumes of poetry during his lifetime, *White Buildings* (1926) and *The Bridge* (1930). He was the subject of great controversy among critics who debated the success or failure of his rich and complex work. Crane was compared to Rimbaud, Whitman, Eliot; he was called a visionary, a mystic, the American Keats. Simultaneously his work was judged by some to be obscure, confusing, a magnificent failure. Whatever labels were pinned on Crane, he did not want for attention from the literary world of America in the 1920s, of which he was a central and vital figure.

The discipline and meticulousness with which Crane approached the craft of writing was missing from his personal life, which was ruled by chaos. Homosexual, he alternated between the casual pursuit of young sailors, and passionate love affairs. Crane was given to heavy drinking bouts and rowdy behavior, his excesses occasionally landing him in jail. Shadowing his behavior was the specter of poverty and chronic financial insecurity. Crane was often broke and out of work, or laboring at a job he despised.

And so it was I entered the broken world

To trace the visionary company of love, its voice
An instant in the wind (I know not whither hurled)
But not for long to hold each desperate choice.[2]

Harold Hart Crane was born on July 21, 1899, in Garrettsville, Ohio, the only child of Clarence Arthur Crane, a successful candy manufacturer, and Grace Hart Crane, a Chicagoan of great beauty. Crane's childhood was marred by his parents' unhappy marriage, their violent quarrels, separations, and passionate reunions. Crane became the go-between, a role he continued to play long after their divorce when he was eighteen. Forced to choose between them, Crane chose his mother over his father, whom he later called "the chocolate maggot," and subsequently became "Hart."

> Employee of C. A. Crane:
> Harold always thought he and his father were worlds apart, but you only had to see the two of them together to know they were father and son. And they both had the same sort of intensity, the same sort of drive; and they were both passionate men. With C. A. it was business and women. With Harold it was poetry and men. But it came to the same thing, really. They both had the same sort of drive.[3]

Crane's interest in and talent for poetry began to reveal itself during his high school years in Cleveland where the family had moved. His first poem was accepted for publication by the Greenwich Village *Bruno's Weekly* in 1916. Crane, who had quit school that year, went to New York in December and quickly made his way into the literary world. His poems began appearing regularly in literary magazines like *The Pagan* and *The Little Review*. He went to work for these magazines when he could, selling ad space or assisting editorially, during his first extended stay in New York and when he returned in early 1919. These early days in New York brought Crane together with Gorham Munson, another young writer and critic, who became a close friend and intimate correspondent.

> To his mother:
> The realization of true freedom is slowly coming to me,

and with it a sense of poise which is of inestimable value. My life, however it shall continue, shall have expression and form. . . . I am fearless. . . . I am determined on a valorous future and something of a realization of life. . . . I am beginning to see the hope of standing entirely alone and to fathom Ibsen's statement that translated is, "The strongest man in the world is he who stands entirely alone." [4]

Life in New York, although exciting, was financially insecure, so Crane accepted an offer from his father, whose business was prospering, to go to work for him. In November, 1919, he returned to Ohio and began selling boxes of Mary Garden Chocolates behind the counter in C. A. Crane's Akron drugstore. He was then transferred to Cleveland where he worked in his father's candy factory. The elder Crane, who believed in the puritan ethic of hard work, starvation wages, and starting at the bottom, was unsympathetic to his son's artistic pursuits and indifference to the business world. Crane suffered in his father's employ: he hated the drudgery of factory work. Their relationship was uncommunicative. During this period, he had an affair with a young man he met in Akron, a passionate involvement which, like others to come, sidetracked him from his creative pursuits.

To Gorham Munson:
This "affair" that I have been having has been the most intense and satisfactory one of my whole life, and I am all broken up at the thought of leaving him. Yes, the last word will jolt you. I have never had devotion returned before like this, nor ever found a soul, mind and body so worthy of devotion. [5]

Crane quit working for his father "for good" in April, 1921. Living with his mother and grandmother in Cleveland, he landed a job as a copywriter for an advertising firm, which left him some energy for his own writing, and he began fashioning a long poem— "For the Marriage of Faustus and Helen."

At times, dear Gorham, I feel an enormous power in me—

that seems almost supernatural. If this power is not too dissipated in aggravation and discouragement I may amount to something sometime. I can say this now with perfect equanimity because I am notoriously drunk and the Victrola is still going with that glorious "Bolero." Did I tell you of that thrilling experience this last winter in the dentist's chair when under the influence of aether and *amnesia* my mind spiraled to a kind of seventh heaven of consciousness and egoistic dance among the seven spheres—and something like an objective voice kept saying to me—"You have the higher consciousness—you have the higher consciousness. This is something that very few have. This is what is called genius"? [6]

Crane returned to New York in March, 1923, first living with the Munsons and then moving into the room of his friend Slater Brown. Many of his poems were now appearing in literary magazines and his friends encouraged him to seek book publication. Crane was just now beginning to conceive of *The Bridge*, the poem that would take him six years to complete. He intended it to be his affirmation of life, a symphonic synthesis of, and new myth for, America.

He had been hired as a copywriter for J. Walter Thompson Company but he resented the demands of his job as well as living conditions in New York City and the difficulty he had finding time for "ecstasy": listening to music, drinking, and writing. New York was a "stupid" place to live for an artist, "writing that damned advertising under that pseudo-refined atmosphere of the office." Crane, his nerves frayed, quit his job and spent the remainder of the year in a house in Woodstock, New York, with friends Slater Brown and Ed Nagle. He successfully pleaded with his mother for some money to tide him over while he restored his health in the country, and worked at his poetry.

Malcolm Cowley:

Five-cent cigar. Hair: bushy hair cropped close to the head. Red face. Rather popping brown eyes. Not a very tall man. I think he was about five-feet-ten, but he gave an impression of being big, and aggressive, and strangely masculine at all times. [7]

Crane's pattern of movement back and forth from city to country was dependent upon his finances, which were in perpetual flux and usually critical. In the spring of 1924 he moved to a room in Brooklyn at 100 Columbia Heights. He could see the Brooklyn Bridge from his window.

In March, the magazine *Secession* published his long poem "For the Marriage of Faustus and Helen" in its entirety and Crane received enthusiastic praise from Gorham Munson and Malcolm Cowley. After rejecting a new proposition from his father to join him in business, he found a job writing copy for Sweet's Catalogue Service, which produced engineering and architectural catalogues.

In November he gave a very successful poetry reading at a gathering attended by many notable figures in American arts and letters including Marianne Moore, Edmund Wilson, Lewis Mumford, and Georgia O'Keeffe.

> To his father:
> Try to imagine working for the pure love of simply making something beautiful—something that maybe can't be sold or used to help sell anything else, but that is simply a communication between man and man, a bond of understanding and human enlightenment—which is what a real work of art *is* . . . I only ask to leave behind me something that the future may find valuable. . . . I shall make every sacrifice toward that end.[8]

In December, 1925, Crane wrote a long letter to Otto H. Kahn, international banker and philanthropist. He explained his writing and his plans for a new, important work, an epic poem entitled *The Bridge*. He described his financial situation and requested a $2,000 loan. After interviewing Crane, Kahn agreed. The money would be paid out to him in installments of $500 each. Crane, with money in his pocket for a change, and a pair of new winter boots, left New York City for Patterson, New York, to spend the winter with poet Allen Tate and his wife.

> Malcolm Cowley:
> Hart drank to write: he drank to invoke the visions that

his poems are intended to convey. But the recipe could be followed for a few years at the most. . . . After that more and more alcohol was needed, so much of it that when the visions came he was incapable of putting them on paper. He drank in Village speakeasies and Brooklyn waterfront dives; he insulted everyone within hearing or shouted he was Christopher Marlowe; then waking after a night spent with a drunken sailor he drank again to forget his sense of guilt.[9]

The house-sharing was a disaster, a result of the clash of three very strong personalities. In the spring, Crane wrote to his mother begging her to permit him to go live in the family's house in Isle of Pines, Cuba. He was low on money again although Kahn had just sent him another $500. The house in Cuba, he explained to his mother, would afford him a refuge from financial worries as well as a place to complete *The Bridge*. After some resistance, Grace Crane relented. He left almost immediately, arriving in Cuba in May, 1926, and remaining until October, when a hurricane destroyed his mother's house. Although he had worked on the poem as planned, he had also indulged in a lot of drinking and island life, and it was still far from finished.

> To William Wright:
> I get awfully exhausted sometimes, trying to achieve some kind of consistent vision of things. But I don't seem to be able to relax—and knowing quite well all the time that most of my energy is wasted in a kind of inward combustion that is sheer nonsense. All else seems boresome, however—so I must continue to kill myself in my own way.[10]

White Buildings, his first collection of poems, was published by Liveright in December, 1926. Ivor Winters, in a review of the poems, named Crane one of "five or six greatest poets writing in English." Waldo Frank called him a "mystical maker." The book's first printing of 500 copies sold out. This success did little for the author, who wanted to avoid another cold winter in Patterson. Crane managed to get $300 more from Kahn. He also got a job as personal secretary to Samuel Wise, a semi-invalid, wealthy Wall Street broker, which took him to southern California. Although the job ended after five months Crane remained in Hollywood where his mother and grandmother now lived. His activities were frenzied. He was drinking heavily and carousing with sailors, and was unable to work on *The Bridge*.

> To Slater Brown:
> A paean from Venusberg! Oy-oy-oy! I have just had my ninth snifter of Scotch. . . . Oh BOY! Try to imagine the streets constantly as they were during that famous aggregation last May in Manhattan. And more, for they are at home here, these western argosies, at roadstead far and near —and such a throng of pulchritude and friendliness as would make your "hair" stand on end. That's been the way of all flesh with me. . . . And wine and music and such nights— WHOOPS!!!!!! [11]

"Excessively hysterical conditions" between Crane and his mother drove him from Hollywood in June, 1928, and back to New York. With his financial situation precarious as usual, once again he endured the ordeal of job hunting, working when and where he could. The death of his grandmother promised him a small inheritance but his mother initially refused to give him the money unless he returned to California. Her actions caused a permanent rupture in their relationship. When she finally relented, Crane took his money and, in December, sailed for Europe.

Crane continued his raucous, drunken behavior in Paris. There he became friends with Harry and Caresse Crosby, expatriate Bostonians with literary interests who were living in high style on family money. They agreed to publish a private edition of *The Bridge* with "sheets as large as a piano score" in their Black Sun Press, and invited Crane to work on the poem at their mill house on the Rouchefoucauld estate outside Paris. More drinking and carousing than writing was done and when he returned to Paris he got himself thrown in jail for his behavior.

> Harry Crosby:
> Hart was magnificent. When the Judge announced that

it had taken ten gendarmes to hold him (the dirty bastards, they dragged him three blocks by the feet) all the court burst into laughter. After ten minutes of questioning he was fined 800 francs and 8 days in prison should he ever be arrested again. . . . Hart said that the dirty skunks in the Santé wouldn't give him any paper to write poems on. The bastards.[12]

The Bridge was finally completed (except for last-minute revisions) amidst much drunken histrionics in December, 1929, after Crane returned to New York. On December 7, he threw a party in celebration that was also a good-bye party for Harry and Caresse Crosby, who were leaving after several weeks in New York. Three days later Harry Crosby committed suicide. Caresse returned to Paris, determined to carry on the work of the Black Sun Press, and soon after Crane mailed her his final revisions of the poem.

Liveright published their edition of the book in America in March, 1930. This time, rather than praise, the reviews were equivocal, and some flatly negative, most notably the review by Ivor Winters, who now pronounced Crane a failure.

> To Ivor Winters:
>   It happens that the first poem I ever wrote was too dense to be understood, and now I find that I can trust most critics to tell me that all my subsequent efforts have been equally futile.[13]

Amidst the Depression and "disintegrating forces" of New York Hart applied for and was granted a Guggenheim Fellowship in March, 1931. Several weeks later he sailed for Mexico where he rented a house in Mixcoac. Unable to get a new work started, Crane found himself suddenly idle without the sustaining force of a work in progress.

> To Waldo Frank:
>   These are bewildering times for everyone, I suppose. I can't muster much of anything to say to anyone. I seem to

have lost the faculty to even feel tension. A bad sign, I'm
sure . . . I'd love to fight for—almost anything, but there
seems to be no longer any real resistance. Maybe I'm only a
disappointed romantic, after all. Or perhaps I've made too
many affable compromises.[14]

Mexico—its warm climate and exotic flora, its beautiful Indians
and plentiful Tequila—wove a spell around Crane. There he could
live like a king on practically nothing. He decided to make the
country his home for some time to come. However, he was not at
peace. He wrote very little, although he managed to complete "The
Broken Tower," one of his finest poems, and send it off to *Poetry*
magazine. His involvement with alcohol was constant; he was restless; he couldn't sleep; he worried about money.

My word I poured. But was it cognate, scored
Of that tribunal monarch of the air
Whose thigh embronzes earth, strikes crystal Word
In wounds pledged once to hope—cleft to despair?[15]

While in Mexico, Crane had his first heterosexual love affair, with
Peggy Baird, the ex-wife of Malcolm Cowley, whom he had known
for twelve years. She moved into his house in Mixcoac and shared
with him a conjugal life that included servants, pets, and flower
gardens. When he wasn't drinking too much, Hart found life satisfying to the point of dispelling his previous loneliness. He and Peggy
discussed marriage.

Crane's father had died in 1931, and he expected to inherit
enough money—about $2,000 a year—to keep him financially secure in
Mexico. However, in April, 1932, he was notified of a complication
regarding his father's estate that would cut him off from his bequest
indefinitely. In panic, Crane got raving drunk, drafted a will, and
swallowed a bottle of Mercurochrome in an unsucessful suicide attempt. Peggy had his stomach pumped and put him to bed. The
following day, they decided it would be best to leave Mexico and
return to the United States to try to work out his financial problems.
He and Peggy sailed from Vera Cruz on the S.S. *Orizaba* on

Crane with Peggy Baird in Mexico

April 25. He was drinking excessively. On April 27, the sun high in the sky, thirty-two-year-old Hart Crane jumped off the ship into the waters north of Havana and was lost at sea.

> Bind us in time, O Seasons clear, and awe.
> O minstrel galleons of Carib fire,
> Bequeath us to no earthly shore until
> Is answered in the vortex of our grave
> The seal's wide spindrift gaze toward paradise.[16]

Notes

1 Crane, "Voyages," *The Complete Poems and Selected Prose of Hart Crane,* p. 35.
2 Crane, "The Broken Tower," *The Complete Poems,* p. 193.
3 Unterecker, *Voyager: A Life of Hart Crane,* p. 16.
4 Weber, *The Letters of Hart Crane (1916–1932),* p. 9.
5 Ibid., pp. 27–28.
6 Ibid., p. 91.
7 Unterecker, op. cit., p. 770.
8 Weber, op. cit., pp. 170–71.
9 Cowley, *Exile's Return,* p. 231.
10 Weber, op. cit., p. 267.
11 Ibid., p. 317.
12 Garmain, Edward, ed., *Shadows of the Sun: The Diaries of Harry Crosby.* Santa Barbara: Black Sparrow Press, 1977, pp. 261–62.
13 Weber, op. cit., p. 301.
14 Ibid., p. 366.
15 Crane, "The Broken Tower," *The Complete Poems,* p. 193.
16 Crane, "Voyages," *The Complete Poems,* p. 36.

Sources

Cowley, Malcolm. *Exile's Return.* New York: Penguin Books, 1976.
Crane, Hart. *The Bridge.* New York: Liveright, 1933.
———. *The Complete Poems and Selected Prose of Hart Crane.* Edited by Brom Weber. New York: Anchor Books, 1966.

Schwartz, Joseph. *Hart Crane: An Annotated Critical Bibliography.* New York: David Lewis, 1970.

Unterecker, John. *Voyager: A Life of Hart Crane.* New York: Farrar Straus & Giroux, 1969.

Weber, Brom, ed. *The Letters of Hart Crane (1916–1932).* Berkeley and Los Angeles: The University of California Press, 1965.

STEPHEN CRANE
1871-1900

I saw a man pursuing the horizon;
Round and round they sped.
I was disturbed at this;
I accosted the man.
"It is futile," I said,
"You can never—"

"You lie," he cried,
And ran on.[1]

STEPHEN CRANE. American novelist, short story writer, and poet. Called the first modern American writer, he introduced a unique brand of social realism into the craft of fiction that later influenced novelists like Theodore Dreiser and James T. Farrell. The key to the effect he achieved lies in his use of contradiction and parody and symbolism. Crane was labeled a realist, an impressionist, a romantic, even a decadent; his work was both highly acclaimed and criticized during his lifetime. He became famous as the author of *The Red Badge of Courage;* he became infamous as a man who would defend a streetwalker from the police, and marry a madam of a house of prostitution. Insulted and abused for his behavior in his own country, Crane sought refuge in England. His accumulated writing filled twelve volumes. His masterpieces were few, however, as he sacrificed quality for quantity in the face of financial pressures resulting from a life-style he could not afford.

To Nellie Crouse (a friend):

So you think I am successful? Well I don't know. Most people consider me successful. At least they seem so to think. But upon my soul I have lost all appetite for victory as victory is defined by the mob. I will be glad if I can feel on my deathbed that my life has been just and kind according to my ability and that every particle of my little ridiculous stock of eloquence and wisdom has been applied for the benefit of my kind.[2]

Stephen Crane was born on November 1, 1871, at the parsonage of the Central Methodist Church in Newark, New Jersey. He was the fourteenth and last child of Reverend Dr. Townley Crane and Mary Ellen Peck. As youngest, his care fell to his fifteen-year-old sister Agnes. Crane's early childhood was spent moving from parsonage to parsonage with his family and he did not go to school until he was eight. His father died when he was nine, and his sister Agnes, whom he adored, died when he was twelve.

At the age of sixteen, Crane went to work as a reporter for his brother Townley's news agency in Asbury Park, New Jersey, writing unsigned articles for the *New York Tribune*. In 1888, he entered Claverack College on the Hudson River where he earned a reputation for vice—the ones his father had preached and written against. He gambled, drank, and smoked, and enjoyed them all. And he read, hungrily devouring Shakespeare and Plutarch's *Lives*.

It has been a theory of mine ever since I began to write, which was eight years ago, when I was sixteen, that the most artistic and the most enduring literature was that which reflected life accurately. Therefore I have tried to observe closely, and to set down what I have seen in the simplest and most concise way.[3]

From Claverack, Crane transferred to Lafayette College in Pennsylvania, flunking out after a year—and flunking out again after a few months at Syracuse University where he played a lot of baseball. The pale, thin young man was a superb bare-handed catcher and briefly considered making this a career. Literature won out, however. During his spell at Syracuse, as well as reporting on local and college news for the *New York Tribune*, he penned the first draft of a short story that would become the novel *Maggie: A Girl of the Streets*.

Jimmie's occupation for a long time was to stand at street

corners and watch the world go by, dreaming blood-red dreams at the passing of pretty women. He menaced mankind at the intersections of streets. At the corners he was in life and of life. The world was going on and he was there to perceive it.[4]

Crane went to New York City in the fall of 1891 where he lived on the lower East Side and frequented the Art Students' League on East Twenty-third Street. Crane was continually hard-up for money and slept in beds borrowed from his artist friends. He explored the life of the streets and life on the Bowery, writing sketches of his impressions which he would try to sell to newspapers. He also continued to write poetry and short stories. When he finished a second draft of *Maggie,* he submitted it to the editor of *Century* magazine; it was rejected as too shocking.

He maintained a belligerent attitude toward all well-dressed men. To him fine raiment was allied to weakness, and all good coats covered faint hearts. He and his orders were kings, to a certain extent, over the men of untarnished clothes, because these latter dreaded, perhaps, either to be killed or laughed at.[5]

After a third draft with still no publisher willing to touch it, Crane decided to publish it himself. He used the pseudonym "Johnston Smith" for safety and reputation's sake. In March, 1893, *Maggie: A Girl of the Streets* was printed, bound in yellow with the title in black letters. The edition of 1,100 copies cost Crane a steep $900 which he paid by selling coal stocks inherited from his mother (who had died in 1891) and borrowing from his brother. He gave away most of the copies.

To Hamlin Garland (writer and mentor):
It is inevitable that you be greatly shocked by this book [*Maggie*] but continue, please, with all possible courage to the end. For it tries to show that environment is a tremendous thing in the world and frequently shapes lives regardless. If one proves that theory, one makes room in Heaven for all

sorts of souls (notably an occasional street girl) who are not confidently expected to be there by many excellent people.[6]

Crane spent the summer of 1893 with his brother Edmund and family in Hartwood, New York, where he first began to fashion out of his imagination a Civil War story that would launch him to fame: *The Red Badge of Courage*. It was first published in a much shortened version in December, 1894, by the Bacheller-Johnson Syndicate and carried in newspapers across the country. Crane received a meager ninety dollars for the sale, but the story's appearance marked the beginning of a slowly mounting wave of recognition for the young writer. Greatly encouraged by the enthusiastic response, Crane submitted the book to Appleton and Company, a New York publisher which agreed to publish it. Then he took off for the West as a journalist on assignment for Bacheller and Johnson.

> Willa Cather (author and acquaintance):
> It occurs to me that all his life was a preparation for sudden departure. I remember once when he was writing a letter he stopped and asked me about the spelling of a word, saying carelessly "I haven't time to learn to spell." Then glancing down at his attire he added with an absent-minded smile, "I haven't time to dress either; it takes an awful slice out of a fellow's life." [7]

The years 1895 and 1896 were critical in Crane's career as a writer. In May, 1895, Copeland and Day published a book of Crane's poems, *The Black Riders and Other Lines*. Although a few critics praised the volume, remarking on the author's originality and genius, the majority made fun of his poems, labeling them silly, eccentric, even decadent. Crane was called the "Aubrey Beardsley of poetry." The failure of *Black Riders* and the insults seriously upset twenty-four-year-old Crane who, in fact, liked his "lines" better than his prose and felt his poems were more ambitious, a truer form of art. Shortly after this disaster, Appleton and Company published *The Red Badge of Courage* in America, and Heinemann's simultaneously published the book in England. Ironically, it was not until the English lauded Crane as a genius and *Red Badge* a masterpiece, that the

American critics and public began to pay attention to the book. Then *Red Badge* began to sell: it was reprinted fourteen times in 1896 and Crane was famous.

> To Nellie Crouse:
> For the first time in my life I began to be afraid, afraid that I would grow content with myself, afraid that willy-nilly I would be satisfied with the little, little things I have done. For the first time I saw the majestic forces which are arrayed against man's true success—not the world—the world is silly, changeable . . . but man's own colossal impulses more strong than chains, and I perceived that the fight was not going to be with the world but with myself.[8]

In November, 1896, the *New York Journal* assigned Crane to cover the Cuban War. With a money belt containing $700 in gold strapped to his waist, Crane traveled to Jacksonville, Florida, to await a ship that would carry him to Cuba. During his wait, he met Cora Taylor, the blond owner and madam of the Hotel de Dream. Cora fell in love with the pale, thin writer whose books and stories she had read. What she lacked in the way of physical attractiveness, she made up for in determination. She steadfastly attached herself to the younger man and soon won him over—"her mouse," as she called him.

The *Commodore*, Crane's ship to Cuba, finally departed from Jacksonville on New Year's Eve, sailing down the St. John's River and out to sea. Two days later, the ship sprung a leak and sank. Crane, the captain, and three other men were the last to abandon ship. They spent thirty hours in a swamped dinghy before managing to get ashore in Daytona, Florida. One of Crane's finest short stories, "The Open Boat," was the result of this aborted journey. He wrote it immediately after the disaster, upon his return to Jacksonville.

> If I am going to be drowned—if I am going to be drowned—if I am going to be drowned, why, in the name of the seven mad gods who rule the sea, was I allowed to come thus far and contemplate sand and trees? Was I brought here merely

to have my nose dragged away as I was about to nibble the
sacred cheese of life? [9]

Unable to get to Cuba, Crane was sent to Greece by the *New
York Journal* to report on the Greco-Turkish War. Cora went with
him as the newspaper's first woman correspondent. The war, however, lasted all of thirty days and by June of 1897 Crane was living
with Cora at Ravensbrook Villa, a damp mansion in the London
suburbs. *The Third Violet,* Crane's novel about the New York City
bohemian art scene, had just been published by Heinemann's and,
once again, the English critics called him a genius while, in America,
the novel was given a decidedly unenthusiastic reception. By now
Crane's name had become associated with scandal in his own country, essentially as a result of his defense in court in October, 1896,
of a streetwalker, Dora Clark, who he felt had been unjustly arrested for soliciting. Newspapers had a field day with the story and
Crane's reputation was permanently damaged. His involvement with
Cora Taylor added to his abuse by the American press.

> To Nellie Crouse:
> For my own part, I am minded to die in my thirty-fifth
> year. I think that is all I care to stand. I don't like to make
> wise remarks on the aspect of life but I will say that it doesn't
> strike me as particularly worth the trouble. The final wall of
> the wise man's thought however is Human Kindness of
> course. If the road of disappointment, grief, pessimism, is
> followed far enough it will arrive there. [10]

The Cranes lived far beyond their means at Ravensbrook, entertaining guests to whom they served expensive wines and food. Fast-
accumulating debts plagued the writer, who, attempting to stay afloat,
turned out numerous stories including "The Monster," "The Blue
Hotel," and "The Bride Comes to Yellow Sky," among the better
ones. That year Crane met Ford Madox Ford, and Joseph Conrad,
with whom he became close friends; the two men spent long evenings
drinking and talking.

Crane soon sought an escape from the confines of domestic life with Cora and its financial responsibilities. The Spanish-American War in Cuba conveniently presented itself. With Conrad's help, Crane managed to borrow enough money to return to the United States, his intention being to enlist in the Navy and get into the battle as a soldier. Departing suddenly, he left Cora to fend for herself in England. When the Navy rejected him as physically unfit, he took an assignment from the *New York World* as a journalist to report on the war.

> I decided that the nearer the writer gets to life the greater he becomes as an artist, and most of my prose writings have been toward the goal partially described by the misunderstood and abused word *realism*.[11]

Crane chased the action, filed dispatches, and as he had yearned to do, saw fighting. He reveled in the excitement and was afraid neither of bullets nor of death, nor of malaria, which he contracted and from which he never fully recovered. At the war's end he remained in Havana for several months; Cora, awaiting him in England, had no idea of his whereabouts as he remained out of touch with her. He began writing *Active Service*, a novel about the war.

> Regarding death thus out of the corner of his eye, he conceived it to be nothing but rest, and he was filled with a momentary astonishment that he should have made an extraordinary commotion out of the mere matter of getting killed. He would die; he would go someplace where he would be understood.[12]

In January, 1899, Crane returned to England, to Cora, to Ravensbrook, to his debts. In February, largely at Cora's prompting for she loved extravagance, they moved to Brede Manor in Sussex, a cold, damp, unfurnished palatial manor inhabited by bats, lacking plumbing, and even more costly than their previous home. Here, with creditors howling at his back, Cora planning extensive improvements of the estate, and freeloaders amusing themselves at the author's expense, Crane wrote frantically, churning out page after page of second-rate material in a futile attempt to restore his crumbling

Crane in his study at Brede Manor, Sussex, 1899

finances. He wrote Cuban war stories (*Wounds in the Rain*); *The O'Ruddy*, a novel that he never completed; *Whilomville Stories*, and more, until, felled by exhaustion, in late December, 1899, Crane had a lung hemorrhage and began to spit blood. His condition deteriorated rapidly and it soon became apparent to him that he was, in fact, dying. In April he wrote his will: Cora was his sole beneficiary.

> Once the line encountered the body of a dead soldier. He lay upon his back staring at the sky. He was dressed in an awkward suit of yellowish brown. The youth could see that the soles of his shoes had been worn to the thinness of writing paper, and from a great rent in one the dead foot projected piteously. And it was as if fate had betrayed the soldier. In death it exposed to his enemies that poverty which in life he had perhaps concealed from his friends.[13]

In a desperate attempt to save Crane's life, Cora borrowed money and arranged to transport him on a long and tedious voyage across the English Channel to a sanitorium in Badenweiler, Germany. Joseph Conrad was at Dover to say good-bye to his friend, who would not be coming back. On May 29, 1900, Crane was carried on a stretcher to a room in a villa near the sanitorium; his favorite dog was at his side. Seven days later, early on the morning of June 5, Stephen Crane died, his body wasted by tuberculosis and malaria. Cora accompanied his body back to the United States where he was buried in the Evergreen Cemetery in Hillside, New Jersey.

> In the desert
> I saw a creature, naked, bestial,
> Who, squatting upon the ground,
> Held his heart in his hands,
> And ate of it.
> I said: "Is it good, friend?"
> "It is bitter—bitter," he answered;
> "But I like it
> Because it is bitter,
> And because it is my heart."[14]

Notes

1 Katz, *The Complete Poems of Stephen Crane*, p. 26.
2 Cady and Wells, *Stephen Crane's Love Letters to Nellie Crouse*, p. 43.
3 Katz, *The Portable Stephen Crane*, p. 534.
4 Stallman, *Stephen Crane: Stories and Tales*, p. 51.
5 Ibid.
6 Katz, *The Portable Stephen Crane*, p. 1.
7 Stallman, *Stephen Crane: A Biography*, p. 130.
8 Cady and Wells, op. cit., p. 44.
9 Katz, *The Portable Stephen Crane*, p. 369.
10 Cady and Wells, op. cit., p. 35.
11 Stallman, *Stephen Crane: A Biography*, p. 95.
12 Katz, *The Portable Stephen Crane*, p. 216.
13 Ibid., p. 212.
14 Katz, *The Complete Poems of Stephen Crane*, p. 5.

Sources

Cady, Edwin H., and Wells, Lester G., eds. *Stephen Crane's Love Letters to Nellie Crouse*. N.Y.: Syracuse University Press, 1954.
Katz, Joseph, ed. *The Complete Poems of Stephen Crane*. Ithaca: Cornell University Press, 1972.
———. *The Portable Stephen Crane*. N.Y.: Penguin Books, 1969.
Stallman, R. W. *Stephen Crane: A Biography*. N.Y.: George Braziller, 1968.
———. *Stephen Crane: Stories and Tales*. N.Y.: Vintage Books, 1955.

HARRY CROSBY
1898-1929

The final refuge is suicide. Here at last, strange to say, thought and imagination conquer instinct. Diogenes is said to have put an end to himself by refusing to breathe—what a victory over the will to live! [1]

HARRY CROSBY. Expatriate American poet and member of the "Lost Generation." He founded the Black Sun Press in Paris, which published lavish editions of works by friends D. H. Lawrence, James Joyce, Archibald MacLeish, Kay Boyle, and Hart Crane as well as six volumes of his own poetry. From 1922 until his death, Crosby kept diaries, *Shadows of the Sun,* in which he recorded the details of his hedonistic literary life, revealing his obsessions with the sun, suicide, and his own death: "A Sun-Death Into Sun." [2]

> For the seekers after Fire and the Seers and the Prophets and the Worshipers of the Sun, life ends not with a whimper, but with a Bang—a violent explosion mechanically perfect . . . while, we, having set fire to the powderhouse of our souls, explode (suns within suns and cataracts of gold) into the frenzied fury of the Sun, into the madness of the Sun into the hot gold arms and hot gold eyes of the Goddess of the Sun! [3]

Harry Crosby was born on June 4, 1898, in the Back Bay area of Boston. His father was Stephen Van Rensselaer Crosby of Albany, Harvard Class of '91. His mother was Henrietta Marion Grew, daughter of a Boston philanthropist and the sister-in-law of J. Pierpont Morgan. Crosby and his younger sister, Kitsa, grew up carefree and untroubled in the family's large house at 95 Beacon Street, their summers spent on the North Shore.

> Geoffrey Wolff (biographer):
> His portrait hung in the salon: his hair was gold and he wore a white smock and white socks and white slippers, and he held a large India rubber ball. His lower lip drooped in a pout, a legacy from his father's mother.[4]

Crosby grew into an unusually beautiful young man. Slim and aristocratic in his bearing, with a full mouth and an intense stare, he had the "look of an old man with a young face." After graduating from St. Mark's, an elite New England prep school, in 1917, Crosby, nineteen years old, eagerly sailed with his friends for France and the war where he served as a volunteer driver in the American Field Services Ambulance Corps. On November 22 in the battle of Verdun Harry miraculously escaped injury when his ambulance exploded under heavy shelling. Crosby was later awarded the Croix de Guerre.

> Ten years ago today the hills of Verdun and the red sun setting back of the hills and the charred skeletons of trees and the river Meuse and the black shells spouting up in columns along the road to Bras and the thunder of the barrage and the wounded and the ride through red explosions and the violent metamorphose from boy into man.[5]

In April, 1919, Crosby returned to his family in Boston ostensibly to resume the life his father had mapped out for him: first Harvard and a "war degree," and then a job at the National Shawmut Bank. Along the way, however, Crosby (who now got drunk quite often and painted his fingernails black[6]) disobeyed all the rules, causing the Boston Brahmins and his father great unease. The climax of his rebellion was a passionate love affair with Mrs. Richard Rogers Peabody, mother of two. Polly Peabody (she would later become "Caresse") was seven years older than Crosby and disarmingly pretty.

He pursued her with determination and finally won her. Their relationship shocked proper Boston society.

> Caresse Crosby:
>   It is difficult to describe Harry completely, for he seemed to be more expression and mood than man—and yet he was the most vivid personality that I have ever known, electric with rebellion. Harry was frail, of middle height, and had an almost ungainly look, but he was taut as a tangent, his eyes blazed like mica, his mouth was large and it quivered ever so slightly when he was nervous, and his hands were like a musician's hands, sensitive, compelling.[7]

Crosby quit his bank job and, in the spring of 1922, quit Boston ("City of Dreadful Night") for Paris where a new bank job awaited, secured for him by his uncle J. P. Morgan. Polly, who had obtained a divorce, eventually joined him until one of Crosby's affairs revealed itself and sent her fleeing back home. He chased after her and they were married in a civil ceremony in New York City on September 9. The Crosbys, with Polly's two children, returned to Paris to live.

> One's innocence deteriorates rapidly: in kindergarten was amazed to hear of kissing; at boarding school was shocked at lewd stories; during the war felt revulsion on hearing of perversion; now worry very little about morals.[8]

With the encouragement of his cousin, Walter Van Rensselaer Berry, international lawyer and a man of letters, Crosby resigned his job at Morgan, Harjes & Co. to devote himself entirely to literature and to living. Rimbaud's *"dérèglement de tous les sens"* and Oscar Wilde's command to yield to every temptation composed his daily catechism: oysters, caviar, champagne, whiskey, cocaine, opium, pretty women, race horses, silk pajamas, furs, and jewels were among the objects of his excesses. He had a sun tattooed between his shoulder blades.

The sun is streaming through the bedroom window, it is

eleven o'clock and I know by my dirty hands, by the torn banknotes on the dressing table, by the clothes and matches and small change scattered over the floor that last night I was drunk. Disgusting! [9]

Crosby inherited a library of 10,000 books from Berry on his death. He began systematically to read and then give away the books, his goal being to reduce his library to one single book. He devoured the poets and read the philosophers on suicide. He copied their words into his diaries, and he wrote his own poetry. He read about the sun, keeping his sun-death fixed in his mind. He contemplated its details, decided on a poison (laudanum), picked out a cemetery, and ordered a gravestone with his name and Polly's (now "Caresse") carved on it in the shape of a cross. They had vowed to die together on October 31, 1942, the day when the earth reached its closest point to the sun.

> I bought a huge drinking glass that will hold two quarts and tonight in Nietzche I read a significant passage: "Die at the right time." Die at the right time, so teacheth Zarethustra and again the direct 31–10–42. Clickety-click clickety-click the express train into Sun.[10]

In the spring of 1927, Harry and Caresse founded the Black Sun Press in Paris at 2 rue Cardinale. Through this enterprise they became acquainted with James Joyce, D. H. Lawrence, and Hart Crane. The press also enabled Crosby to publish his own poems in small, beautifully bound editions: *Red Skeletons* (1927), *Chariot of the Sun* (1928), *Transit of Venus* (1928), *Mad Queen* (1929), *Sleeping Together* (1929), and *Shadows of the Sun*.

> Built a bonfire and burned eight copies of *Red Skeletons* a rotten book. There were four copies left and these we shot full of bullet holes—they made a very nice target.[11]

In July, 1928, while staying at the Lido in Venice, he met twenty-year-old Josephine Rotch, a fashionable, rich, and darkly pretty Bostonian who was very willing to become erotically entangled with

Crosby. They began an affair, one of several that he carried on simultaneously. She became his "Fire Princess." (There also were the "Sorceress" and the "Lady of the Golden Horse".) Josephine, unlike the others, was unwilling to be just a casual romance.

Crosby and Caresse rented a mill house on the estate of Armand de Rochefoucauld as a retreat where they could go for rest and quiet. (At this time, Caresse knew all about his latest infatuation with Josephine.) The mill house provided little peace as it became the focal point for a constant stream of visitors, wine-soaked lunches, drunken parties, and donkey races.

> Bored and *very* restless. What is it I want? Who is it I want to sleep with? Why do I *hate* society? [12]

In August, 1929, he took up flying, soloing for the first time on November 11, Armistice Day. He wrote in his diary of the appeal of a "sun-death" from an airplane "for when the body strikes the ground Bang, Twang flies the Arrow of Soul to and into the Sun for Eternity!" [13] On November 16, he and Caresse sailed on the *Mauretania* for the United States. During the trip he copied out sixty-four dreams that make up the volume he called *Sleeping Together* and dedicated the work to Caresse.

Soon after their arrival in Boston, Crosby met secretly with Josephine, now Mrs. Albert Bigelow, having recently married a young Harvard student from a proper Boston family. Even so, she was possessive and demanding. Harry and Josephine carried on their clandestine meetings in Boston and New York, and spent two days in a Detroit hotel on opium "catapulting through space in each other's arms." Eventually he returned to Caresse in New York. In their room, high up in the Savoy Plaza, he asked her to jump out the window with him: "Let's meet the sun together." Caresse refused.

> I like our room 2702 at the Savoy Plaza I like living in one room more concentrated for the poet and high up 27 stories and the round disc of the Sun miraculous place for the sun-death room of the rising sun.[14]

Hart Crane gave Crosby and Caresse a going-away party at his

Crosby with Caresse, Le Bourget, 1928

apartment in Brooklyn on December 7 (they were scheduled to leave for Paris in a week). On the afternoon of December 10 Crosby and Josephine appeared unexpectedly at his friend Stanley Mortimer's studio in the Hotel des Artistes, an apartment building on the West Side of Manhattan. Mortimer went out for the afternoon, leaving the couple alone. Later that evening, Harry Crosby and Josephine were discovered in Mortimer's bed. They lay side by side, fully clothed. Each had been shot in the temple. Crosby's hand still held the gun. It was engraved with a sun. And, on the soles of his feet, the toenails of which were painted red, there was a tattoo of a pagan sun and a tattoo of a cross. He was thirty-one years old.

> we desire to die together
> we desire to be cremated together
> we desire that our ashes be mingled
> and taken up in an aeroplane at sunrise
> and scattered to the four winds
> let a cannon be fired as a symbol of our
> explosion into Sun [15]

Notes

1 Germain, *Shadows of the Sun: The Diaries of Harry Crosby*, p. 125.
2 Ibid., p. 132.
3 Cowley, *Exiles Return*, p. 272.
4 Wolff, *Black Sun: The Brief Transit and Violent Eclipse of Harry Crosby*, p. 20.
5 Germain, op. cit., p. 162.
6 Wolff, op. cit., p. 73.
7 Caresse Crosby, *The Passionate Years*, p. 83.
8 Germain, op. cit., p. 38.
9 Ibid., p. 55.
10 Ibid., p. 197.
11 Ibid., p. 240.
12 Ibid., p. 256.
13 Ibid., p. 197.
14 Ibid., p. 286.
15 Ibid., p. 153.

Sources

Cowley, Malcolm. *Exiles Return*. New York: Penguin Books, 1976.

Crosby, Caresse. *The Passionate Years*. New York: The Dial Press, 1953.

Germain, Edward, ed. *Shadows of the Sun: The Diaries of Harry Crosby*. Santa Barbara, Ca.: Black Sparrow Press, 1977.

Wolff, Geoffrey. *Black Sun: The Brief Transit and Violent Eclipse of Harry Crosby*. New York: Vintage Books, 1977.

JAMES DEAN
1931-1955

The problem for this cat—myself—is not to get lost.[1]

JAMES DEAN. Movie star and idol of the adolescents of the 1950s. He was petulant, insecure, and rebellious. The Dean legend and cult was born with *East of Eden* and mushroomed after his car-crash death and the release of *Rebel Without a Cause*. A year after his death Warner Brothers was receiving 8,000 fan letters a week. *Photoplay* magazine named him number one in their popularity poll. Effigies of his face in Miracleflesh were selling at a rate of 300 a week. James Dean, who had made only three pictures in his career (*Giant* was the third), had become a posthumous industry.

    George Stevens (director):
        Here was a boy just on the rise. He'd hardly broken water, flashing into the air like a trout. A few more films and the fans wouldn't have been so bereft. He shortly would have dimmed his luster.[2]

   James Byron Dean was born in Marion, Indiana, on February 8, 1931, the only child of Winton Dean, dental technician, and Mildred Wilson Dean, farm girl. The family moved to Santa Monica, California, when Dean was five. Four years later, his mother suddenly dead of cancer, Dean was taken back to Indiana to be raised by his

Aunt Hortense and Uncle Marcus Winslow on their farm in Fairmount. His father remained in California.

> My mother died on me when I was nine years old. What does she expect me to do? Do it all alone? [3]

Treated with special love and care by his aunt and uncle, Dean had an all-American boyhood: 4-H clubs, pet pigs and prize-winning cows, motor bikes, BB guns, and even drawing and dancing lessons. In high school, it was basketball (although he was short, only five-foot-seven) and track (the pole vault), and the usual teenage pranks. Dean also showed a flair for dramatics and attracted the attention and encouragement of Adeline Nall, the dramatics coach. In his senior year, he won a statewide dramatic speaking event. In his performance he screamed and fell down on the stage. He went on to participate in a nationwide contest but was disqualified because he refused to shorten his twelve-minute speech to the allotted ten.

> I don't want to be just a good actor. I don't even want to be the best. I want to grow, grow so tall nobody can reach me.[4]

Although Dean wanted to pursue the theater, his practical-minded father, who was orchestrating his son's life from afar, wanted him to study law. Dean obeyed. Leaving Fairmount in the summer of 1949, he traveled to California where he lived uneasily with his father and stepmother in Santa Monica. That fall he entered Santa Monica City College as a law student. Not for long, however; in his sophomore year he transferred to UCLA, which had a large, professional theater department. That year he played Malcolm in *Macbeth*. Although the critics didn't think much of him, he was spotted by an agent who got him his first professional job in a Pepsi-Cola commercial.

Ivan Moffat (screenwriter):
He was quite slight of build and, I would say, about five-foot-six or seven at the most in height. He had these pale, rather unexpectedly pale, eyes and a very small nose. And he gave the impression of dispersed energy, diffused energy. He would never walk straight, you know, he was often hunched,

hunched shoulders. And he had a funny laugh. A most improbable laugh, like a goat.[5]

Dean and his father soon parted company. In 1951, unwilling to tolerate campus fraternity life, he was sharing an apartment with William Bast, another theater arts major. He was looking for work as an actor, struggling to pay the rent and have enough left over to eat, and cutting most of his college classes. That spring he appeared as John the Baptist in "Hill Number One," a television drama, and the first James Dean fan club was formed by a group of high school girls.

> William Bast:
> He was my crazy roommate, moody, unpredictable, not yet sure of what he had, not yet ready for the role destiny had chosen for him.[6]

Dean dropped out of UCLA in his second year. Unkempt and unshaven, he worked in a parking lot and hung around Hollywood. Rogers Brackett, an account supervisor and a CBS-TV director, entered his life at this time. Fifteen years his senior, Brackett was a good-looking, sophisticated man with the right connections. Dean was soon living with Brackett, who was pushing the young actor's career. Brackett later described their father-son relationship as "somewhat incestuous." [7]

> Rogers Brackett:
> I have often thought I should have left "Hamlet" in the parking lot.[8]

Bit parts in movies such as the comedy *Sailor Beware* (with Dean Martin and Jerry Lewis) fell short of satisfying Dean's ambitions or his talent. New York, his friends advised him, was the place to go if he was really serious about acting. Brackett arranged for Dean to have a room at the Iroquois Hotel when he arrived and provided names of people to look up. He was soon signed with an agent, Jean Deacy, and had a "job" rehearsing contestants for "Beat the Clock." Thereafter, bit parts on live television shows such as "Studio One" and "Kraft Theater" kept him going. And Dean became a member of the Actor's Studio, where Lee Strasberg taught the "Method" to an elite workshop of promising talent.

> Acting is the most logical way for people's neuroses to express themselves, in this great need we all have to express ourselves. To my way of thinking, an actor's course is set even before he's out of the cradle.[9]

During the early period in New York, Dean led a nomadic life. When Brackett arrived in town, he stayed in his studio. At other times he shared an apartment with friends. He was always shifting around. He dated different women and had a close relationship with Elizabeth Sheridan, a dancer who was also struggling to make it.

In October, 1952, Dean got the lead part in a Richard Nash play, *See the Jaguar*, produced by Lemuel Ayers, whom he had met through Brackett. The play opened and closed within a week. James Dean, however, had been noticed. His performance was called "extraordinary" by Walter Kerr. Thereafter, work began to come steadily and, over the next year, Dean appeared in many television parts. In spite of the prevailing opinion in the business that he was undisciplined and unprofessional (he was often late for rehearsals, had temper tantrums, fussed over directions, fell asleep) his career had taken an important turn. James Dean was on the rise.

> Dennis Stock (photographer):
> Jimmy was an insomniac . . . so at odd times and in odd places he would simply pass out, for a few minutes or a few hours, then wake up and set out again. He lived like a stray animal; in fact, come to think of it, he was a stray animal.[10]

In November, Dean landed the part of Bachir, the homosexual Arab houseboy in Gide's *The Immoralist*. The production of the play starred Geraldine Page and Louis Jourdan. Rehearsals were strenuous and Dean, as usual, was difficult to work with. The play opened in New York on February 8, 1954. After turning in an excellent performance, Dean gave his three-weeks' notice: Elia Kazan had tapped the twenty-three-year-old actor for the part of Cal Trask in his new movie, *East of Eden*. Dean won the Daniel Blum Theater Award that year as "the best newcomer of the year" for his portrayal of Bachir. He also bought a motorcycle.

> Ruth Goetz:
> We go into rehearsal [for *The Immoralist*] and the little son of a bitch was one of the most unspeakably detestable fellows to work with I ever knew in my life.[11]

The filming of *East of Eden* began in Hollywood in the spring. Elia Kazan housed Dean in an elaborate dressing room on the lot right next door to him in order to keep an eye on the unpredictable young actor. Dean had a habit of staying out all night and going off on reckless motorcycle rides which Kazan had strictly forbidden.

During filming, the movie magazines were crammed with stories about Dean's love affair with Pier Angeli. A serious relationship had, in fact, blossomed but the affair ended badly a few months later when Pier, under pressure from her family to marry, wed singer Vic Damone.

> Elia Kazan (director):
> He was never more than a limited actor, a highly neurotic young man. But he had a lot of talent and he worked like hell. He was the perfect boy for the part. He did a swell job, you know. And yet he was obviously sick. I don't know what was the matter with him. He just got more so.[12]

East of Eden premiered in New York on March 10, 1955. Dean, who had refused to attend the opening night, read the reviews the following morning in Hollywood. He was, he discovered, "the screen's most sensational male find of the year." James Dean was a new star. Even so there were a few dissenting voices. Bosley Crowther, the most vehement, called Dean "a mass of histrionic gingerbread." But the overwhelming verdict was favorable. Overnight, Dean became big news, from his pranks, his eccentric behavior, his sloppy dress, his in-

Dean in Giant

somnia, to his resemblance to Marlon Brando, his love life, his philosophy. The media were having a feast, and Dean responded to the attention.

> Ezra Goodman (reporter, *Life* magazine):
> Dean became impossible. If he thought he was not getting enough attention in a restaurant, he would beat a tom-tom solo on the tabletop, play his spoon against a water glass with a boogie beat, pour a bowl of sugar into his pocket, or set fire to a paper napkin. He collected a small crew of sycophants and what gaucheries he couldn't think of, they could.[13]

East of Eden quickly became number one on *Variety's* list of top-grossing films. And Dean was soon signed to a new contract with Warner Brothers calling for nine pictures for a six-year period at a minimum guarantee of $15,000 per picture. With his newly acquired wealth, Dean purchased a $4,000 Porsche Speedster and entered his first sports car race in Palm Springs. In spite of his lack of experience, he won the amateur class and placed third in the professional class, driving like a daredevil, mad for speed. "Racing is the only time I feel whole,"[14] he said.

On March 28, 1955, Dean went to work on his next film, *Rebel Without a Cause*, directed by Nicholas Ray and costarring Natalie Wood and Sal Mineo. He played the role of the rebellious teenager, Jim Stark. This role would become inextricably tied to his own identity in the public mind. James Dean *was* Jim Stark. He was the rebel without a cause.

After finishing the movie, he went right into what would be his last film, *Giant*, directed by George Stevens. He played the part of Jet Rink, an angry, tough Texas ranch hand who makes millions in an oil strike. He ages from twenty-five to about forty-five by the end of the film. Once again, Dean, who was getting known for his thirst for speed, was forbidden by the director to drive. The car on loan to him by the studio was confiscated. *Giant* was completed in September, 1955, and Dean had preserved his growing reputation of being difficult to work with.

I'm a serious-minded intense little devil, terribly gauche and so tense I don't see how people stay in the same room with me. I know I wouldn't tolerate myself.[15]

On September 30, 1955, Dean, in his new Porsche Spyder (he had traded in his Speedster) with his expert mechanic Rolf Wuertherich at his side, drove off for a race to be held in Salinas the next day. On the way he was stopped for speeding and given a ticket for doing 65 MPH in a 45-MPH zone. Several hours later, the sun setting in his eyes, he collided with an oncoming car. It was 5:45 P.M. and James Dean was dead at the age of twenty-four.

If a man can bridge the gap between life and death, if he can live after he's died, then maybe he was a great man. Immortality is the only true success.[16]

Notes

1 Howard Thompson, "Another Dean Hits the Big League," *New York Times,* March 13, 1955.
2 Ezra Goodman, "Delirium Over a Dead Star," *Life,* September 24, 1955, p. 76.
3 Herndon, *James Dean, A Short Life,* p. 9.
4 Martinelli, *The James Dean Story,* p. 32.
5 Derek Marlowe, "Soliloquy on James Dean's Forty-fifth Birthday," *New York Magazine,* November 8, 1976, p. 42.
6 Goodman, op. cit., p. 79.
7 Martinelli, op. cit., p. 45.
8 Ibid., p. 44.
9 Thompson, op. cit.
10 Stock, *James Dean Revisited,* p. 82.
11 Herndon, op. cit., p. 89.
12 Marlowe, op. cit., p. 42.
13 George Scullin, "James Dean: The Legend and the Facts," *Look,* October 16, 1955, p. 128.
14 Martinelli, op. cit., p. 125.
15 Goodman, op. cit., p. 86.
16 Marlowe, op. cit., p. 46.

Sources

Herndon, Venable. *James Dean, A Short Life*. New York: New American Library, 1975.

Martinelli, Ronald. *The James Dean Story*. New York: Pinnacle Books, 1975.

Stock, Dennis. *James Dean Revisited*. New York: Penguin Books, 1979.

SERGEI ESENIN
1895-1925

I greet everything, I accept everything,
I am glad and happy to abandon my soul.
I have come on this earth
To leave it soon.[1]

SERGEI ESENIN. Russian lyric poet. He is considered, with Maya-kovsky, his counterpart and rival, one of the two major poets of the Russian Revolution. Called Don Quixote of the village, Esenin was a Romantic poet, a poet of the Motherland, and of a way of life that was dying out.

Extremely ambitious, hungry for fame, Esenin's goal was to be-come Russia's greatest poet, the one who spoke for the people. He achieved this to a great extent. He was loved, adored, and indulged in the different parts he played on his road to fame, from peasant poet, innocent and cherubic, to hooligan poet garbed in the clothes of a dandy for whom public scenes and scandals were the food of life.

Today he is the most popular poet in Russia. A living legend, his suicide crowned his life. Lyric poets, he said, should not live too long.

> Boris Pasternak:
> Esenin treated life like a fairy tale. . . . He also wrote his poems in a fairy-tale manner: he would either play the game of patience with words or write with his heart's blood. His most valuable asset was the vision of nature from his na-tive land—woody, middle-Russian Ryazan—rendered with daz-zling freshness, as he experienced it as a child.[2]

Sergei Esenin was born on October 3, 1895, in Konstantinovo, a small village in the Ryazan province, the first child and only son of Alexander Esenin and Tatyana Fyodorovna Titova (two sisters would be born in 1905 and 1911). As his parents' marriage was unstable, at the age of four Esenin was sent to live with his maternal grandparents, well-to-do peasants, who raised him in a lively atmosphere. His grandfather read him the Bible, his grandmother sang songs to him and told him fairy tales. Esenin began to write poems at the age of eight.

> Anatoly Mariengof (poet and friend):
> The basic thing in Esenin: fear of loneliness.[3]

Fourteen-year-old Esenin was sent to the Church boarding school at Spas-Klepiki where he trained to be a parish teacher. However, he wanted to be a poet, a *famous* poet. After graduation, he went to Moscow where he spent three years working in a bookstore, a printing factory, a butcher shop. He studied literature at the Shanayavsky University and joined an organization of proletarian peasant writers. By nineteen, he had quit his last nonpoetic job and had his first poem published in a children's journal. He was living with a girl he had met in a factory who soon became pregnant with his child.

> Listen, my rotten heart,
> My dog's heart.
> For you, as for a thief,
> I have hidden a knife in my sleeve.[4]

In March, 1915, Esenin left Moscow, his girl friend, and his newborn child, for Petrograd, literary capital of Russia, "to take glory and fame by the horns." He quickly made contact with poet Alexander Blok, who was impressed with the verse of the self-taught peasant poet and put him in touch with poets Murashov and Gorodetsky. In blue peasant coat and Russian boots, his blue eyes and cherubic face topped by golden curls, Esenin was swiftly accepted into the literary salons and drawing rooms where he recited his lyrical poems, dreamy and gay, which evoked the region where he had spent his youth.

Hopes, painted by the autumn cold, are shining;
My steady horse plods on as calm as Fate;
His dun lip twitches moistly at the lining
Of my blown coat; he does not change his gait.

On a far road the unseen traces, leading
Neither to rest nor battle, lure and fade;
The golden heels of day will flash, receding,
And labors in the chest of years be laid.[5]

Esenin became the protégé of Nikolai Klyuev, a peasant poet of significant reputation, eleven years his senior, and homosexual, whom he met in Petrograd in October, 1915. Klyuev masterminded the younger poet's career. Together they began appearing at the salons and literary taverns of the city. Outfitted in peasant costumes, they recited poetry and sang folk songs. Although Esenin's choice of mentor and choice of path alienated him from some of his other literary friends, it did not hurt his career. The journals were now publishing his poetry. Klyuev arranged for his own publisher to issue in 1916 Esenin's first book of verse: *Radunitza* (*Mourning for the Dead*), thirty-three selected poems written between 1910 and 1915. It was received as the work of a gifted poet.

Vladimir Mayakovsky:
The first time I saw him he was dressed in a shirt embroidered with some crosses and had bast moccasins on his feet. . . . Knowing how eagerly a genuine—as opposed to a theatrical—peasant changes his attire to town jackets and shoes, I did not believe Esenin.[6]

The Army called Esenin up in 1916, but the intervention of literary friends of influence kept him from the front lines. Instead, Esenin was sent to Tsarskoe-Selo where he served in the office and infirmary of Military Sanitary Train Number 143, which was under the jurisdiction of the Empress Alexandra. Several times the poet was called upon to write and recite poetry for the Empress and her daughters. Esenin obliged and received gifts for his efforts. He was lonely, bored, and unhappy, however, with the restrictions of Army life. He got drunk whenever he could obtain enough beer or wine.

> Sooner or later I'll stick
> The cold steel into my ribs.
> No, I cannot strive
> Towards the eternal rotten horizon.[7]

While serving at Tsarskoe-Selo, Esenin met Ivanov-Razumnik, an intellectual and social historian, and fell under the influence of his revolutionary socialist philosophy. Although he was essentially politically naive, even indifferent, Esenin responded to his ideas and his championing of the people over all.

Esenin deserted from the Army in March, 1917, after the abdication of the Tsar, and spent the next months wandering about Russia and writing poetry. Under the influence of Ivanov-Razumnik and his group, "The Scythians," including Blok and Klyuev, he tried to imbue his poetry with the correct socialist spirit for the people of the Revolution. Esenin greeted the October Revolution with excitement. It coincided with his poetic vision of the coming new order in which the peasants would be triumphant, and he, as poet of the peasants, would play an important role.

> The moon is the tongue
> In the bell of the sky
> My country's my mother,
> A Bolshevik, I.

> That all may be brothers
> Is cause for me
> To rejoice in your death,
> My own country.[8]

At twenty-three, Esenin was a well-published and well-read poet living in Moscow. He was both popular and controversial. He called himself a Bolshevik, but, at the same time, he wrote in his poem "Inoniia!" about a city that is a paradise on earth for the Russian peasantry, a city invulnerable to the steel and iron of technology. Esenin's vision of revolution was religious and spiritual rather than political.

Early in 1919 he aligned himself with the Imaginist literary movement, one of the many schools that proliferated during the early years of the Soviet era. This group of artists and poets—including dandy Anatoly Mariengof, who would become his most intimate friend over the next four years—published a declaration in January in *Soviet Land,* a Moscow newspaper, that aroused a storm of controversy. The group was accused of writing antiproletarian verse; at the same time, it was praised for its daring originality and vitality. An Imaginist publishing company was founded, and Esenin and Mariengof opened a bookshop in which they sold Imaginist books. Despite the civil war that was disrupting the country and inflicting severe hardship on most people, Esenin prospered. These would be the most productive and happy years of his life.

> Imaginist Declaration:
> We assert that the only law of art, its only and incomparable method, is the revelation of life by means of the image and the rhythm of images. . . . The image and nothing but the image. . . . Notice how lucky we are. We have no philosophy. We propose no logic of thoughts. The logic of our certitude is more powerful than anything.[9]

Esenin found personal freedom in the Imaginist's code of rebellion and anarchy in art. He began to play a new part, that of "hooligan" poet, and he was an extremely successful performer. In the cafés and taverns of Moscow he sought the attention that would bring him the notoriety and fame he craved. He became the star attraction at the Stall of Pegasus, the Imaginist café, reading his poetry to adoring fans. He created scandal wherever he could and was often arrested for his public scenes. He began drinking heavily and became rowdy and destructive when intoxicated.

> On purpose I go uncombed,
> With my head, like an oil lamp, on my shoulders.
> I like to light up in the dark

The leafless autumn of your souls.
I like it when the stones of insults
Hit me, like hail in a howling storm.
I only press more firmly then with my hands
The rocking bubble of my hair.[10]

Esenin had married Zinaida Raikh, a beautiful, pale-faced Jew-
ess—who later became a famous actress and married the director
Meyerhold—in 1917. By 1920, their marriage was coming apart.
Zinaida gave birth to a son that year, their second child, but Esenin,
questioning her fidelity, refused to believe it was his. He lived like a
nomad, moving from flat to flat.

I didn't know that love is an infection,
I didn't know that love is the pest,
She came with narrowed eyes.
She drove the hooligan to insanity.[11]

That summer Esenin made a visit to Konstantinovo, where he had
grown up, and realized for the first time the effects of the Revolution.
In essence, village life was becoming obsolete, dying out; technology
was replacing flesh with iron. Esenin, whose entire identity as a poet
was connected to this old and simple way of life, the land, the peasants,
declared himself the "last poet of the village."

In 1921, Esenin wrote *Pugachov*, a long historical verse play about
an eighteenth-century rebel peasant. He considered the work his masterpiece. But when it was published most critics condemned the play
as a complete failure, accusing Esenin of a complete lack of understanding of history.

To Zenja (girl friend):
I am very sad at the moment, for history goes through a
difficult period of murder of the personality, as far as it is alive.
For this is not at all Socialism as I had expected it to come,
but a determined and deliberate Socialism . . . without any
glory and without dreams. In this Socialism the living person
feels hedged in.[12]

Later that year, Esenin, who had divorced Zinaida, met the woman who would be his next wife.

Isadora Duncan, the famous American dancer, was in her forties, aging and overweight. She had come to Moscow to give dance recitals and to found a dancing school. Although Esenin and Duncan had few words with which to communicate (she did not speak Russian, he did not speak anything but Russian) they carried on a boisterous affair conducted in an atmosphere of heavy drinking and partying. Their relationship was volatile, Esenin often packing up and leaving Duncan only to give in to the older woman's pleas to return.

In order to facilitate visas for a trip to Europe and the United States, Esenin and Duncan were married on May 2, 1922. The purpose of the trip was to raise money through dance recitals for Duncan's school. Esenin, however, had his own reason to go abroad. His fame in Russia a certainty, he believed he could become an international poet by traveling abroad.

> Ilya Ehrenburg (novelist, journalist):
> It is difficult to imagine a more unhappy man. He could not stay in one place. Love bored him; he suspected his friends of intrigues, was a hypochondriac, thought constantly he would die soon.[13]

Their travels gained Esenin more infamy than fame. Frustrated by language barriers and by the lack of interest in him except as Isadora's young, handsome husband, Esenin reacted by drinking heavily and brawling in public. After he was hospitalized several times in Europe, Duncan managed temporarily to force him to stop drinking.

The four months the couple spent in America, however, furthered Esenin's deterioration. Unable to speak English, unable to play the role of a famous poet in America, trapped into following his wife around like a pet, Esenin took out his misery and frustration in the speakeasies where he consumed volumes of poisonous prohibition booze. His relationship with Duncan was marked by noisy fights and brawls. When the couple returned to Russia in August, 1923, they separated and divorced. From abroad Esenin had brought back trunks of new European clothes: silk underwear, shirts, exotic powders and

Esenin with Isadora Duncan

perfumes. His physical appearance, however, was that of a burnt-out man.

> Oh fatherland! How ridiculous I've become.
> On sunken cheeks a dry blush spreads.
> The speech of my compatriots has become strange
>   to me,
> In my own country I am like a foreigner.[14]

On his return from Europe Esenin's standing as a poet was in question. While many editors still supported his work and published him, he was attacked by Marxist critics for his political irrelevancy and unsophisticated verse. He was not a "Communist poet." In 1924, a volume of poems written by Esenin before and during his trip was published in Moscow entitled *Moscow the Tavern City*. The poems depicted the life in the taverns of the city and emphasized drunkenness and decadence. Esenin's deterioration continued. He was hospitalized for "nerves" in late 1923, and again in February, 1924, after falling through a window and severely cutting his arm.

> Ilya Ehrenburg:
>   The saddest thing of all was to see, next to Yesenin, a random group of men who had nothing to do with literature, but simply liked . . . to drink somebody else's vodka, bask in someone else's fame, and hide behind someone else's authority. It was not through this black swarm, however, that Yesenin perished. He drew them to himself. He knew what they were worth; but in his state he found it easier to be with people he despised.[15]

In the summer of 1924, Esenin went home to Konstantinovo once again. On this trip he concluded that he had lost his place as poet of the village and was truly homeless. He spent September through March traveling in the Caucasus trying unsuccessfully to master an understanding of Communist philosophy in order to be able to write poetry for the new generation. He wrote *Anna Snegina*, a long, autobiographical poem about unrequited love, which he read to a group of writers upon his return to Moscow. Its indifferent reception made

him unhappy, and he soon returned to the Caucasus. He resumed
drinking heavily and fell ill, coughing up blood. He was hospitalized
with a lung infection.

> To Volf Erlikh (poet and friend):
> I have simply ruined my voice by drinking. In the Cau-
> casus I ran in the snow with an open shirt. I wanted to catch
> cold but I didn't succeed. . . . But as for dying, I'll die any-
> how. And very soon.[16]

When Esenin returned to Moscow in May he looked gravely ill.
In June he abruptly declared that he was going to marry Sofya
Tolstaya, the rather plain granddaughter of Leo Tolstoy. This plan
puzzled his friends, who regarded the couple as ill-matched.

In June, Gosizdat, the state publishing company, decided to issue
a large collection of Esenin's poetry—10,000 lines—for which Esenin
would be paid a rouble a line, a substantial amount of money. Hardly
ever sober, Esenin's preparation of the manuscript was hampered by
the disorganization and chaos that ruled his life. And despite this
official acceptance of his old work, his new poems were criticized and
insulted.

> My friend, my friend,
> I am very, very sick!
> I don't know myself from where
>   this sickness has come.
> Is it the wind whistling
> Over the empty and lonely field,
> Or is it the alcohol scattering
>   my brain,
> Like leaves in September?[17]

On November 26, 1925, Esenin, in desperate condition, hospi-
talized himself in the psychiatric clinic of the University of Moscow.
He was unwilling, however, to complete a treatment there and on
December 21 checked out and got drunk.

To start a new life, to begin all over again, became his goal. On
December 23, he left his newly wed Sofya. After visiting Zinaida

Raikh and their two children, and Anne Izryadnova, his factory girl friend, and their son to say good-bye, he left Moscow by train for Leningrad.

In Leningrad, Esenin checked into the Angleterre Hotel and spent a few days visiting friends. He paid a visit to his old mentor Klyuev, who was unfriendly and insulting. On December 27 Esenin wrote his last poem. Lacking a pencil, he slashed his wrist and wrote the lines in blood. Later that day he calmly presented the poem to his friend Volf Erlikh, but forbade him to read it. Erlikh put the poem in his pocket unread.

> Now good-bye, my friend, no hand clasped,
> no word spoken,
> Do not let me vex or sadden you.
> In this life there's nothing new in dying
> And, in truth, to live is nothing new.[18]

Early in the morning of the following day, using a cord from one of his trunks, Sergei Esenin, thirty years old, hanged himself from a heating pipe in his hotel room.

> Vladimir Mayakovsky ("To Sergei Esenin"):
> To die—
> in life
> is not so hard
> To make life—
> harder by far.[19]

Notes

1 De Graaff, *Sergej Esenin, A Biographical Sketch*, p. 29.
2 Woroszyski, *The Life of Mayakovsky*, p. 385.
3 McVay, *Esenin, A Life*, p. 147.
4 De Graaff, op. cit., p. 35.
5 Yarmolinsky, *An Anthology of Russian Verse, 1812–1960*, p. 194.
6 Woroszyski, op. cit., p. 386.
7 De Graaff, op. cit., p. 35.
8 Yarmolinsky, op. cit., p. 195.

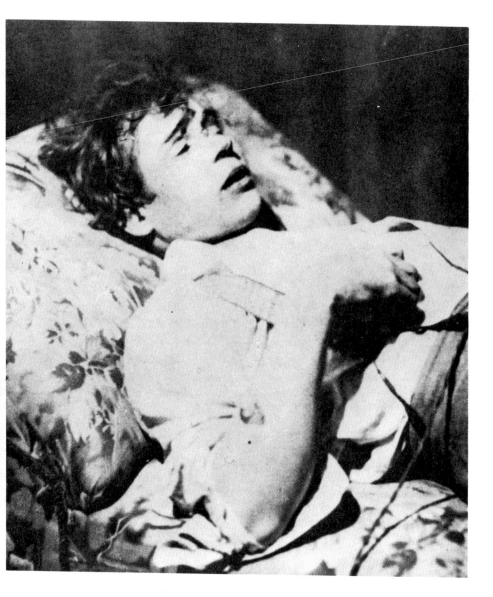

Esenin a few hours after his death

9 McVay, op. cit., p. 113.
10 De Graaff, op. cit., p. 80.
11 Ibid., p. 35.
12 Ibid., pp. 82–83.
13 Woroszyski, op. cit., p. 389.
14 De Graaff, op. cit., p. 125.
15 Woroszyski, op. cit., p. 393.
16 De Graaff, op. cit., p. 147.
17 Ibid.
18 Bowra, *A Second Book of Russian Verse*, p. 137.
19 Woroszyski, op. cit., p. 398.

Sources

Bowra, C. M., ed. *A Second Book of Russian Verse*. London: Macmillan & Co., 1948.

De Graaff, Frances. *Sergej Esenin, A Biographical Sketch*. The Hague: Mouton & Co., 1966.

McVay, Gordon. *Esenin: A Life*. Ann Arbor: Ardis, 1976.

Ponomareff, Constantin V. *Sergey Esenin*. Boston: Twayne Publishers, 1978.

Woroszyski, Wiktor. *The Life of Mayakovsky*. Translated by Boleslaw Taborski. New York: The Orion Press, 1970.

Yarmolinsky, Avrahm, ed. *An Anthology of Russian Verse, 1812–1960*. New York: Anchor Books, 1962.

F. SCOTT FITZGERALD
1896-1940

He had come a long way to this blue lawn; and his dream must have seemed so close that he could hardly fail to grasp it. He did not know that it was already behind him, somewhere back in that vast obscurity beyond the city, where the dark fields of the republic roll on under the night.[1]

F. SCOTT FITZGERALD. American novelist and short story writer. He is placed high on the list of twentieth-century American writers. He was both star of and spokesman for the decade he called the "Jazz Age," the 1920s, "the greatest, and gaudiest spree in history," which saw "a whole race going hedonistic, deciding on pleasure." Like the age, he flourished in its exuberant abandon, participating in its madnesses and excesses and transforming its rites and passages into a successful literary career. At twenty-three, he was a best-selling author (*This Side of Paradise*). His popular short stories as well as his much publicized life with his wife, Zelda, made him the darling of college students and flappers to whom he was "a sort of oracle." That age in which he flourished, however, took him with it when it crashed.

> If personality is an unbroken series of successful gestures, then there was something gorgeous about him, some heightened sensitivity to the promises of life, as if he were related to one of those intricate machines that register earthquakes ten thousand miles away. This responsiveness had nothing to do with that flabby impressionability which is dignified under the name of the "creative temperament"—it was an extraordinary gift for hope, a romantic readiness.[2]

Francis Scott Key Fitzgerald was born on September 24, 1896, in St. Paul, Minnesota. His father, Edward Fitzgerald, scion of an aristocratic Southern family, was elegant, ineffectual, of "tired stock," a failure. His mother, Mollie McQuillan, was the daughter of a wealthy Irish Catholic businessman. She was gauche, practical, and not very pretty. Scott Fitzgerald, their only son, arrived in the world shortly after an epidemic claimed his two sisters. Annabel, his baby sister and only sibling, arrived in 1901.

> To John O'Hara:
> I am half black Irish and half old American stock with the usual exaggerated ancestral pretensions. The black Irish half of the family had the money and looked down upon the Maryland side of the family who had . . . that . . . certain series of reticences and obligations that go under the poor old shattered word "breeding.". . . So being born in that atmosphere of crack, wisecrack and countercrack I developed a two-cylinder inferiority complex. . . . I spent my youth in alternatively crawling in front of the kitchen maids and insulting the great.[3]

Fitzgerald's early childhood years were spent in Syracuse and Buffalo, New York, until 1908, when his father lost his job as salesman at Procter and Gamble. The family returned to St. Paul and the McQuillan fold. There they lived on Mollie McQuillan's inheritance in a house at the edge of the fashionable Summit Avenue community. Fitzgerald attended private Catholic schools in St. Paul and in New Jersey. He began to write, his stories and poems appearing in the school paper; he also played football, which was a better way to become a hero, despite his smallish build. He believed himself to be "marked for glory," no matter how he would make his mark in life.

> Andrew Turnbull (biographer):
> What he saw in the mirror was cause for hope. Handsome, pert, fresh, blond, he looked—as someone said at the time—like a jonquil. He parted his hair in the middle . . . and though he slicked it down for formal occasions, it was usually

windblown from his energetic life. His pale, clear skin was
the kind that grows rosy with cold or exertion.[4]

Fitzgerald entered Princeton University in September, 1913.
Although a poor student, he distinguished himself as a writer of
humorous pieces published in the *Tiger* and as lyricist for the musical
productions of the Triangle Club. Popular, he was admitted to the
prestigious and exclusive Cottage Club. In his junior year, Fitzgerald
was placed on academic probation. As a result, he was ineligible for
any extracurricular activities including performing in Triangle Club
productions, a bitter disappointment to the promising young writer.
In November, 1915, he fell ill with malaria (later discovered to have
been TB) and dropped out for the rest of the year.

At Princeton he met two young men who would be important
friends and influences in his early writing career: John Peale Bishop
and Edmund Wilson; he had his first serious love affair, with Gin-
erva King, a brunette beauty, and daughter of a wealthy Chicago
businessman; he also began to drink, often to the extent of passing out.

Drunk at 20, wrecked at 30, dead at 40.
Drunk at 21, human at 31, mellow at 41, dead at 51.[5]

In November, 1917, the Army called and Fitzgerald reported
for training at Fort Leavenworth, Kansas. Although he did not take
the Army very seriously, he hoped to get into the war. In the meantime, he took his writing ambition seriously, working on a novel on
weekends which he mailed to Shane Leslie, a young Irish author
Fitzgerald had met at the Newman School in New Jersey. The novel,
entitled *The Romantic Egoist,* was an autobiographical account
about himself, his friends, and his life at Princeton. Leslie sent it to
Scribner's, who eventually rejected it in both the original and revised
form.

Fitzgerald's regiment had by now moved to Camp Sheridan near
Montgomery, Alabama. Here, at a country club dance, he met Zelda
Sayre. The daughter of a judge, the youngest child, she was a spoiled
Southern beauty with a wild streak that made her extremely enticing.
They fell in love and became engaged. Fitzgerald wanted to marry

her but not until he was certain of his future as a successful writer. In February, 1919, discharged from the Army, Fitzgerald went to New York City to get a job on a newspaper and sell his short stories. He had arrived in "the land of ambition and success."

> Zelda Sayre:
>   Scott—there's nothing in all the world I want but you— and your precious love. All the material things are nothing. I'd just hate to live a sordid, colorless existence—because you'd soon love me less—and less. . . . I don't want to live—I want to love first, and live incidentally.
>   I want you to wear me, like a watch—charm or a button hole bouquet—to the world. And then, when we're alone, I want to help—to know that you can't do *anything* without me.[6]

Fitzgerald rented a room in Morningside Heights. Unable to get a job on a paper, he worked in the copywriting department of an ad agency for ninety dollars a month. He wrote short stories at night, submitted them to magazines, and collected rejection slips for his efforts. He pined for Zelda, who was not behaving like an engaged woman at home. As a result, Fitzgerald traveled to Montgomery for a confrontation which resulted in a broken engagement.

In 1919, after a three-week bender, he quit his job in New York and went home to write. Months later, he had rewritten and reworked *The Romantic Egoist*, which he sent off to Maxwell Perkins at Scribner's, with a new title, *This Side of Paradise*. Scribner's accepted the novel ten days later. Soon after, Zelda agreed to marry Fitzgerald. His dreams were coming true—he was twenty-three years old.

> The dream had been early realized and the realization carried with it a certain bonus and a certain burden. Premature success gives one an almost mystical conception of destiny as opposed to will power. . . . The man who arrives young believes that he exercises his will because his star is shining.[7]

This Side of Paradise was published on March 26, 1920. When Zelda and Scott were married in New York City on April 3, the novel was already in its second printing, the critics having praised it loudly and enthusiastically for its youthful exuberance. The couple, who would epitomize the decade of the twenties, honeymooned at the Biltmore Hotel, where they snacked on champagne and fresh spinach, cartwheeled down the halls, and dived in the fountain at the Plaza until their outrageous and disruptive antics and pranks caused them to be expelled. Their scenes provided welcome tidbits for gossip columns.

Scott Fitzgerald earned $18,850 from his book, stories, and picture rights during that first year. However, his life-style with Zelda, extravagant and careless, saw him begin the dangerous practice of having money advanced to him from Scribner's and from his agent, Harold Ober, to meet his expenses, which were always greater than his cash on hand. They always lived beyond their means and except for one brief spell, Fitzgerald would never be out of debt for the rest of his life.

> When bored we took our city with a Huysmans—like perversity. An afternoon alone in our "apartment" eating olive sandwiches and drinking a quart of Bushmill's whiskey . . . then out into the freshly bewitched city, through strange doors into strange apartments. . . . At last we were one with New York, pulling it after us through every portal. . . . I remember riding in a taxi one afternoon between very tall buildings under a mauve and rosy sky; I began to bawl because I had everything I wanted and knew I would never be so happy again.[8]

After spending a drink-soaked, gay party summer in a rented house in Westport, Connecticut, Scott and Zelda traveled in Europe for a few months before returning to St. Paul. Zelda was pregnant, Fitzgerald was working on a new novel, *The Beautiful and the Damned*, which was close to completion. Their only child, Frances Scott Fitzgerald, was born on October 26, 1921. The new novel was published in April, 1922. Eerily prescient of his own life to come, it told the story of a young and glamorous couple and their alcoholic fall from grace. Not as well received by the critics as *This Side of Paradise*, its sales did not match those of its predecessor.

In October, 1922, Scott and Zelda moved to a rented house in Great Neck Estates on Long Island. Although he began working on his third novel, the next months were largely spent entertaining or being entertained in an alcoholic haze and he made little progress. The schedule of their days included several hours for recovering from the hangover from the previous night's party. When necessary Fitzgerald would knock off short stories for badly needed money. (He was now being regularly published by *The Saturday Evening Post* and his price had gone from $30 to $1,500 per story; it would eventually rise to $3,500.)

> To Maxwell Perkins:
>
> It is only in the last four months that I've realized how much I've—well, almost *deteriorated* in the three years since I finished *Beautiful and Damned*. The last four months of course I've worked but in the two years . . . before that, I produced . . . an average of about *one hundred* words a day. If I'd spent this time reading or traveling or doing anything—even staying healthy—it'd be different but I spent it uselessly, neither in study nor in contemplation but only in drinking and raising hell generally.[9]

In April, 1924, Scott and Zelda left New York for Europe where they lived for the next two and a half years in Paris or on the Riviera in a spacious rented villa high above the Mediterranean. Soon after their arrival, Fitzgerald got back to writing. While he worked, Zelda had a brief affair with a French aviator until it was ended by Fitzgerald's discovery. This incident permanently scarred their marriage.

By October, Fitzgerald had largely completed his third novel, *The Great Gatsby*, which he considered his masterpiece, "a purely creative work," "a consciously artistic achievement." He had fervent hopes that it would sell 80,000 copies. The novel, published in April, 1925, received excellent reviews. In the eyes of the critics, Fitzgerald had matured into a full-blown artist. He received letters of praise from T. S. Eliot, Edith Wharton, and Gertrude Stein. Ironically, the sales of the novel were a great financial disappointment, only half that of his earlier books: about 22,000 copies were sold.

Fitzgerald, who had wanted to be "extravagantly admired again," returned to writing the short stories that were so easy to sell to *The Saturday Evening Post* for $2,500 apiece.

Gertrude Stein:

You write naturally in sentences and one can read all of them and that among other things is a comfort. You are creating the contemporary world much as Thackeray did in his *Pendennis* and *Vanity Fair* and this isn't a bad compliment. You make a modern world and a modern orgy strangely enough it was never done until you did it in *This Side of Paradise*. . . . This is as good a book and different and older and that is what one does, one does not get better but different and older and that is always a pleasure.[10]

Scott and Zelda Fitzgerald spent the summer of 1925 at Cap d'Antibes, a time of "1,000 parties and no work." They became close friends with Sara and Gerald Murphy, a wealthy American couple who were building a villa there. Fitzgerald had also met Ernest Hemingway, a young writer whom Fitzgerald helped in whatever ways he could, Hemingway becoming something of an idol to the older man. Hemingway told Fitzgerald that Zelda was crazy; Zelda thought Hemingway was a phony.

Throughout this year and the next the Fitzgeralds moved around —from the south of France to an apartment in Paris; they traveled in Italy, and returned to the Riviera. Zelda was frequently ill with various ailments such as appendicitis and chronic colitis. Fitzgerald, at work on his new novel, was often drunk, as was Zelda. They were both out of control and sometimes destructive.

Gerald Murphy:

[Zelda's] beauty was not legitimate at all. It was all in her eyes. They were strange eyes, brooding but not sad, severe, almost masculine in their directness. She possessed an astounding gaze. . . . If she looked like anything it was an American Indian. . . . You know in their early days they

Fitzgerald with Zelda and their daughter, Scottie, 1926

were two beauties . . . Scott's head was so fine, really unbelievably handsome. They were the flawless people.[11]

The Fitzgeralds returned to the U. S. in 1927. In need of money as usual, Fitzgerald spent two months in Hollywood on a screenwriting venture: his script was rejected. In March, 1927, they rented a palatial house in Wilmington, Delaware, where Fitzgerald hoped to finish his novel. Instead, they hosted drunken weekend parties to which they would import their New York friends. Zelda began to take dancing lessons in Philadelphia. Fitzgerald began to drink while he was working and wasn't making headway. They began to clash.

The Fitzgeralds returned to Europe and the Riviera in the summer of 1929, and were living in Paris when the stock market crashed. Zelda had her first breakdown in April, 1930, and again in May when she was sent to a sanitorium in Switzerland and diagnosed as schizophrenic. Fitzgerald put his novel aside and churned out short stories to support her hospitalization. She was released in September, 1931, and Fitzgerald brought her back to the U. S. and Montgomery. In October, 1931, he made a second trip to Hollywood to work on a screenplay—also rejected—although he was paid $1,200 a week for five weeks.

> To Scottie Fitzgerald (daughter):
> I was a man divided—she wanted me to work too much for *her* and not enough for my dream. She realized too late that work was dignity, and the only dignity.[12]

Zelda had another breakdown in January, 1932, and was hospitalized at Phipps Clinic in Baltimore. In May, Fitzgerald rented a house, La Paix, in the countryside and Zelda was well enough to join him there. He got back to work on his novel, but there was a great deal of tension between Fitzgerald and Zelda. In February, 1934, she returned to Phipps.

> Arthur Mizener (biographer):
> In June, Zelda accidentally set La Paix on fire . . . and before the fire was under control the third floor had burned

out. . . . He would never have the house repaired because, he said, he could not endure the noise, and the macabre disorder of the place with its burnt-out and blackened upper story was a kind of symbol of the increased disarray of his own life.[13]

Tender Is the Night, Fitzgerald's fourth novel, which he had begun writing nine years before, was finally published by Scribner's in April, 1934. It concerns the relationship between a psychiatrist and one of his patients, a wealthy woman, whom he marries. The novel was not well received: even Fitzgerald's close friends were critical of the book (later, it came to be considered one of his most interesting works) and it sold only 13,000 copies. Fitzgerald was sick from drink and deeply in debt with Zelda hospitalized and a young daughter growing up and requiring schooling.

Ernest Hemingway:
You see, Bo, you're not a tragic character. Neither am I. All we are is writers and what we should do is write.[14]

Nineteen thirty-six was Fitzgerald's lowest year since 1926. He sold only four stories and eight *Esquire* pieces, and he had been ill with turberculosis and alcoholism. He was in debt to both his agent and his publisher.

In 1937, Harold Ober got him a six-month contract as a scriptwriter with MGM for $1,000 a week. After moving to Hollywood, he met Sheilah Graham, Hollywood columnist, with whom he fell in love. She would be his companion until his death.

While the scriptwriting proved to be demoralizing, Fitzgerald persevered at it for two years and paid off some of his debts. In 1939, a drinking binge landed him in the hospital. He only curtailed his drinking when Sheilah Graham threatened to leave him.

The horror has come now like a storm—what if this night prefigured the night after death—what if all thereafter was an eternal quivering on the edge of an abyss, with everything base and vicious in oneself urging one forward and the baseness and viciousness of the world just ahead. No choice, no road, no hope—only the endless repetition of the sordid and the semitragic.[15]

In a final year and a half of sobriety, although worn out and aged from the effects of his alcoholism and tuberculosis, Fitzgerald set to work on a novel about the Hollywood movie industry: *The Last Tycoon*. In November, 1940, he had a cardiac spasm. On December 21, while reading the *Princeton Alumni Weekly* in the apartment he shared with Sheilah Graham, he dropped dead of a heart attack. He was forty-four years old.

All of Fitzgerald's novels were out of print when he died. *The Last Tycoon*, unfinished, was published a year later.

John Dos Passos:
The fact that at the end of a life of brilliant worldly successes and crushing disasters Scott Fitzgerald was engaged so ably in a work of such importance proves him to have been the first-rate novelist his friends believed him to be.[16]

Notes

1 Fitzgerald, *The Great Gatsby*, p. 182.
2 Ibid., p. 2.
3 Turnbull, *The Letters of F. Scott Fitzgerald*, p. 503.
4 Turnbull, *Scott Fitzgerald*, p. 48.
5 Fitzgerald, "The Note-Books," *The Crack-Up*, p. 196.
6 Milford, *Zelda*, p. 41.
7 Fitzgerald, "Early Success," *The Crack-Up*, p. 89.
8 Fitzgerald, "My Lost City," *The Crack-Up*, pp. 28–29.
9 Turnbull, *Letters*, pp. 162–63.
10 Fitzgerald, *The Crack-Up*, p. 308.
11 Milford, op. cit., p. 124.
12 Turnbull, *Letters*, p. 33.
13 Mizener, *The Far Side of Paradise*, p. 230.
14 Ibid., p. 239.
15 Fitzgerald, "Sleeping and Waking," *The Crack-Up*, p. 67.
16 Fitzgerald, *The Crack-Up*, p. 343.

Sources

Fitzgerald, F. Scott. *The Beautiful and the Damned.* New York: Charles Scribner's Sons, 1950.

———. *The Crack-Up.* New York: New Directions, 1956.

———. *The Great Gatsby.* New York: Charles Scribner's Sons, 1953.

———. *The Last Tycoon.* New York: Charles Scribner's Sons, 1941.

———. *Tender Is the Night.* New York: Bantam Books, 1951.

———. *This Side of Paradise.* New York: Charles Scribner's Sons, 1948.

Milford, Nancy. *Zelda.* New York: Harper & Row, 1970.

Mizener, Arthur. *The Far Side of Paradise.* Boston: Houghton Mifflin Co., 1951.

Turnbull, Andrew. *Scott Fitzgerald.* New York: Charles Scribner's Sons, 1962.

———, ed. *The Letters of F. Scott Fitzgerald.* New York: Charles Scribner's Sons, 1963.

JUDY GARLAND
1922-1969

How strange when an illusion dies
It's as though you've lost a child
Whom you've cherished and protected
Against the wilds of the storms and hurts
In this frightening world.[1]

JUDY GARLAND. American singer and film actress. "Born in a trunk," she became a teenage movie star and eventually a legend in her own time. Called a "Phoenix" during the last decade of her life, she came back, again and again, to give memorable and record-breaking performances at the Palladium and Carnegie Hall. Garland is considered one of the greatest live entertainers the show business world has ever seen.

Her public success was subtly connected with the components of her unhappy personal life: severe drug and alcohol abuse, divorces, financial problems, and suicide attempts. She became a symbol of bravery and survival. Even in her last appearances, Garland, gaunt and frail, was irresistible to her fans.

> Ray Bolger (actor):
> Judy Garland never found that land, never really heard that lullaby, never saw a rainbow that wasn't manufactured in a studio. Judy's world was the Wicked Witch's World. Bubble, bubble, toil and trouble. Oh yes, she had her triumphs. But, while she triumphed on the stage, the pot was boiling for Judy. She never had a chance.[2]

Judy Garland was born Frances Ethel Gumm on June 10, 1922, in Grand Rapids, Minnesota. She was the third child, third girl, of Frank and Ethel Gumm, a vaudeville team who ran the New Grand, the only theater in the small town. As "Baby Gumm," she made her theatrical debut three years later at the New Grand: between movie showings, she sang "Jingle Bells" and danced with her sisters, Virginia and Mary Jane. She was a precocious performer with a big voice and an obvious talent; she charmed and delighted the audience.

> My job is entertaining. Fortunately I'm mad about an audience. I really truly appreciate anyone taking time out and spending money to hear me sing. And, believe me, I love singing for them. No matter how many people hurt me, when that orchestra starts playing . . . I sing! [3]

In 1927, the Gumms moved to Lancaster, California, north of Los Angeles. Once again, Frank Gumm took over the only theater in town. Frances and her sisters appeared regularly there. As a juvenile trio, they also made frequent radio broadcasts and appeared in stage extravaganzas in Los Angeles. Baby Gumm's reputation grew and she began making solo appearances, including several at the Coconut Grove in 1932 at the age of ten.

> You stand there in the wings . . . and sometimes you want to yell because the band sounds so good. Then you walk out and if it's a really great audience, a very strange set of emotions can come over you. You don't know what to do. It's a combination of feeling like Queen Victoria and an absolute ass. [4]

In 1933, Ethel Gumm took Frances and Virginia to live in Los Angeles, enrolling them in a school for theatrical children. Frank Gumm remained in Lancaster with Mary Jane. The Gumms' marriage was in trouble, possibly due to Frank's apparent bisexuality. Frances was close to her father, and the separation made her unhappy.

The following summer Ethel and her three daughters embarked on a long road tour of the States. During a booking at the Oriental Theater in Chicago, George Jessel, the M. C., suggested that the

Gumm sisters change their name to the "Garland Sisters." Soon after, the Garland Sisters were signed by the William Morris Agency and "Baby Gumm" became "Judy Garland."

> *Variety,* November 4, 1934:
> Hardly a new act, this trio of youngsters has been kicking around the coast for two years, but has just found itself. As a trio it means nothing, but with the youngest . . . featured, it hops into class entertainment . . . the girl is a combination of Helen Morgan and Fuzzy Knight. Possessing a voice that, without a PA system, is audible throughout a house as large as the Chinese, she handles ballads like a veteran and gets every note and word over with a personality that hits audiences . . . she has never failed to stop the show.[5]

Family vaudeville life ended for Judy Garland in the fall of 1935 when she auditioned for Louis B. Mayer, President of MGM. She sang "Zing Went the Strings of My Heart," and she had a screen test. Garland, at thirteen, was signed up as a contract player; her starting salary was $100 a week. A month later, Frank Gumm died suddenly.

The MGM lot became Judy Garland's universe. It provided her with schooling, and dancing and singing lessons; there she found her friends and boyfriends and went to parties and on chaperoned dates. She was a plump teenager and so she was put on a diet and sent to exercise classes. In addition she was given diet pills, the dangers of amphetamine addiction then unknown. From the studio's standpoint it was a practical move. Louis Mayer, who referred to her as "fat one," and "hunchback," wanted to get his money's worth out of the young player.

> *Chicago Sun Times:*
> Anslinger said Judy told him she was taking amphetamines (pep pills) when she got out of bed in the morning, minor stimulants during the day, a shot of morphine before fulfilling nighttime engagements, and finally, a sleeping pill to help her sleep.[6]

Although she had appeared in two movies—*Every Sunday* with Deanna Durbin, and *Pigskin Parade* (for which she was loaned out to Twentieth Century–Fox) her first significant part was playing Sophie Tucker's daughter in *Broadway Melody of 1938*, in which she sang "Dear Mr. Gable." Her talent and commercial appeal were acknowledged by enthusiastic reviews. MGM went ahead full throttle with their new singing sensation. During her fifteen years with the studio, she would make thirty movies.

After a sequence of Andy Hardy movies (*Thoroughbreds Don't Cry; Love Finds Andy Hardy; Babes in Arms*) that paired her with Mickey Rooney, Garland was lifted by a tornado that spun her into another realm. Her hair dyed red, her breasts flattened, caps on her front teeth, her nose reshaped by rubber discs, her barely five-foot frame costumed in a blue gingham dress, sixteen-year-old Judy Garland became Dorothy in *The Wizard of Oz*, singing and dancing down the Yellow Brick Road surrounded by Munchkins. When the picture was released in the summer of 1939, Judy Garland landed in stardom—so heavily, in fact, that she would never leave Dorothy behind. Not a glamour-girl type, Garland would in fact be the eternally adolescent Dorothy in the minds of her fans. Just before her death, she would tell an audience that she had performed "Over the Rainbow" 12,380 times.

> I was always lonesome. The only time I felt accepted or wanted was when I was onstage performing. I guess the stage was my only friend, the only place where I could feel comfortable. It was the one place where I felt equal and safe.[7]

With the grand success of *The Wizard of Oz*, Garland's career accelerated and became more demanding. Along with an increase in her work schedule, and the pressure, came an increase in her need for drugs, the pills that enabled her to keep up with it all: to awake at dawn and to sleep at night. Insomnia was a chronic problem.

In 1940, Garland was awarded a special Oscar for *The Wizard of Oz*. She was now earning $2,000 a week at MGM, and the movie magazines were filled with stories about the eighteen-year-old girl and her dates with Jackie Cooper and Robert Stack.

In 1941, she eloped with a thirty-one-year-old musician, David Rose. The impulsive marriage was short-lived, and she was separated from Rose a year and a half later. In the meantime, she starred in the musical *Meet Me in St. Louis,* which was one of her best films, as well as the beginning of her relationship with Vincente Minnelli, the director. Garland and Minnelli were married in 1945, and a year later, Liza Minnelli was born.

Although Garland had displayed signs of temperamental behavior at the studio, sometimes showing up late, sometimes not showing up at all, her conduct seemed to be out of control when she was working on *The Pirate,* which Minnelli was directing. Although she had made a pact with Minnelli to stay off pills, she hadn't been able to keep it. Her condition became serious enough for her to be admitted to a sanitorium in Los Angeles and then sent to the Riggs Foundation in Massachusetts for treatment.

> Someone came to interview me this afternoon and said that people are saying I hit the bottle. Now, what does that mean —hit the bottle? Does it literally mean smacking the bottle? Or does it mean I like to drink? I told the girl that I like to drink iced tea, like to drink soup, like to drink vodka and tonic. And, anyway, what kind of question is that? [8]

After recovering, Garland went back to the studio and made *Easter Parade* with Fred Astaire. However, in her next picture, *The Barkleys of Broadway,* she was habitually late on the set and was eventually replaced. In May, 1949, she was suspended by MGM during the filming of *Annie Get Your Gun.* She was admitted to a Boston hospital where she was detoxified of the amphetamines and barbiturates that were poisoning her system. She returned to work in *Summer Stock.* Overweight, she had been instructed by the studio to lose fifteen pounds, and began dieting with the help of pills. The film was completed with a great deal of trouble, mostly caused by Garland's temperamental behavior. Ironically, MGM tapped her to star in *Royal Wedding* soon after, despite evidence that she was in no condition to work.

On June 17, 1950, she was suspended from the film, the last time she would be so dismissed. Her life at MGM had ended after sixteen

Billie Burke as the Good Witch and Judy Garland as Dorothy,
The Wizard of Oz, 1939

years. She had earned millions of dollars for the studio, but she was broke. Three days later newspaper headlines announced that Judy Garland had tried to commit suicide: she had slashed her neck with a piece of glass, but the wound was superficial. MGM released her from her contract. At the same time, her marriage to Minnelli ended.

> Louis B. Mayer:
> I couldn't have done more for her if she had been my own daughter.[9]

Soon she was paired with Sidney Luft, a producer, who would also serve as her manager and advisor. With his encouragement, she made her first personal appearance as a free agent in a stage show at the Palladium in London in 1951. She was a sensation and played to a full house for four weeks. Next came an engagement at the RKO-Palace Theater in New York where Garland opened on October 16, 1951. By the time the show closed on February 24, 1952, an all-time-long-run record of nineteen weeks had been set. Her dressing room was affixed with a gold plaque commemorating the event. Garland was making her "comeback."

> Vincente Minnelli:
> If she could never belong to one man, Judy would always belong to the people. She might exasperate them or try their patience, but she would remain a national addiction.[10]

Garland and Luft were married in 1952 and their first child, Lorna Luft, was born in December. Judy Garland's mother died suddenly in January, 1953, and her death was the cause of speculation in the press concerning her relationship to her famous daughter: had Ethel Gumm been an evil stage mother? did Judy Garland abandon her mother's support, forcing her to earn a living working in a factory? Thus, the Garland legend was slowly being created.

After four years away from films, in 1953 Garland made *A Star Is Born* for Warner Brothers, with her husband as producer. As Esther Blodgett, the unknown singer who rises to fame, Garland, under the direction of George Cukor, was superb. Both she and

James Mason, who played her alcoholic husband, were nominated for Academy Awards in 1954. But Garland, who had just given birth to Joseph Luft, lost the Oscar to Grace Kelly for *Country Girl.*

> George Cukor:
> Toward the end of shooting we had to do a scene when she's in a state of total depression after her husband's suicide. . . . We'd talked about the scene only a little, but we both had a general idea of what it should be. The basic note was her melancholia, her state of total depression. Just before the take I said to her very quietly, "You know what this is about. You really know about this." She gave me a look. . . . That was all. We did a take. . . . She loses her head. She gets up and screams like somebody out of control, maniacal and terrifying! She had no concern with what she looked like, she went much further than I expected, and I thought it was great.[11]

Garland did a television special in 1955 and, for the next few years, continued to appear around the country in live performances. It was soon evident that she was not in good health—she was approaching obesity and she appeared to be shaky. Audiences and critics received her less kindly than in the past.

> Kenneth Tynan (critic):
> Miss Garland is a squat woman now, and it takes some effort of puckering and wrinkling for her face to achieve the hopeful, trusting smile that first transfixed us. But she can still do it, because she incarnates a dream. She embodies the persistence of youth so completely that we forbid her to develop, and permit her no maturity. Even in middle age, she must continue to sing about adolescence and all the pain and nostalgia that go with it.[12]

Drug abuse, once again, resulted in her hospitalization in New York, followed by a period of recuperation. To test her wings she returned to the Palladium in London. And, on April 23, 1961, Judy Garland came back again, this time to Carnegie Hall. A magnificent one-night-stand performance was the first stop on a tour of sixteen cities.

Garland received another Academy Award nomination for the part of Irene Hoffman in *Judgment at Nuremberg*, a part she had been grateful to get. Her marriage with Sid Luft broke up, ending in divorce and a custody fight over the children. She hosted "The Judy Garland Show" on CBS in 1963, which was a strain on her as well as a commercial failure. She was barely holding herself together.

> Let me tell you, legends are all very well if you've got some-one around who loves you, some man who's not afraid to be in love with Judy Garland!
> I mean I'm not in the munitions business! Why should I always be rejected? All right, so I'm Judy Garland. But I've been Judy Garland forever.[13]

In the last years of her life, Garland experienced few highs and many lows, including a disastrous trip to Australia with a new beau, Mark Herron, a young actor. She left the stage after a concert in Melbourne to a chorus of boos: her voice had given out. She eventually landed in a Hong Kong hospital. Then she married Mark Herron: the marriage lasted six months.

She was hired and then fired from the movie *Valley of the Dolls* because of her erratic behavior. She returned to the Palace once more in August, 1967, for a four-week run.

> William Goldman:
> They had been after her flesh for a long while, but it is only now, after she is done and it is ended, that she allowed them contact. Just the barest gaze. Her finger tips to theirs as she moved, as always, jerkily, parallel to the footlights, first right to left, then back . . . the din, already painful, some-how went up a notch, now almost completely covering the noise from the pit where the band went wearily on with "Over the Rainbow," over and over, "Over the Rainbow" over again.[14]

Garland in concert, c. 1964

In May, 1968, Judy Garland was thrown out of her St. Moritz hotel room for failure to pay a $1,800 bill. Ex-husband Sid Luft explained to the press that she was heavily in debt and that the government was collecting back taxes. In 1969, looking an ancient forty-seven years old, she married a much younger man, Mickey Deans, a restaurant manager. She had just finished a run at the Talk of the Town in London. Despite her health, now visibly broken, she made a brief concert tour of Scandinavia.

Judy Garland died on June 22, 1969. She was discovered by Mickey Deans locked in the bathroom of their cottage on Cadogan Lane in London. The coroner ruled her death accidental, the result of a barbiturate overdose.

> Ray Bolger:
> Judy Garland died. Suicide? *No!* She just *wore out!* W-o-r-e o-u-t.[15]

Notes

1 Edwards, *Judy Garland*, p. 310.

2 Ray Bolger, "Judy Garland," *Cue*, March 28, 1970, p. 55.

3 John Gruen, *Close Up*, New York: The Viking Press, 1968, p. 43.

4 Shana Alexander, "Judy's New Rainbow," *Life*, June 2, 1961, p. 108.

5 *Variety*, November 4, 1934, p. 13.

6 Art Petaque, "Ex-Narcotic Chief Tried to Get Judy Off Drugs," *Chicago Sun Times*.

7 Edwards, op. cit., p. 22.

8 Gruen, op. cit., pp. 41–42.

9 Edwards, op. cit., p. 132.

10 Vincente Minnelli, *I Remember It Well*, New York: Doubleday & Co., 1974, p. 250.

11 Gavin Lambert, *On Cukor*, New York: G. P. Putnam's Sons, 1972, p. 125.

12 Kenneth Tynan, *New Yorker*, May 23, 1959, p. 172.

13 Gruen, op. cit., p. 43.

14 William Goldman, *The Season*, New York: Harcourt, Brace & World, 1968, p. 3.

15 Bolger, op. cit., p. 55.

Sources

Edwards, Anne. *Judy Garland*. New York: Pocket Books, 1975.

Finch, Christopher. *Rainbow: The Stormy Life of Judy Garland*. New York: Ballantine Books, 1975.

Frank, Gerold. *Judy*. New York: Dell Publishing Co., 1976.

BILLIE HOLIDAY
1915-1959

When I die people can maybe cry for me because
they'll know they're going to start me off in hell
and move me from bad to worse.[1]

BILLIE HOLIDAY. American singer. Called the greatest jazz vocalist who ever lived, she was a pioneer in the field; there is hardly a jazz musician or vocalist who has not been influenced by her: Sarah Vaughan, Ella Fitzgerald, Cleo Laine, Lena Horne, to name a few. Although she received praise and laudatory reviews, she never had a hit record or the mass popularity that she craved while she lived.

She was called "Lady Day" and, at her peak, she was a robust beauty: golden brown skin, full red mouth, a white gardenia in her hair, and a voice she played like a horn, always with her unique timing and phrasing. She was also temperamental, unreliable, insecure. She suffered from stage fright, eased only by heroin, to which she became addicted, or alcohol. She was an outlaw of sorts, and a victim: persecuted, framed, and manipulated.

> I knew that nobody understood my singing. They didn't like me; they didn't hate me either. They just didn't have any enthusiasm either way, like they hadn't been told by anybody yet whether I was good or bad. And when you're doing something new, you got to have somebody tell people.[2]

Before she became Billie Holiday, she was Eleanora Fagan, born on April 7, 1915, in East Baltimore, Maryland. In her autobiography, she says that her mother, Sadie Fagan, was thirteen and scrubbing floors in a hospital; her father, Clarence Holiday, was fifteen and a musician. Her grandfather was half Irish, both son and slave of a plantation owner.

The family did not hold together, scattering for survival. She was left with her grandparents in Baltimore while her mother went up North to work as a maid and her father went on the road, playing guitar with Fletcher Henderson's Band.

> When I was thirteen I got real evil one time and set in my ways. I just plain decided one day I wasn't going to do anything or say anything unless I meant it. Not "Please, sir." Not "Thank you, ma'am." Nothing. Unless I meant it.[3]

By the time she left Baltimore to go up North to join her mother she had heard her first jazz records—Louis Armstrong and Bessie Smith—on a victrola in the front parlor of a neighborhood whorehouse. She had changed her name to "Billie Holiday," after her movie idol, Billie Dove. And she had been locked up in a Catholic institution for wayward girls after a neighbor tried to rape her.

> According to the judge, I was supposed to stay there until I was dead or twenty-one. But they finally got me out.[4]

Up North, Billie worked as a maid, and spent four months on New York's Welfare Island for prostitution before she discovered that she could earn money doing something she had been doing all her life and enjoyed: singing in the supper clubs and late-night spots that made 133rd Street in Harlem the center of jazz. She landed her first paying job at a club called Pod and Jerry's.

> I asked him to play "Trav'lin All Alone." That came closer than anything to the way I felt. And some part of it must have come across. The whole joint quieted down. If someone had dropped a pin, it would have sounded like a bomb. When I finished, everybody in the joint was crying in their beer, and I picked thirty-eight bucks up off the floor.[5]

Holiday was discovered by John Hammond, a young jazz writer and producer, who first heard her sing at Monette's Supper Club on 133rd Street in Harlem. Hammond became a key figure in her career: he arranged for her to make her first recordings with Benny Goodman's Band. ("I got thirty-five bucks for the sessions but nothing happened with the record." [6]) Later, Hammond got her together with pianist Teddy Wilson. The recordings Holiday made with Wilson—"What a Little Moonlight Can Do" and "I Wished on the Moon" among others—would become classics. Enthusiastically received, especially in England, they laid the groundwork for her growing reputation. In April, 1935, Holiday made her debut on Amateur Night at the Apollo Theater in Harlem and was so well received that she was asked to return in August.

> If you find a tune and it's got something to do with you, you don't have to evolve anything. You just feel it, and when you sing it other people can feel something too. With me, it's got nothing to do with working or arranging or rehearsing. Give me a song I can feel, and it's never work. There are a few songs I feel so much I can't stand to sing them, but that's something else again. [7]

Count Basie's Band arrived in New York City late in 1936, and one of its members, Lester Young, a tenor-saxophone player, met up with Billie Holiday at a recording session. Holiday admired Young's playing and he admired her singing; together, their musical styles and needs meshed. They became very close friends (although never more than that) and Young eventually moved in with Holiday and her mother in their Harlem apartment. Lester nicknamed her "Lady Day"; her mother Sadie became "Duchess." Holiday named him "Prez"—he was to her "the top man."

In 1937, Holiday went on the road with Count Basie and his band, touring the country in the Blue Goose Bus, and making her debut in Philadelphia singing "I Can't Get Started with You." Excited at first, she soon became disenchanted with the one-night stands and the discomfort of bus travel. Less than a year later, Holiday was fired.

Willard Alexander (executive, MCA):

It was John Hammond who got Billie the job with Count Basie, and he was responsible for Basie keeping her. In fact, if it hadn't been for John Hammond, Billie would have been through six months sooner. . . . The reason for her dismissal was strictly one of deportment, which was unsatisfactory, and a distinctly wrong attitude toward her work. Billie sang fine when she felt like it. We just couldn't count on her for a consistent performance.[8]

Soon afterward, she went on the road again with "sixteen white cats, Artie Shaw and his Rolls Royce—and the hills were full of white crackers."[9] She stayed with Shaw's band for more than a year although at the time a black female singer with an all-white band was daring and unconventional, and there were racial incidents in the South. She left Shaw's band, however, because of an incident that took place in New York City: the band was engaged to play at the Lincoln Hotel, and the management forced Holiday to use the back door and instructed her not to mingle with the guests.

The next thing I knew, I was singing less and less. Some nights I'd only be on for one song all night—and that would be before or after the band had been on the air.

Finally when they cut me off the air completely, I said to hell with it. I just fired myself.[10]

In 1939, Holiday began a very successful run at the Café Society, a new club on Sheridan Square, New York City. Here she came into her own, singing "Strange Fruit" for the first time, the song written by poet Lewis Allen about lynching. It became her personal song of protest. Holiday recorded it soon after for a small jazz label and it became her best-selling record.

John Chilton (biographer):

Its release gained enormous publicity for Billie, but despite the wide press coverage she still felt that she was no nearer to receiving acceptance from the general public . . . she felt that she was as far as ever from the glamorous fame for which she was striving.[11]

In 1942, despite the warnings of her mother and her agent, Holiday eloped with Jimmy Monroe, the brother of a club owner and "the most beautiful man" she had seen in a long time. Holiday had a weakness for beautiful men. Monroe, already once married, had a reputation for spending time with white women. He was not the ideal match for Holiday, and their marriage barely got off the ground. It was during this time that she met another partner—heroin. Holiday, who had always enjoyed marijuana and could drink like one of the boys, nurtured a drug habit that slowly began to take its physical toll, seriously affecting her career, as well as swallowing up her earnings. At first, however, she performed superbly. Like alcohol, the drug helped her to conquer her stage fright.

> I had the white gowns and the white shoes. And every night they'd bring me the white gardenias and the white junk.[12]

By 1947, her drug habit had become a serious problem. Holiday and her manager, Joe Glaser, agreed that it was time for her to take a "cure." She spent three weeks in an expensive New York clinic, and temporarily freed herself of the habit. This effort, however, resulted in bringing her drug problems to the attention of the FBI and the New York Police Narcotics Squad, who began to look into her affairs with great interest. After a Philadelphia engagement, Holiday was trailed by detectives to New York where she was arrested for illegal drug possession. She pleaded guilty at her trial and was sentenced to "a year and a day" in the Federal Reformatory for Women in West Virginia.

> All I know is that when I was on nobody bothered me; no law, no cops, no federal agents. And nobody tailed me. I didn't get heated up until I made an honest-to-God sincere effort to kick. Whoever did that to me changed the whole course of my life. I'll never forgive them.[13]

Holiday served nine months of her sentence. When she was

paroled she was free of drugs, she had gained twenty badly needed pounds, and she looked once again like the beautiful Lady Day. Ten days after her release, on March 27, 1948, she made a spectacular comeback at a midnight concert at Carnegie Hall. The audience demanded six encores. Everything was like it had been, except for one difference—she could sing her heart out at Carnegie Hall, but because of her narcotics conviction a New York law prohibited her from singing in any New York City establishment that served liquor. Without a cabaret card the small, intimate nightclubs where she had blossomed were closed to her. Holiday appealed the ruling but with no success.

> I could play in theaters and sing to an audience of kids in their teens who couldn't get in any bar. I could appear on radio or TV. I could appear in concerts at Town Hall or Carnegie Hall. That was O.K. But if I opened my mouth in the crummiest bar in town, I was violating the law.[14]

John Levy, the manager of the Ebony Club on Broadway, arranged for her to work there undisturbed. Soon, Holiday had become romantically involved with Levy, and, as she was prone to do with the men in her life, entrusted him with her personal management and the management of her money. Holiday performed that year as part of the stage show at the Strand, a Broadway theater. She also sang in nightclubs outside New York from coast to coast.

In January, 1949, while she and Levy were in San Francisco for several club engagements, the hotel room in which they were staying was raided by narcotics agents, and a small amount of opium discovered in Holiday's possession. She was charged with narcotics possession and released on bail in time to fulfill an engagement at the Café Society in the Fillmore district of San Francisco. The story of her arrest was carried in the papers and drew SRO audiences to hear her sing. In May, 1949, Holiday was tried and found innocent; the implication of the court's findings was that she had been framed. Her relationship with Levy ended soon after.

The next man in her life was Louis McKay, whom she had known since her early days in Harlem. She "gave herself over" to him and, like Levy, he became her manager and handled her money affairs. Their relationship was turbulent, but McKay was successful at managing Holiday's career.

In the early fifties Holiday was singing to capacity crowds and record-breaking audiences in America and Europe. In spite of her exile from New York clubs, she was making more money than ever before in concert, and she was more in demand than ever. Her old magic seemed to be working. Jazz concerts and festivals, as well as nightclubs and television specials, gave her top billing.

> The stuff they wrote about me in Europe made me feel alive. Over here some damn body is always trying to embalm me. I'm always making a comeback, but nobody ever tells me where I've been.[15]

In February, 1956, while in Philadelphia for an engagement, she was again arrested and charged with narcotics possession. Released on bail, when she returned to New York she entered a hospital to get off heroin. Although she succeeded, temporarily, she began to use gin by the bottleful as a substitute, and her deterioration was accelerated. She and McKay separated. On October 5, 1957, Holiday, thin and haggard, sang at the First Monterey Jazz Festival. In 1958, she went to Europe and performed so poorly that she was booed off the stage in Milan. In the spring of 1959, she was back in New York, living alone on West Eighty-seventh Street, when she heard the news of Lester Young's death. Alcoholism and heart failure had killed him.

Holiday sang her last concert at the Phoenix Theater in Greenwich Village. She collapsed after two numbers. Billie Holiday was admitted to Metropolitan Hospital in Harlem on May 31, suffering from cardiac failure and liver problems.

> I'm not supposed to get a toothache; I'm not supposed to get nervous; I can't throw up or be sick to my stomach; I'm not supposed to get the flu or have a sore throat. I'm supposed to go out there and look pretty and sing good and smile and I'd just better. Why? Because I'm Billie Holiday— and I've been in trouble.[16]

Even the hospital and serious illness could not protect Holiday

Holiday being booked on narcotics charges in San Francisco, 1949

from indignity. On June 12, her hospital room was searched by police who allegedly discovered a packet of heroin. Once again, she was charged with possession of narcotics. She was photographed and fingerprinted in her bed. Her personal possessions, her flowers, and her comic books were confiscated.

Billie Holiday died in her hospital bed on July 17, under arrest. She was forty-four years old. She had seventy cents in the bank, and $750 strapped to her leg.

Three thousand people attended her funeral. Benny Goodman, John Hammond, Leonard Feather, and Gene Krupa were among those who came to mourn. After her death, sales of her records began to climb.

> I've fought all my life to be able to sing what I wanted the way I wanted to sing it. Before I die I want a place of my own where nobody can tell me *when* to go on. I might go on at nine, or four in the morning; I might sing forty-nine songs or one song. I might even get up and stop the band in the middle of a number and sing something I felt like singing.[17]

Notes

1   Holiday, *Lady Sings the Blues*, p. 110.
2   Ibid., p. 63.
3   Ibid., p. 86.
4   Ibid., p. 18.
5   Ibid., p. 34.
6   Ibid., p. 37.
7   Ibid., p. 39.
8   Chilton, *Billie Holiday: The True Story of the Immortal Billie Holiday*, p. 51.
9   Holiday, op. cit., p. 70
10 Ibid., p. 81.
11 Chilton, op. cit., p. 73.
12 Holiday, op. cit., p. 116.
13 Ibid., p. 118.
14 Ibid., p. 148.

15 Ibid., p. 181.
16 Ibid., p. 170.
17 Ibid.

Sources

Chilton, John. *Billie Holiday: The True Story of the Immortal Billie Holiday.* New York: Quartet Books, 1975.
Holiday, Billie. *Lady Sings the Blues.* New York: Avon Books, 1976.

JANIS JOPLIN
1943-1970

I just made love to 25,000 people, and I'm goin'
home alone.[1]

JANIS JOPLIN. American singer. Queen of rock music. She called herself "Pearl"; her purpose in life was to "feel things." Befeathered, beaded, and swathed in satin and velvet, she sang soulful blues that captured the imagination of the hippie counterculture of the 1960s and the respect of music critics like Ralph Gleason and Nat Hentoff, and turned her into a major cult heroine.

Joplin made only three records during her short career. Her power was in live performance: onstage, stirring an audience into a frenzy, her writhing, shrieking, and moaning were contagious. Onstage she was no longer fat, ratty-haired, bad-complexioned; she was the leading lady, both wanted and adored. Offstage she had whiskey and heroin to comfort her.

> I can't sleep! I go to bed worrying and I wake up worrying every morning, worrying that they'll have found out I really can't sing! [2]

Janis Joplin was born on January 19, 1943, in Port Arthur, Texas, a middle-class oil refinery town near the Louisiana border. Her father, Seth Joplin, was an engineer employed by Texaco. Her mother, Dorothy, was registrar at Port Arthur College. She was their first child. Her sister Laura would arrive six years later and her brother Michael when she was ten. Her early childhood was happy. She was bright, she enjoyed painting and reading, interests her parents encouraged, and she was cute, an angel-faced, golden-haired child.

> Like I was raised in Texas, man, and I was an artist and I had all these ideas and feelings that I'd pick up in books, and my father would talk to me about it, and I'd make up poems and things. And, man, I was the only one I'd ever met. There weren't any others. There just wasn't *anybody*, man, in Port Arthur. There were a couple of old ladies who used to do watercolors and paint still lives and that was it. . . . There's nobody there. Nobody.[3]

Janis Joplin began emerging from her protective coloring during her years at Thomas Jefferson High School. Her body rebelled in puberty with severe acne that left her face permanently scarred; her hair turned brown and wild; she gained weight. She became a tomboy and a troublemaker. Her friends were a gang of rowdy boys. In sweatshirt and blue jeans, her hair uncombed, she drove fast, drank too much beer, and was generally rowdy. Her behavior earned her the disapproval of Port Arthur.

> Seth Joplin (father):
> One night she had a painting she wanted to do, on a great big canvas, six or eight feet long. So she took it out into the garage. It was a cold winter night and she ran the clothes dryer for heat and painted out there all night long.[4]

Although Joplin listened to music during those years, especially the records of Bessie Smith and Leadbelly, she did not become seriously interested in singing until she was nineteen and an art major at the University of Texas. There, as a member of a trio called the Waller Creek Boys, she performed every week at Threadgill's, a hillbilly bar. She drank a lot of beer to get up her courage, then she played an autoharp and sang. It was a bluegrass sound, high and sometimes shrill. Soon singing and music replaced painting for her.

>I was just a young chick, I just wanted to get it on. I wanted
>to smoke dope, take dope, lick dope, suck dope, fuck dope,
>anything I could lay my hands on I wanted to do it, man.[5]

In January, 1963, Joplin abruptly left Austin with friend Chet
Helms and headed for San Francisco: she had just been voted
"Ugliest Man on Campus" at the University of Texas. The next year
and a half was divided between North Beach in San Francisco,
where Joplin sang in coffee houses and passed the hat, and New
York's East Village where she joined the blossoming hippie culture.
Her unshakable partners had become liquor and amphetamines, the
latter gaining such a dangerous hold on her that in the summer of
1965 twenty-two-year-old Joplin went back home to Port Arthur.
She stayed a year, during which time she returned to college and saw
a psychologist. She also pursued her singing, performing regularly in
Austin at the Eleventh Door. She was improving: audiences began
to respond to her.

>I wasn't planning any of this, I wasn't planning on sitting
>in cold dressing rooms all my life, I didn't even know it
>existed. Even when I was a singer I never wanted to be a
>star. I just liked to sing because it was fun, just like people
>like to play tennis: it makes your body feel good. Everybody
>gave you free beer.[6]

In May, 1966, Travis Rivers arrived in Port Arthur with a message for Joplin from Chet Helms in San Francisco who was managing
Big Brother and the Holding Company, a four-member male group
that needed a female singer. Helms wanted Joplin to join them. She
accepted his offer and arrived in San Francisco on June 4, 1966.
Six days later, still wearing her drab Port Arthur clothes, she made
her debut at the Avalon ballroom singing the gospel song "Down on
Me." At first, no one knew quite what to make of her.

The group performed regularly that summer at the Avalon. In
August they went to Chicago for a four-week engagement; there
they were signed up by Mainstream Records to make their first album.

Nick Gravenites (songwriter and friend):

They were just too freaky! This chick had this hair hanging down and she was dressed in this *bedspread!* And the
jewelry! Chickenbones! Voodoo shit! And this patchouli per-
fume, *reeking!* Her complexion was a wipe-out. She had this
sore throat and she was screeching like a wounded owl! . . .
They were aliens and they were sticking it out.[7]

By early 1967 Janis Joplin was becoming something of a star in
the San Francisco area. She was working well with the band and
staying away from drugs. For several months she also had a steady
relationship with Joe McDonald of Country Joe and the Fish. This
proved to be a rare and short-lived period of security in her romantic
life. Their bond, however, was not strong enough to endure the
pressures of the music and the road. After this affair she pursued
pretty young boys—or girls—to stave off her loneliness. When that
failed, she drank.

> The one thing I've learned about being on the road, that
> music and that hour you get onstage is *all*. The rest of it's
> fucked up . . . people trying to get something out of you,
> trying to talk to you, trying to sleep, you can't sleep, at two
> the bars are closed, it ain't really a rocking good time. The
> rocking good times you create, you bring the bottle your-
> self. . . . The road is just a hassle.[8]

Janis Joplin with Big Brother and the Holding Company was
officially "discovered" in June of 1967 at the Monterey Pop Festival. In a dazzling silver-white lamé pantsuit, her hair flying, twenty-
four-year-old Joplin belted out "Love Is Like a Ball and Chain."
The response of the audience was so enthusiastic that Joplin and
Big Brother were asked to perform again that night for a crowd of
40,000, including Clive Davis, President of Columbia Records, and
Albert Grossman, renowned rock star manager. They gave an equally
exciting performance at the Monterey Jazz Festival three months
later.

> Ralph J. Gleason (music critic):
> The first thing she did was to say "shit" and that en-

deared her right away. Then she stomped her foot and shook her hair and started to scream. They held still for a couple of seconds, but here and there in the great sunlit arena, longhairs started getting up and out into the aisles and stomping along with the band. By the end of the first number the Monterey County Fairgrounds arena was packed with people writhing and twisting and snaking along in huge chains.[9]

Janis Joplin's career moved swiftly toward its crest. In February, 1968, she and Big Brother, now managed by Albert Grossman, arrived for their East Coast debut at the Anderson Theater in New York's East Village. The concert and Joplin received rave reviews. Columbia Records signed them up. They went on to play in Boston, Providence, then appeared in the Midwest, returning to New York in March for the opening of Bill Graham's Fillmore East. The media showered Joplin with attention; she was reviewed, interviewed, and photographed. She was fast becoming the biggest star in American rock and roll.

Cheap Thrills (Joplin wanted to call the album *Sex, Dope, and Cheap Thrills*) was recorded in New York during the spring and summer of 1968. By the album's August release, a rift had developed between Joplin and Big Brother, and the decision was made to split up.

Cashbox defined Janis Joplin as "a mixture of Leadbelly, a steam engine, Calamity Jane, Bessie Smith, an oil derrick, and rotgut bourbon funneled into the twentieth century somewhere between El Paso and San Francisco." *Cheap Thrills* sold a million dollars' worth of copies.

Peter Albin (bass player of Big Brother):
It was in New York that she made the decision to split. There were several gigs where all of us would feel down. She'd have done her part with an amount of self-assurance, but there was a whole time when the waves started separating. The kind of performance she would put out would be a different trip than the band's. I'd say it was a star trip, where she related to the audience like she was the only one on the stage.[10]

Joplin at the San Jose Pop Festival

By now, Joplin was driving a Day-Glo-painted Porsche and costuming herself in bright-colored feathers and beads, silk, velvet dresses, and gold shoes. She was also supporting a fairly expensive heroin habit, which she alternated with liberal doses of Southern Comfort.

> Country Joe McDonald:
> Some people need a lot of convincing that love is around them and she—her excuses were running out. Her game was running out because her dreams were all coming true. I mean she was getting rich, she was getting famous, she could have anything she wanted to and the only thing left for her to have was love, to give it and take it.[11]

Joplin's departure from Big Brother angered many of her fans and altered the momentum and direction of her career. Her second band (she introduced it at their debut at the Fillmore on February 11, 1969, as "Janis and the Jack-Offs") was heavy on horns, and disparate in spirit. They never came together enough to win the devotion of the fans or the praise of the critics. However, in the spring they managed to complete a successful European tour which culminated in an exciting concert at Albert Hall in London before returning to the States to record the *Kozmic Blues* album.

> Paul Nelson (music critic):
> The first song made a number of things both painfully and delightfully clear. The potential to become a genuinely great rock singer is still there, but so are the infamous and disheartening Joplin tendencies toward vocal overkill. Indeed, Janis doesn't so much sing a song as to strangle it to death right in front of you . . . it would seem to belong more to the realm of carnival exhibition than musical performance.[12]

At the Woodstock Festival in August, 1969, Joplin was beginning to show signs of her chronic self-abuse: her voice was strained and her former electric energy was missing. The tone of her performances was becoming one of belligerence and desperation. At a concert in Tampa, Florida, in November, she was arrested for shouting obscenities after the police took exception to her exhortations to the audience to get up and dance. She repeated this new routine at a peace rally in Madison Square Garden, badgering the unresponsive audience into dancing. That month, her friend (and later biographer) Myra Friedman persuaded her to see a doctor regarding her heroin addiction. Joplin admitted to the doctor that she had overdosed six times and agreed to a treatment of Dolophine.

> I'm here to have a party, man, as best I can while I'm here on this earth. I think it's your duty to. When I'm ready to retire I'll tell you about it. If I start worrying about everything I'm doing . . . I'd just as soon quit now. If that's what I got to do to stick around another forty years, you can have it.[13]

Full-Tilt Boogie, Joplin's third band, which many felt to be her best musically, was formed in April, 1970. She had ended a brief but serious relationship with a law student. She was off drugs but drinking heavily, often to the point of blacking out. After a rowdy trial run at a Hell's Angels concert, Joplin and her new band embarked on a tour through the South and Midwest. The concerts were poorly promoted and as a result the halls were often only half filled. The small, quiet audiences greatly disappointed Joplin, who nevertheless gave her all.

> I know me, I've been around a long time. . . . I was the same chick because I've been her forever, and I know her, she ain't no star—she's lonely, or she's good at something. I have to get undressed after the show, my clothes are ruined, my heels are run through, my underwear is ripped, my body's stained from my clothes, my hair's stringy. I got a headache and I got to go home and I'm lonely . . . and I'm pleading with my road manager to please give me a ride home . . . please, please, just so I can take these fuckin' clothes off, and that ain't no star, man, that's just a person.[14]

On August 12 she gave a sensational concert for 20,000 people at Harvard Stadium. She was in top form despite the fact that she had been getting drunk all summer. The audience was in the palm of her hand, dancing in the aisles and demanding encore after encore. This was her last concert. The next day she went home for a tenth reunion of her high school class.

As far as Port Arthur was concerned, nothing had changed.

> Maybe my audiences can enjoy my music more if they think I'm destroying myself.[15]

In September, Joplin went to Los Angeles to record *Pearl*. During these last few weeks of her life she was caught in a revolving door: she was seriously considering marrying a young man from the East who would fly to Los Angeles to see her for weekends; she had also reestablished contact with Peggy Caserta, an old friend.

> Jerry Garcia (member, the Grateful Dead):
> She was on a real hard path. She picked it, she chose it. . . . She was doing what she was doing as hard as she could. . . . She did what she had to do and closed her books.
>
> It was the best possible time for her death. If you know any people who passed that point into decline . . . really getting messed up, old, senile, done in. But going up, it's like a skyrocket, and Janis was a skyrocket chick.[16]

On September 18, the death of Jimi Hendrix from the effects of a barbiturate overdose in London was announced in the news. Less than a month later, on October 4, in the early morning hours, Janis Joplin mainlined heroin for the last time. She was alone in her hotel room after spending a long evening at the recording studio. Her body was discovered by her road manager. She was twenty-seven years old.

In her will Joplin allocated $2,500 to be spent on a party in the event of her death: several hundred guests drank and danced all night, compliments of Pearl. Her body was cremated and her ashes scattered on the Pacific.

> I went to a doctor the other day because one of the people in

my office thinks I have a drinking problem, so I went to the doctor for special problems and I told him, "I did this when I was twenty-two, and I did this when I was twenty-five, and I took this when I was twenty-six, and I started this at fourteen, I started this at eighteen, whatever they are, and I've been drinking a lot lately." He looked at me and said, "Man, I don't think you have a drinking problem, I think you're doing great." Most of my biggest problems now are what color scheme to use on my next string of beads.[17]

Notes

1 Dalton, *Janis*, p. 57.
2 Friedman, *Buried Alive*, p. 270.
3 Dalton, op. cit., p. 89.
4 Ibid., p. 220.
5 Ibid., p. 36.
6 Ibid., p. 38.
7 Friedman, op. cit., p. 95.
8 Dalton, op. cit., p. 65.
9 Ibid., p. 236.
10 Ibid., p. 201.
11 Ibid., p. 239.
12 Ibid., p. 258.
13 Ibid., p. 113.
14 Ibid., p. 39.
15 Friedman, op. cit., pp. 200–01.
16 Dalton, op. cit., p. 45.
17 Ibid., p. 65.

Sources

Carey, Gary. *Lenny, Janis & Jimi*. New York: Pocket Books, 1975.
Dalton, David. *Janis*. New York: Popular Library, 1971.
Friedman, Myra. *Buried Alive*. New York: Bantam Books, 1974.

JACK KEROUAC
1922-1969

The only people for me are the mad ones, the
ones who are mad to live, mad to talk, mad to be
saved, desirous of everything at the same time,
the ones who never yawn or say a commonplace
thing, but burn, burn, burn like the fabulous
yellow roman candles exploding like spiders
across the stars.[1]

JACK KEROUAC. American novelist and poet, and one of the leaders of the Beat Generation of the 1950s. In his autobiographical novels, especially *On the Road,* his most famous, he articulated the rebellion of the post-World War II bohemian counterculture and avant-garde, capturing its quintessence in his spontaneous prose. Fueled with Benzedrine, or alcohol, Kerouac's vision was all troubles and ecstasies on freedom's path. He was called a seer and a shaman; he called himself a religious wanderer, a dharma bum. Others called him a fool, and infantile, not a writer but a drunken typist with a photographic memory.

> My name is Jack ("Duluoz") Kerouac and I was born in Lowell, Mass. on 9 Lupine Road on March 12, 1922. "Oh you're putting me on." I wrote this book *Vanity of Duluoz.* "Oh you're putting me on." It's like that woman . . . who wrote me a letter awhile ago saying, of all things, listen to this:
> "You are not Jack Kerouac. There is no Jack Kerouac. His books were not even written." [2]

Kerouac's parents were working-class people. His father, Leo, was a job printer and often away from home. His mother, Mémère, worked part-time in a shoe factory. Kerouac was their third and last child. His brother, Gerard, five years older, died of rheumatic fever when Jack was six. His sister Caroline would commit suicide many years later. Kerouac remembered all of his growing-up, and even the anguish of his brother's death would somehow be made sweet in his autobiographical works.

> The boy, me, Jacky Duluoz, kid of writeups, track teams, home and believing goodheartedness with just a touch of the Canuck half-Indian doubt and suspicion of all things non-Canuck, non-half Indian—a lout—the order of the lout on my arm—They saw this boy well-brushed though not combed consciously, still a kid, suddenly big as a man, awkward, etc. —with serious blue-eyed pensive countryboy countenance sitting in gray high school halls in button-down sweater no water on his hair as photographer snaps line of home roomers.[3]

Kerouac grew up dark-haired and handsome. Of average height, he was strong and muscular. At the age of sixteen he won a scholarship to Columbia University: his ambition was to become a football star and the greatest writer that ever lived. Kerouac spent a year at Horace Mann High School in the Bronx making up credits and entered Columbia in 1940. His football career was immediately aborted by a cracked tibia in an early game. Kerouac spent the remainder of the year as a wounded athlete, smoking a pipe and reading Thomas Wolfe. In his sophomore year he quit both football and Columbia and jumped on a southbound bus.

> This was the most important decision of my life so far. What I was doing was telling everybody to go jump in the big fat ocean of their own folly. I was also telling myself to go jump in the big fat ocean of my own folly. What a bath![4]

He returned to Columbia the following year but dropped out again to go on the road, eventually going home to wait for a call from the Navy to serve in World War II. Most of Kerouac's Navy time was spent in the "mad ward." He told the Navy doctors that he was "old Samuel Johnson." Both he and a handwritten novel he called *The Sea Is My Brother* were under observation. After six months, he was released, "honorable discharge, indifferent character."

> Not a warrior, Doctor, please, but a coward intellectual . . . but only in the sense that I feel I have to defend a certain portion of Athenian ethos, as might we say, and not because I'm yellow, because certainly, I *am* yellow, but I just can't take that business of telling me how to be day in and day out. . . . I cannot live with your idea of discipline, I'm too much of a nut, and a man of letters.[5]

After a spell as merchant seaman on the S.S. *Weems* Kerouac returned to New York City and hovered around the Columbia campus. Enter the characters and props of his future: Lucien Carr, William Burroughs, Allen Ginsberg, morphine, marijuana, Benzedrine, Rimbaud, Yeats, Nietzsche, Lautréamont. Kerouac initiated his career as literary artist with a blood oath and began taking so much Benzedrine that he was eventually hospitalized with thrombophlebitis. He returned home to recuperate and help his mother care for his father, who was dying of cancer.

In the evenings he wrote a novel while sitting at the kitchen table. Influenced by the novels of Thomas Wolfe, Kerouac watched his manuscript, *The Town and The City*, grow to 1,200 pages.

> "Where are we going, man?"
> "I don't know but we gotta go." [6]

In 1946, Neal Cassady, twenty-year-old "jail kid shrouded in mystery," arrived in New York City and entered Kerouac's life. Cassady looked like a cowboy, thin and wiry; he was sharp-eyed and hawk-nosed. A stream of words poured from his mouth. Cassady quickly mesmerized Kerouac.

In the summer of 1947, his novel half done, Kerouac left home and bussed and hitchhiked out to Denver where Cassady and Allen Ginsberg were living. From there, he continued to San Francisco, hoping to ship out on a round-the-world freighter.

I was a young writer and I wanted to take off.

Somewhere along the line I knew there'd be girls, visions, everything; somewhere along the line the pearl would be handed to me.[7]

Kerouac could not get on a ship, so he took a job as a night watchman. He was soon fired. After an amorous interlude with a Mexican girl, he returned to Mémère, who was living in an apartment in Ozone Park, New York. This was the first of a series of periodic, compulsive trips that Kerouac took cross-country and home again. He was either chasing after, running with, or running from Neal Cassady, the holy con man and his overexcited ecstasies.

"What's your road, man?—holyboy road, madman road, rainbow road, guppy road, any road. It's an anywhere road for anybody anyhow. Where body how?"[8]

Kerouac completed *The Town and the City* and submitted it to Charles Scribner's Sons, Thomas Wolfe's publisher, who rejected the novel. Little, Brown & Company also declined the book. Meanwhile, Allen Ginsberg, acting as informal agent for the book, gave a copy to Robert Giroux, editor in chief at Harcourt Brace, who accepted it for publication and paid Kerouac an advance of $1,000. The novel was published in 1950: reviews were mixed, and it did not sell many copies.

Suddenly I had a vision of Dean, a burning shuddering frightful Angel, palpitating toward me across the road, approaching like a cloud, with enormous speed, pursuing me like the Shrouded Traveler on the plain, bearing down on me. I saw his huge face over the plains with the mad bony purpose and the gleaming eyes; I saw his wings; I saw his old jalopy chariot with thousands of sparking flames shooting out from it; I saw the path it burned over the road. . . . It came like the wrath to the West.[9]

In October, 1950, Kerouac, nearly twenty-eight, was back home again with Mémère, recuperating from a drug-filled trip he had taken with Neal to Mexico City to visit William Burroughs. A month later he abruptly married Joan Haverty, a young and beautiful member of Allen Ginsberg's crowd whom Kerouac had occasionally dated. This was his second marriage. His first, in 1944, was to Edie Parker, a wealthy Michigan girl he had met at Columbia; their marriage was annulled after six months. His marriage to Joan Haverty would also end after six months. In the meantime, while Joan worked as a waitress, Kerouac sat in their loft on West Twenty-first Street in New York City and struggled with writing *On the Road*.

> Something, someone, some spirit was pursuing all of us across the desert of life and was bound to catch us before we reached heaven . . . death will overtake us before heaven. The one thing that we yearn for in our living days, that makes us sigh and groan and undergo sweet nauseas of all kinds, is the remembrance of some lost bliss that was probably experienced in the womb and can only be reproduced . . . in death. But who wants to die? [10]

According to legend, his friend Lucien Carr gave Kerouac a roll of teletype paper from the wire service office where he worked which solved his writing problems. Feeding the roll into his typewriter, Kerouac was able to type the book nonstop in a three-week burst of Benzedrine-aided creativity. He had discovered what he called his "spontaneous style." The result was a single-spaced paragraph one hundred feet long. In the novel, Neal Cassady becomes "Dean Moriarty," and Kerouac "Sal Paradise," narrator of the story of the Beat Generation whose "one and noble function of the time" was "to *move*."

> Nothing could stop me from writing big books of prose and poetry for nothing, that is, with no hope of ever having them published—I was simply writing them because I was an "Idealist" and I believed in "Life" and was going about justifying it with my earnest scribblings—Strangely enough, these scribblings were the first of their kind in the world, I was originating . . . a new way of writing about life, no fiction,

no craft, no revising afterthoughts, the heartbreaking discipline of the veritable fire ordeal where you can't go back.[11]

On the Road would eventually become a best-seller, and Kerouac's most famous (and infamous) work. Yet it took five years for a publisher to decide to buy it and two more years after that for the book to be published. Robert Giroux turned it down right away: he was put off by the teletype roll. Writer John Clellon Holmes gave the book to his agent, who sent it to Viking Press. There, editor Malcolm Cowley was intrigued enough not to say "no," although Viking's acceptance did not come for several years. In the meantime other publishers read and rejected the book.

> Malcolm Cowley:
>   Well, Jack did something that he would never admit to later. He did a good deal of revision, and it was very good revision. Oh, he would never, never admit to that because it was his feeling that the stuff ought to come out like toothpaste from a tube and not be changed, and that every word that passed from his typewriter was holy.[12]

During those years Kerouac, like the characters in *On the Road*, swung back and forth like a pendulum across the United States and Mexico. He lived with Neal Cassady and his new wife Carolyn in San Francisco, writing *Visions of Cody* and working as a brakeman on the railroad.

He spent time in Mexico City with Burroughs where he wrote *Dr. Sax* in a urinal. Periodically he went home to Mémère where, in quiet, clean security, he wrote *Maggie Cassidy* and *The Subterraneans*. He practiced Buddhism with poet Gary Snyder in a cabin in Mill Valley, California. He spent eight sober weeks alone on Desolation Peak in Washington writing in his journal. He participated with Ginsberg, Philip Whalen, Gary Snyder, and Gregory Corso in the San Francisco Poetry Renaissance, reading poetry at Gallery Six.

> Gary Snyder:
>   Jack's touching back with his mother was a function of

the way he was, and it was understood by most of his friends because they felt that that was, in some way, part of the quality of his genius. . . . The mystique of the Beat Generation or . . . the liberating thing that we felt in our lives about that time . . . was the sense that you can actually do what you want to do. . . . Jack kind of led the way, it was his style, but no woman, or other man, say, that wanted to really be together with him in anything could hope to do it. He had an inability to be together on that plane.[13]

On the Road was finally published by Viking Press in September, 1957. Gilbert Millstein, reviewing the book for the *New York Times*, called it "the most beautifully executed, the clearest, and the most important utterance yet made by the generation Kerouac himself named years ago as 'beat' and whose principal avatar he is." [14] Other reviewers were much less laudatory, but the novel quickly became a best-seller. And Jack Kerouac was suddenly a star, a celebrity, King of the Beats. He was assumed to be Dean Moriarty by most of his fans, and therefore was expected to act like Dean Moriarty. Kerouac found himself overwhelmed and playing a part he did not like. In his lumber jacket and black jeans, drinking from a bottle, he found himself at literary parties, in television appearances and radio interviews being heralded as either a prophet or a freaky clown. But he was not, after all, Dean Moriarty. He was Ti Jean, shy Canuck. And he was "already sick of the subject."

When my books became notorious . . . and interviewers tried to ask me questions, I just answered with everything I could think of—I had no guts to tell them to leave me alone.[15]

Grove Press published *The Subterraneans* shortly thereafter, and in 1958, Viking published *The Dharma Bums*, which Kerouac had written a month after *On the Road* was published. Kerouac was attacked and misunderstood; fame was uncomfortable, dulled only by his continual drinking. The money he was now making did not seem to make his new situation as public figure any less painful.

Kerouac at work

Kerouac finally retreated with Mémère to a house in Northport, on the north shore of Long Island.

By the early 1960s, Kerouac's reputation as a serious writer had further diminished with the unfavorable critical reception of his novels *Dr. Sax, Maggie Cassidy, Visions of Cody.* Neal Cassady was serving a five-year sentence for a drug conviction, and Kerouac was becoming more alcoholic and desperate. In August, 1960, he made one more trip to San Francisco which turned into a nightmare of delirium tremens and hallucinations He recorded the experience in *Big Sur*, a novel published in 1962.

> I later had adventures in Big Sur down there that were really horrible and only as horrible as you get when you get older and your last moment impels you to test *all*, to go *mad*, just to see what the Void'll do.[16]

Kerouac gradually retreated from the world, avoiding his old friends and his old ways that, he said, bored him. The changes wrought by the 1960s had made the world a place he no longer understood, or felt a part of. Through a haze of alcohol, he wrote when he could, which was not very often.

> Does it matter to five thousand sneering college writing instructors that I wrote seventeen novels after a youth of solitary practice amounting to over two million words, by the window with a star in it at night, the bedroom window, the cheap room window, the nut ward window, the porthole window, eventually the jail window? I saw that little winding dirt road going west to my lost dream of being a real American Man.[17]

Mémère suffered a stroke in 1966 that left her severely paralyzed and needing constant care. That fall Kerouac married Stella Sampos, whom he had known since his Lowell boyhood, his friend Charlie Sampos's older sister. She looked after Mémère while he drank and tried to write. In 1968, Kerouac learned that Neal Cassady had been found dead by the railroad tracks in Mexico. He refused to believe it.

Kerouac spent the last year of his life in St. Petersburg, Florida, where he moved his wife and Mémère to escape the harsh New

England winter. Late at night, sentimental on liquor, he called his old friends—Carolyn Cassady, Allen Ginsberg, John Clellon Holmes—to reminisce. He stayed home, watching television, steadily drinking, occasionally working on an old story, "Pic." There, on October 20, 1969, he began hemorrhaging blood from his mouth. Stella rushed him to the hospital where he died the following day. Kerouac was forty-seven years old.

> "The fog'll fall all over you, Jacky, you'll wait in fields— You'll let me die—you won't come save me—I don't even know where your grave is—remember what you were like, where your house, what your life—you'll die without knowing what happened to my face—my love—my youth—You'll burn yourself out like a moth jumping in a locomotive boiler looking for light—Jacky—and you'll be dead—and sink—and you'll be dead—and lose yourself from yourself—and forget—and sink—and me too—and what is all this then?" [18]

Notes

1 Kerouac, *On the Road*, p. 9.
2 Kerouac, *Vanity of Duluoz*, p. 12.
3 Kerouac, *Maggie Cassidy*, p. 30.
4 Kerouac, *Vanity of Duluoz*, p. 95.
5 Ibid., p. 167.
6 Kerouac, *On the Road*, p. 196.
7 Ibid., p. 11.
8 Ibid., p. 206.
9 Ibid., p. 212.
10 Ibid., p. 103.
11 Kerouac, *Desolation Angels*, p. 229.
12 Gifford and Lee, *Jack's Book*, p. 206.
13 Ibid., p. 212.
14 Gilbert Millstein, "Books of the Times," *New York Times,* September 5, 1957, p. 27.
15 Kerouac, *Desolation Angels*, p. 229.
16 Ibid., p. 363.
17 Kerouac, *Vanity of Duluoz*, pp. 171–72.
18 Kerouac, *Maggie Cassidy*, p. 184.

Sources

Charters, Ann. *Kerouac*. San Francisco: Straight Arrow Books, 1973.
Gifford, Barry, and Lawrence Lee. *Jack's Book: An Oral Biography of Jack Kerouac*. New York: St. Martin's Press, 1978.
Kerouac, Jack. *Big Sur*. New York: Farrar, Straus and Cudahy, 1962.
————. *Desolation Angels*. New York: G. P. Putnam's Sons, 1978.
————. *The Dharma Bums*. New York: New American Library, 1959.
————. *Maggie Cassidy*. New York: McGraw-Hill Book Co., 1978.
————. *On the Road*. New York: New American Library, 1957.
————. *The Subterraneans*. New York: Ballantine Books, 1973.
————. *Vanity of Duluoz*. New York: G. P. Putnam's Sons, 1978.
McNally, Dennis. *Desolate Angel*. New York: Random House, 1979.

ROSS LOCKRIDGE
1914-1948

We Americans make the modern error of dignify-
ing the Individual. We do everything we can
to butter him up. We give him a name . . . as-
sure him . . . he has certain inalienable rights
. . . educate him . . . let him pass on his
name to his brats, and when he dies we give him
a special hole in the ground and a hunk of stone
with his name on it. But after all, he's only a seed,
a bloom and a withering stalk among pressing
billions. Your Individual is a pretty disgusting,
vain, lewd little bastard. . . . By God, he has
only one right guaranteed to him in Nature, and
that is the right to die and stink to Heaven.[1]

ROSS LOCKRIDGE, JR. American author of a single novel, *Raintree County,* his ambitious attempt at the Great American Novel, and his attempt at the Great American Dream. The success of the book became Lockridge's albatross. On the evening before the newspapers announced that *Raintree County* had made the best-seller list, he took his own life.

> For as he lay on the bank of the Shawmucky, he knew that he too would be a great poet. It seemed to him that he must be a greater poet even than Shakespeare because there was some essence of what he was that Elizabethan England couldn't possibly compose. He . . . was perhaps the bearer of the sacred fire of poetic genius that is given from mind to mind like a regenerating torch.[2]

Ross Lockridge, Jr., was born on April 25, 1914, in the small town of Bloomington, Indiana, the youngest by seven years of four children. His father, Ross Lockridge, Sr., was a book salesman and local historian with several books to his credit. His mother, Elsie Shockley, was an Indiana girl, a practical no-nonsense woman whose main concern was the proper education of her children for whom she had high expectations, especially her youngest.

> A whole world of creation seemed waiting. He had only to set pencil to paper in the sunlight of the Shawmucky. And wandlike, the pencil would touch immortal poems into being.[3]

After high school Lockridge spent a year in Paris studying at the Sorbonne on scholarship. He finished with top honors and returned to Bloomington where he attended the University of Indiana as had his parents. He graduated in 1935 Phi Beta Kappa. In 1937 he married his hometown sweetheart, Vernice Baker, and moved into a small cabin in Bloomington. A year later their first child was born. Teaching and studying for his master's degree, Lockridge labored in his spare time over a long narrative poem he called "The Dream of the Flesh of Iron." The manuscript grew to 400 pages.

> This was a season of gorgeous dreams by day and night. . . . He memorized whole books of poetry, read everything he could find, aspired to have all human knowledge. . . . At night, his dreams, always vivid, were enriched with his bardic obsession.[4]

In 1940, having been awarded a scholarship to Harvard to complete his Ph.D., he moved Vernice and baby son to Cambridge, Masachusetts. At this point he tried out "The Dream" on an editor at Houghton Mifflin. The response was unencouraging so he put away the poem and began to concentrate on a novel about Indiana in the late 1800s which he had begun several years before.

The novel quickly took hold of him. Eventually he gave up working toward his Ph.D. and got a teaching job at Simmons College to support his family. Writing the novel became his main occupation, his obsession. The family moved from Cambridge to a small apartment in Boston where they lived in near poverty for five years while he worked on the book. By fall, 1944, the Lockridge family had grown to three children. The novel, which had been entirely rewritten once, was now in its second draft and 600,000 words long. Vernice spent the next eighteen months typing it (as well as having a fourth child). When she finished, Lockridge christened the 2,000-page manuscript *The Riddle of Raintree County* and submitted it, in five spring binders, to Houghton Mifflin. He was convinced he had written a masterpiece.

> *Time* magazine:
> As in *Ulysses*, the formal setting is one community and the time of one day. The community is the small town of Waycross, Indiana, and the date July 4, 1892. The hero, John Wickliff Shawnessy, is both family man and poet. . . . Mr. Shawnessy, fifty-three, schoolteacher and county scholar, moves through the day as a leading citizen in the local celebrations. At intervals the day's events or reflections, like firecrackers, touch off flashbacks to the significant events of Mr. Shawnessy's life.[5]

Five weeks later Houghton Mifflin responded: they would like to publish his novel, provided certain cuts and revisions were made, and they offered him an advance of $3,500. Jubilant and confirmed, Lockridge quit his job at Simmons College and the family returned to Bloomington. Temporarily housed with his parents, he went to work on the agreed-upon revisions. As he worked, his expectations for the novel continued to grow. His fertile imagination churned out publicity schemes and angles for launching the book, which was scheduled for publication in the spring of 1947.

Shortly after he completed the first set of revisions, Houghton Mifflin asked for more revisions, including some actual cutting. This time Lockridge went to Boston to be near his editor and completed the revisions while staying at his old apartment on Montfort Street. He was emotionally and physically exhausted by the time he had finished the work.

The galley proofs were ready in April and sent to him in Manistee, Michigan, where the family had moved the previous summer. In the meantime he had learned that MGM was having a contest for new novels with a fat purse for the winner. He agreed to allow Houghton Mifflin to submit *Raintree County* for the prize.

In America, we've found a quick way to express all values.

Everything here fits into the price system. Everybody goes
around wearing a pricetag of one kind or another. . . . The
whole cockeyed civilization is a series of pricetags hanging
out for people to read each other by. And life in America
consists of trying to accumulate more and more spectacular
pricetags. Everything is on the block in America and can be
had for a price.[6]

Houghton Mifflin announced to Lockridge that they were delay-
ing publication of the book from July to January, 1948: it conflicted
with the publication of another important novel. This was a frustrat-
ing disappointment for him. An extra $1,000 advance was offered
by the publisher to appease him. In the meantime, MGM announced that it was considering making *Raintree County* the contest
winner, provided the author agreed to cutting the novel. Lockridge
was called to New York for a meeting with a representative of MGM,
who made it clear to him that the prize would not be his unless he
agreed to cut a minimum of 50,000 words from the book. After some
initial resistance, he agreed.

His worst dreams were those in which it seemed to him that
he had come back to Raintree County, sick, lonely, perhaps
dying, and no one paid any attention to him.[7]

The division of the MGM prize money soon became a bitter
bone of contention between Lockridge and Houghton Mifflin. According to the rules of the contest, the publisher was awarded a sum
of $25,000 and the author $150,000. But by their contract, of the
$150,000 to go to Lockridge, Houghton Mifflin was entitled to 15
percent. Lockridge considered this to be extortion. He threatened to
go to another publisher with his next book, but was eventually
placated by certain minor concessions made by Houghton Mifflin.
The revisions, the cutting, the prize, the publicity, the waiting, the
negotiating were taking their toll on him.

Perhaps it was right after all to worry about himself. If he
fell and came apart, all things fell and came apart. Who
else could save the streambegotten girl or find beauty by the

river? . . . If he triumphed, there would be triumphs for all, but if he died there would be deaths for all. It was still his legend and they couldn't take it away from him.[8]

While awaiting publication of *Raintree County*, Lockridge found himself unable to get started on a new book. Obsessed with the fate of his first novel, he suffered from insomnia, and was losing weight. In October, he learned that the novel had been selected by the Book-of-the-Month Club. However, once again, there was a call for cuts to be made and, once again, he excised several thousand words from the book.

In November, Lockridge and his wife went to Los Angeles both to get away from winter weather and to investigate MGM's operations with regard to *Raintree County*. Their visit was a disappointment; nothing concrete was being done at the studio. When they returned to Indiana in December, Lockridge's depression had worsened. He agreed to undergo a series of shock treatments, but they failed to help.

> Johnny knew then that the War was over for him. He sank back into fever and dull pain. For days and nights thereafter he lay, dreaming of Raintree County, seeing the earth of it ravaged and dry as if the source of its life had been scorched to a trickle.[9]

Raintree County was finally published on January 5, 1948. The first reviews were excellent and the book quickly went into a second printing. However, a second set of reviews in the *New Yorker* and *Newsweek* attacked the novel. And in early March, the story of an attack on the book by Father A. J. Barrett, Jesuit priest, appeared in the *New York Times*.

The *New York Times*:

The Reverend Alfred J. Barrett of Fordham University described *Raintree County* as "1,066 pages of bombast, rank obscenity, materialistic philosophy, and blasphemous impudicity" which "patently falls within the general prohibition of the Index." . . . Father Barrett said the book was

Lockridge with family, 1947

inimical to faith and morals and announced he was giving up his B. O. M. C. subscription because the book had been chosen for distribution.[10]

The novel was strongly defended by Houghton Mifflin, who explained that the intent of *Raintree County* was "to give the world a legend of moral and spiritual regeneration in an era when hatred and materialism appear to be enveloping the world—or much of it —in fear and religious despair." Lockridge, nevertheless, was deeply wounded by Barrett's attack. He became depressed and couldn't work.

> Was it possible that all the beauty, life, and loyalty, the brave dreams and the young hopes had to die, after all! Was it so easy to dispose of that intense young person who went by the name of Johnny Shawnessy? This young man had held up whole worlds by his single strength. He had floated a universe by a simple expedient of filling his lungs with air. With a very sensitive pencil he had wrought the fairest republic since the beginning of time.[11]

On Saturday evening, March 6, 1948, Ross Lockridge, Jr., locked himself in the garage of his new home, got into the front seat of his Kaiser, and turned on the engine. His wife discovered his body several hours later. Lockridge was thirty-three years old. The next morning, *Raintree County* appeared for the first time in the number one position on the best-seller list of the *New York Herald Tribune*.

> Died. Ross Lockridge, Jr., 33. Author of the ambitious, partly successful, best-selling attempt at a great American novel, *Raintree County*; by his own hand; in Bloomington, Indiana.[12]

Notes

1 Lockridge, *Raintree County*, p. 272.
2 Ibid., p. 99.

3 Ibid.
4 Ibid., p. 100.
5 *Time*, January 12, 1948, p. 85.
6 Lockridge, op. cit., p. 848.
7 Ibid., p. 957.
8 Ibid., p. 1046.
9 Ibid., p. 735.
10 *New York Times*, March 8, 1948, p. 15.
11 Lockridge, op. cit., p. 1046.
12 *Time*, March 15, 1948, p. 86.

Sources

Leggett, John. *Ross and Tom: Two American Tragedies.* New York: Simon & Schuster, 1974.
Lockridge, Ross F. *Raintree County.* Boston: Houghton Mifflin Co., 1948.

JACK LONDON
1876-1916

Ah, it is growing dark and darker. It is the darkness of death, the ceasing to be, the ceasing to feel, the ceasing to move, that is gathering about you. . . . Your eyes are becoming set. They are glazing. My voice sounds faint and far. You cannot see my face. And still you struggle in my grip. You kick with your legs. Your body draws itself up in knots like a snake. Your chest heaves and strains. To live! To live! To live! [1]

JACK LONDON. American novelist and short story writer. He was a spokesman for the Socialist Labor Party and, at the same time, the embodiment of the American dream. A self-made man, London became the highest-paid living writer in history, the world's first "millionaire novelist." Although critics ignored him for long periods of time, London remains today one of the most popular writers in the world: his novels and stories have been translated into over forty languages. His vital, unique, and important contribution to the art of fiction is now recognized.

> I believe that life is a mess. . . . It is like yeast, a ferment, a thing that moves and may move for a minute, an hour, a year, or a hundred years, but that in the end will cease to move. The big eat the little that they may continue to move, the strong eat the weak that they may retain their strength. The lucky eat the most and move the longest, that is all.[2]

He was born John Chaney, an illegitimate child, on January 12, 1876, in a San Francisco slum, the result of the passion of W. H. Chaney, an Irish astrologer, who would later deny his paternity, and Flora Wellman, a Wisconsin girl of Welsh descent who was fond of spiritualist seances and schemes for getting rich.

> I was five years old the first time I got drunk.[3]

Soon after his birth, Flora married John London, a widower with two girls of his own, who gave the boy his new name: John Griffith London. He grew up in a succession of homes as the family moved around San Francisco and across the bay to Oakland in search of a living. They tried growing olive trees, potato farming, and running a boarding house, none with great success.

> I had found my way to the free public library, and was read-ing myself into nervous prostration. . . . I read everything, but principally history and adventure, and all the old travels and voyages. I read mornings, afternoons, and nights. I read in bed, I read at the table, I read as I walked to and from school, and I read at recess while the other boys were playing. I began to get the "jerks." To everybody I replied: "Go away. You make me nervous."[4]

Work was a major element in London's life from his earliest years. He was delivering papers when he was ten. After grammar school he worked long hours in a cannery. When he was not working, he sailed his small boat in the Bay, and learned the rough and drunken ways of the men who robbed the oyster beds. At fifteen, he was "Prince of the Oyster Beds," having borrowed money to purchase his own sloop for robbing. A year later, he switched allegiances and went to work for the Fish Patrol of San Francisco Bay.

London grew into a very appealing young man, his head crowned with a mop of light, curly hair, large blue eyes in a well-formed face, his expression a mixture of passionate openness and intense shyness. His five-foot-seven frame was strong and athletic.

> In the saloon, life was different. Men talked with great voices, laughed great laughs, and there was an atmosphere of great-ness. Here was something more than common every-day where nothing happened. Here life was always very live, and, some-

times, even lurid, when blows were struck, and blood was shed, and big policemen came shouldering in.[5]

At seventeen, he shipped out as an able-bodied seaman on the *Sophia Sutherland*, a sealing ship bound for the north Pacific, and spent five months at sea and in foreign ports on drinking sprees with his mates. When he returned home he wrote a piece for a competition in the *San Francisco Call* and won the $25 first prize.

> I no longer read my library books. I made no dates with the girls. I was a proper work beast. I worked, and ate, and slept, while my mind slept all the time. The whole thing was a nightmare.[6]

A job in a jute mill, working ten hours a day, was replaced by a job shoveling coal for an electric company, until he had enough and escaped, beating his way east on the railroads. In Reno, he joined Kelly's Army of unemployed workers marching to Washington. On the way he was thrown in jail in Pennsylvania for vagrancy. The experience frightened him and set him on the road to socialism.

> His puppyhood was a period of foolish rebellion. He was always worsted, but he fought back because it was his nature to fight back. And he was unconquerable. Yelping shrilly from the pain of lash and club, he none the less contrived always to throw in the defiant snarl, the bitter vindictive menace of his soul which fetched without fail more blows and beatings. But his was his mother's tenacious grip on life. Nothing could kill him.[7]

Back in Oakland, Jack London was determined to develop his brain and become more than a workhorse. He stopped drinking, and attended Oakland High School for a year, studying and writing pieces for the school paper. Upon graduation he went to a cramming school to prepare for entrance exams to the University of California. He began to make friends with fellow students, who helped him with his studies.

London entered the University in the fall of 1896 and stayed for two semesters before dropping out, impatient with the leisurely pace. He went right to work writing essays and short stories, submitting them to magazines with no success. By April, 1896, he had joined the Socialist Labor Party in Oakland. His politics were evolving into a mix of survival of the fittest, individualism on one hand, and the "people," the brotherhood of man on the other.

> He was confused, painfully conscious of his inarticulateness. He felt the bigness and glow of life in what he had read, but his speech was inadequate. He could not express what he felt, and to himself he likened himself to a sailor, in a strange ship, on a dark night, groping about in the unfamiliar running rigging.[8]

In 1897, Jack London, twenty-one years old, sailed from San Francisco for the Klondike. He returned a year later with less than five dollars' worth of gold dust, sick with scurvy, but with a head full of adventures to be written down. With his mother's encouragement, he once again sat down to write, submitting his stories to magazines, and keeping careful records: from August, 1898, to May, 1900, fifteen stories were accepted while eighty-eight others were rejected more than 400 times.[9]

> He began to doubt that editors were real men. They seemed cogs in a machine. That was what it was, a machine. He poured his soul into stories, articles, and poems, and entrusted them to the machine. He folded them just so, put the proper stamps inside the long envelope along with the manuscript, sealed the envelope, put more stamps outside, and dropped it into the mailbox. It traveled across the continent and after a certain lapse of time the postman returned him the manuscript in another long envelope, on the outside of which were the stamps he had enclosed. There was no human editor at the other end, but a mere cunning arrangement of cogs that changed the manuscript from one envelope to another and stuck on the stamps.[10]

In October, 1899, the *Atlantic Monthly* bought his short story "An Odyssey of the North" and paid him $120. Houghton Mifflin wanted to publish his Alaskan stories, and the Hearst Press hired him to write articles for their paper. London was on his way to becoming a successful writer with a name everyone soon would know.

> He struggled in the dark, without advice, without encouragement, and in the death of discouragement. . . . Martin had faith in himself, but he was alone in this faith.[11]

London married Bess Maddern, a young woman he had met while at the University of California, in April, 1900. At the time he was passionately in love with Anna Strunsky, a fellow socialist and radical. However, he reasoned that marriage to Bess would give his life stability and respectability; it would be an anchor for him. Bess agreed to his proposal; she, too, was in love with another. Soon after their marriage, Houghton Mifflin published *The Son of Wolf,* a collection of his Alaskan stories, that was very well received. London was now being paid a monthly retainer of $125 by the S. S. McClure newspaper syndicate to write his first novel.

By 1902, London had fathered two girls and was shouldering the upkeep of both his own and his mother's household. His novel *Daughter of the Snows* was rejected by McClure and his retainer terminated. A second volume of short stories, *Children of the Frost,* was published that year, as well as a children's book. London was feeling the oppression of marriage and its trappings and he openly renewed his pursuit of Anna Strunsky. A writing assignment from the American Press Association enabled him to escape his personal entanglements and go to London where he spent seven weeks in the East End writing *The People of the Abyss.*

> This long sickness of pessimism . . . I had it very bad. I meditated suicide cooly, as a Greek philosopher might. . . . Success—I despised it. Recognition—it was dead ashes. Society, men and women above the ruck and muck of the water-front and the forecastle—I was appalled by their unlovely mental mediocrity.[12]

His finances were restabilized by George Brett of Macmillan who offered to pay him $150 a month for two years in exchange for the right to publish his books. In the winter of 1903, despite his domestic unhappiness, London sat down and, in a six-week spell, wrote *The Call of the Wild.* He sold the short novel to the *Saturday Evening Post* for $2,000, and to Macmillan for the same amount, outright, unwilling to wait for possible royalties. The book sold a million copies, and, had he waited, he would have earned a sizable income, probably enough to ease considerably the amount of hack writing he would later do to survive.

> So it was . . . that Martin questioned the validity of his popularity. It was the bourgeoisie that bought his books and poured its gold into his money-sack, and from what he knew of the bourgeoisie it was not clear to him how it could possibly appreciate or comprehend what he had written. His intrinsic beauty and power meant nothing to the hundreds of thousands who were acclaiming him and buying his books. He was the fad of the hour, the adventurer who had stormed Parnassus while the gods nodded. . . . Fawn or fang, it was all a matter of chance.[13]

That year, with some of the money from the sale of *Call of the Wild,* London bought a small sloop which he anchored in the bay. He spent many hours on the boat; it was his refuge from his marriage, a place where he could meet with friends, or write in peace, or drink. On board he wrote *The Sea Wolf,* which later became a classic.

After his relationship with Anna Strunsky terminated, London sought other passionate involvements and found one with Charmian Kittredge, five years his senior, one of a new breed of liberated women who was part of "the Crowd," a group of San Francisco bohemians he associated with. Soon after meeting her, London separated from Bess and their children, and moved to an apartment in Oakland. By 1905, he had married Charmian and they were living on a small ranch near Glen Ellen, California. This initial acquisition of land marked the beginning of London's expanding domain as well as his expanding debts. He would be over his head financially for the rest of his life and forced to write to pay for his extravagant, and often disastrous, ventures.

> In my brain every thought was at home. Every thought, in its little cell, crouched ready dressed at the door, like prisoners at midnight waiting a jail-break. And every thought was a vision, bright-imaged, sharp-cut, unmistakable. My brain was illuminated by the clear, white light of alcohol.[14]

On April 23, 1907, London, Charmian, and a small inexperienced crew set sail from San Francisco on the *Snark*, a boat that he had built for an expensive $30,000. The voyage, as he had planned it, would last for seven years and take them around the world. Less than two years later, however, London, having contracted a variety of tropical diseases—malaria, yellow fever, yaws—was hospitalized in Sydney, Australia. Formerly a healthy and strong man, he never fully recovered from the effects of these illnesses. This marked the beginning of his physical decline.

> I am aware that within this disintegrating body which has been dying since I was born I carry a skeleton; that under the rind of flesh which is called my face is a bony, noiseless death's head.[15]

After returning to their California ranch in 1909, Charmian became pregnant and London embarked on a new venture, the construction of Wolf House, a large stone house that would cost $70,000. *Martin Eden* was published and, although the critics panned it, it sold 250,000 copies. London bought more land, borrowing money from his publisher and writing to pay the bills that kept piling up.

Charmian gave birth to a baby girl; it died a few days later.

> Hanging by his hands, his feet would be in the water. He could slip in noiselessly. No one would hear. A smother of spray dashed up, wetting his face. It tasted salt on his lips and the taste was good. He wondered if he ought to write

London with Charmian in Australia, 1909

a swan-song, but laughed the thought away. There was no time. He was too impatient to be gone.[16]

London was appalled by the deterioration of his health, which he had taken for granted. Although he had always been an excessive drinker, he began to drink more to relieve the pain of his various ailments. He also began treating himself with a drug containing arsenic, which resulted in severe and serious side effects. Nevertheless, he continued writing, completing *John Barleycorn*, an autobiographical novel about his own experience with alcoholism.

> He let himself go and sank without movement, a white statue, into the sea. He breathed in the water deeply, deliberately, after the manner of a man taking an anaesthetic. When he strangled, quite involuntarily his arms and his legs clawed the water and drove him up to the surface and into the clear sight of the stars.[17]

In 1913, a few weeks before it was scheduled to be completed, Wolf House burned to the ground. "My home—one of my dreams —is destroyed," he wrote to a daughter, Joan.[18]

He and Charmian went to Mexico to report on the revolution for *Collier's*. London went on a heavy drinking spree and contracted a severe case of dysentery that nearly killed him, and would recur periodically.

> Down, down, he swam till his arms and legs grew tired and hardly moved. He knew that he was deep. His endurance was faltering, but he compelled his arms and legs to drive him deeper until his will snapped and the air drove from his lungs in a great explosive rush.[19]

By 1915, the war had deflated the writing market in the United States and London was having trouble paying off the large debts he had accumulated. He sought refuge in Hawaii where he and Charmian were able to live like wealthy people. To appease his creditors, London wrote two novels about dogs. All the while, his health continued to decline and he was plagued by pain and discomfort; he was suffering from nephritis and pyorrhea.

> His willful hands and feet began to beat and churn about, spasmodically and feebly. . . . He was too deep down. They could never bring him to the surface. He seemed floating languidly in a sea of dreamy vision.[20]

When London returned to California in August, he began to work on a novel entitled *How We Die*. The condition of his kidneys and bowels worsened; he was instructed by his physician to follow a strict diet. Ignoring this, he dieted on raw fish and nearly raw duck, and treated himself with a variety of drugs.

On November 22, 1916, he was discovered comatose on the floor, after apparently injecting himself with an overdose of morphine. Jack London died later that evening. He was forty years old.

> What was that? It seemed a lighthouse; but it was inside his brain—a flashing bright white light. It flashed swifter and swifter. There was a long rumble of sound and it seemed to him that he was falling down a vast and interminable stairway. And somewhere at the bottom he fell into darkness. That much he knew. He had fallen into darkness. And at the instant he knew, he ceased to know.[21]

Notes

1 London, *The Sea Wolf*, p. 75.
2 Ibid., p. 35.
3 London, *John Barleycorn*, p. 16.
4 Ibid., pp. 40–42.
5 Ibid., p. 42.
6 Ibid., p. 199.
7 London, "Batard," *Great Short Works of Jack London*, p. 3.
8 London, *Martin Eden*, p. 10.
9 Andrew Sinclair, *Jack*, p. 53.
10 London, *Martin Eden*, p. 118.

11 Ibid., p. 119.
12 London, *John Barleycorn*, pp. 253–54.
13 London, *Martin Eden*, p. 374.
14 London, *John Barleycorn*, p. 5.
15 Ibid., p. 314
16 London, *Martin Eden*, p. 409.
17 Ibid., p. 410.
18 London, *Letters from Jack London*, King Hendricks and Irving Shepard, eds., New York: The Odyssey Press, 1965, p. 394.
19 London, *Martin Eden*, p. 411.
20 Ibid.
21 Ibid.

Sources

London, Jack. *The Best Short Stories of Jack London*. Greenwich, Conn.: Fawcett, 1962.
———. *The Call of The Wild and Selected Stories*. New York: New American Library, 1960.
———. *Great Short Works of Jack London*. Edited by Earle Labor. New York: Harper & Row, 1970.
———. *John Barleycorn*. New York: D. Appleton-Century Co., 1938.
———. *Martin Eden*. New York: Grosset & Dunlap, 1909.
———. *The People of the Abyss*. Westport, Conn.: Lawrence Hill & Co., 1977.
———. *The Sea Wolf*. New York: Bantam Books, 1963.
Sinclair, Andrew. *Jack*. New York: Harper & Row, 1977.

MALCOLM LOWRY
1909-1957

You cannot trust the ones who are too careful. As
writers or drinkers. Old Goethe cannot have been
so good a man as Keats or Chatterton. Or Rimbaud. The ones that burn.[1]

MALCOLM LOWRY. English novelist, short story writer, poet. His public reputation rests on a single work, *Under the Volcano*, which is regarded as one of the important novels of the twentieth century.

Lowry was a dipsomaniac, pursued by "The Furies singing over their victim sending him mad." [2] His elements were water—the sea on which he sailed and in which he swam, and the liquids, the beer, mescal, and wine, in which he drowned—and fire, which he said followed him everywhere.

> Help me to write,
> Show me the gates
> Where the orders are,
> And the cage
> My soul stares at,
> Where my courage
> Roars through the grates. [3]

Clarence Malcolm Lowry was born on July 28, 1909, in Birkenhead, Cheshire, England, into a well-to-do middle-class family. He was the last child of four boys. His father, Arthur Osborne Lowry, a prosperous cotton broker, was an authoritarian figure with strict rules of behavior for his sons. Lowry's relationship with him was never easygoing, although he depended upon him for financial support for most of his life. His mother, Evelyn Boden Lowry, the daughter of an English shipowner, was a quiet woman and often absent from home on trips with her husband, leaving her children in the care of nurses.

> (Oh Lord God, look down upon your unworthy and un-
> washed servant, Hilliot, the seaman, the Liverpool-Norwegian,
> whose knees knock together at thunder, whose filthy hands
> tremble always in impotent prayer; Oh Thou who createst my
> eyes from the green mantle of the standing pool, who createst
> everything, the weak and the strong, the tender with the cruel,
> the just and the unjust, pity his small impulses of lust, and
> see that little beauty in his life, which so soon shall be among
> the green undertow of the tides; and as he stands alone, naked,
> weaponless, deliver him from his bondage and bring him out
> of the darkness and the grief and the pain into sunlight.) [4]

Lowry was stocky and muscular with a powerful chest and arms that appeared too short for his body. His brown hair uncombed, his clothes perpetually rumpled, he was an awkward youth. But he had a flair for words, and he wanted to write. He began at the Leys School in Cambridge as a teenager, writing poems and stories that were published in the school magazine.

When he was seventeen he went to sea for six months as a cabin boy on a tramp steamer bound for the Far East. He kept a journal when he wasn't too drunk to write (for the voyage was filled with drink) from which he culled his first novel, *Ultramarine.*

> First, I am a strange man, or I would like to be a strange
> man, which is nearer the truth—you will have seen that: some
> might say, almost, the fool.[5]

It took Lowry six years to write the novel, a period he spent in school at Cambridge (St. Catherine's College) fulfilling his father's wishes, and in London. Vacations were spent with Conrad Aiken in Rye, Sussex. The two had met as a result of Lowry's worshipful admiration of Aiken's novel *The Blue Voyage*. In the coming years, Aiken served as his mentor and surrogate father.

> Clarissa Lorenz (Mrs. Conrad Aiken):
>   A creature of extremes, he either starved himself or gorged . . . I kept fearing he would absentmindedly set fire to his mattress or break a leg falling downstairs. He moved like a somnambulist, his blue blazer spotted and rumpled, a necktie holding up his trousers.[6]

Ultramarine was published by Jonathan Cape in 1933 and unmemorably received. Shortly after, Lowry married Jan Gabrial in Paris. She was a glamorous, dark-haired American woman he had met while traveling with the Aikens in Spain. They were not well-matched. Lowry drank excessively. She periodically left him and eventually returned alone to New York City. Lowry followed and they tried to make their marriage work, living in a small apartment on Central Park West. In 1935, Jan committed him to Bellevue Hospital for three weeks of drying out after a bout of continuous drinking. Lowry survived the ordeal of his confinement and wrote "The Last Address" when he was released, a short story that he later expanded into the novella *Lunar Caustic*.

In September, 1936, Lowry persuaded Jan to go with him to Los Angeles where he sought employment as a screenwriter. Having no success, he and Jan went on to Mexico and moved into a house in Cuernavaca. There, in the shadows of the volcanoes, he completed a short story that would serve as the basis for *Under the Volcano*. During this period, Jan left Lowry for good. His drinking had become uncontrollable. During a trip to Oaxaca he was thrown in jail three times for his disturbances. On the verge of a nervous breakdown, Lowry was rescued by lawyers dispatched by his father and escorted by train to Los Angeles. He was declared mentally incompetent and placed under the legal guardianship of an employee hired by his father to take care of him. By now Lowry, at the age of twenty-seven, was obviously living for two reasons: to drink and to write.

> Clarisse Francillon (friend and translator):
>   To drink or not to drink, that *was* the question. On the

one hand you had the most vigorous, lucid, sanest man that ever walked the earth, of exceptional strength, an outstanding capacity for work going as far as asceticism; on the other, the maniac, the madman, a victim pursued by demons, the plaything of evil forces, who lets himself be driven out of the gardens of this world, to totter at the brink of the abyss outside. All his life, he had been that pendulum increasingly and relentlessly impelled from one extreme to the other. Only Death put an end to this swinging back and forth.[7]

While living in Los Angeles, he fell in love with Margerie Bonner, an ex-actress, scriptwriter, and author of mystery novels. Four years older than Lowry, she became a crucial force of stability and sanity in his emotional and creative life. She had strength and control where he lacked them, and she had absolute faith in his genius. Their relationship was an intimate collaboration. They were married and moved to British Columbia where, in pioneer simplicity, they lived in a squatter's shack at the edge of the forest, and on the Pacific in Dollarton, a fishing community. These were the good years. Lowry worked on a third draft of *Under the Volcano*, which he sent to his agent, Harold Matson, in July, 1940. This draft would be rejected by thirteen publishers. But in the meantime, Lowry, an incessant reviser, began a fourth draft. His work was interrupted when a fire completely destroyed their shack and all their belongings, except for the manuscript of *Under the Volcano*, which he rescued, and the clothes on their backs. Undaunted, they soon rebuilt the shack, and in the summer of 1945, sent the new draft of the novel to Matson.

> Harold Matson:
>   Your novel has for me a peculiar fascination, sometimes aggravatingly. It is full of wonderful potentialities, in my judgement, but it needs a great deal of work to bring it down to size and proportion within the limits of its own worth. Perhaps I have become impatient with it and that may be the reason why this novel is much too long, and much too full of talk—for me.[8]

In December, 1945, still without a publisher for *Under the Vol-*

cano, Lowry and his wife went to Mexico and rented an apartment in Cuernavaca. On Christmas eve, Lowry received a letter from Jonathan Cape, the English publisher, who offered to publish his novel if Lowry would agree to revise it. According to Douglas Day, his biographer, Lowry "took the letter from Cape as a challenge. Cape, he felt, was asking him to defend his book, and to say why it should be left as it was." He worked on a reply. After two weeks his answer to Cape had become "a document absolutely unique in literary history: a thirty-one-page exegesis which demonstrated in every page that Lowry knew precisely what was going on in every chapter of his novel, why it was all there as it was, and what it meant." [9] In April, 1946, Cape agreed to publish the English edition without revision. The same day, Lowry got word that Reynal and Hitchcock had accepted the book for publication in America.

> *He was lying face downward drinking from a lake that reflected the white-capped ranges. . . . Yet his thirst still remained unquenched. Perhaps because he was drinking, not water, but lightness and promise of lightness—how could he be drinking promise of lightness? Perhaps because he was drinking, not water, but certainty of brightness—how could he be drinking certainty of brightness? Certainty of brightness, promise of lightness, of light, light, light, and again, of light, light, light, light, light!* [10]

During the long months between the writing of the letter and the novel's acceptance, Lowry had periodic bouts with alcohol, especially mescal, which made him dangerously drunk and sometimes violent. He got into trouble with the Mexican police over an unpaid fine from his visit in 1938, and as a result he and Margerie were escorted to the border and forced to leave the country in the spring of 1946. They returned to Dollarton.

Under the Volcano was published in America on February 19, 1947. It received highly laudatory reviews. It was called a work of genius, and one of the most original and creative novels of the time. It was not, however, a great financial success: fewer than 30,000 copies sold by the end of the 1940's. Its reception in England when it was published several months later was far less enthusiastic.

The novel is a complex, symbol-laden, autobiographical work, Lowry's vision of hell on earth. Set in Mexico, the action takes place in one day, the Day of the Dead, November, 1939, and the last day in the life of British Consul Geoffrey Firmin, dipsomaniac. In his exegesis for Cape Lowry described the novel as being concerned with the "forces in man which cause him to be terrified of himself . . . with the guilt of man, with his remorse, with his ceaseless struggling toward the light under the weight of the past, and with his doom." [11]

> The truth is, the beastly book seemed to go off like a hundred skyrockets at once and I am still trying to dodge the sparks and sticks falling on my head which is, I hope, so far from being swollen that it still has the wit to suggest that such success, if this can indeed be called such, may be the worst possible thing that could happen to any serious author. [12]

Lowry's life went steadily downhill after the publication of his novel. His disintegration over a period of ten years was marked by alternating periods of depression and breakdown, and periods when he was able to control his drinking and immerse himself in creative work. Although he was at work on several major projects, only a few short stories and poems were published during these years.

His other works were all published after his death: *Hear Us O Lord from Heaven Thy Dwelling Place* (1961), a collection of short stories; *Selected Poems* (1962); *Dark As the Grave Wherein My Friend Is Laid* (1968), an unfinished novel; *Lunar Caustic* (1968), based on three weeks he spent in Bellevue; and *October Ferry to Gabriola* (1970).

He and Margerie remained in Dollarton until July, 1954. Lowry, often drunk, was frequently the victim of minor accidents: "It is the suspicious element of the possibly suicidal in all these constant small accidents that have plagued me which frightens me." [13] In August, when the authorities began to serve eviction notices on the people living in the squatters' shacks, he and Margerie packed up and left.

They traveled to Europe and to London where Lowry spent four months in 1955 in a psychiatric hospital, undergoing drug therapy and shock treatments. Although he was improved when released, he did not remain so.

> Everything written about drink is incidentally absurd. Have to do it all over again, what about conflict, appalling sadness that can lead equally to participation in the tragic human condition, self-knowledge, discipline. Conflict is all-important. Gin and orange juice best cure for alcoholism real cause of which is ugliness and complete baffling sterility of existence as sold to you, otherwise it would be greed.[14]

On the evening of June 27, 1957, Lowry became violently drunk, forcing his wife to flee the small cottage where they were living in Sussex, England. When she returned the following morning, she discovered him lying dead on the floor. A bottle of her sleeping pills was missing. It was soon discovered, empty, hidden in a drawer. The coroner's ruling was "death by misadventure." Malcolm Lowry was forty-seven years old.

> Malcolm Lowry
> Late of the Bowery
> His prose was flowery
> And often glowery
> He lived, nightly, and drank, daily,
> And died playing the ukelele.[15]

Notes

1 Margerie Lowry, *Malcolm Lowry: Psalms and Songs*, p. 121.
2 Lowry, *Ultramarine*, p. 58.
3 Day, *Malcolm Lowry*, p. 268.
4 Lowry, *Ultramarine*, pp. 72–73.
5 Ibid., p. 93.
6 Margerie Lowry, op. cit., p. 60.
7 Ibid., p. 89.
8 Lowry, *Selected Letters*, p. 420.

Lowry in Dollarton, 1953

9 Day, op. cit., p. 295.
10 Lowry, *Under the Volcano*, pp. 125–26.
11 Lowry, *Selected Letters*, p. 66.
12 Day, op. cit., p. 355.
13 Ibid., p. 422.
14 Margerie Lowry, op. cit., p. 96.
15 Day, op. cit., p. 15.

Sources

Day, Douglas. *Malcolm Lowry*. New York: Dell Publishing Co., 1975.

Lowry, Malcolm. *Dark As the Grave Wherein My Friend Is Laid*. Edited by Douglas Day and Margerie Bonner Lowry. New York: New American Library, 1968.

———. *Hear Us O Lord from Heaven Thy Dwelling Place*. Philadelphia: Lippincott, 1961.

———. *October Ferry to Gabriola*. Edited by Margerie Lowry. New York: New American Library, 1970.

———. *Selected Letters*. Edited by Harvey Breit and Margerie Bonner Lowry. Philadelphia: Lippincott, 1965.

———. *Selected Poems*. Edited by Earle Birney with the assistance of Margerie Bonner Lowry. San Francisco: City Lights Books, 1962.

———. *Ultramarine*. Middlesex, England: Penguin Books, 1974.

———. *Under the Volcano*. New York: New American Library, 1966.

Lowry, Margerie, ed. *Malcolm Lowry: Psalms and Songs*. New York: New American Library, 1975.

VLADIMIR MAYAKOVSKY
1893-1930

All I have ever done—
                    is yours—
rhymes,
        themes,
                diction,
                        bass!
What is there
            that turns to ashes
                                faster
                                    than fame?
Shall I take it
                to the grave after death? [1]

VLADIMIR MAYAKOVSKY. Russian poet and playwright, later canonized poet laureate of the Revolution by Stalin, he was literary star of the post-Revolution period of the 1920s. (He and rival Sergei Esenin contended for the role of spokesman for the proletariat and the new order.) Although never a member of the Communist Party, Mayakovsky became the troubador of the Revolution and Bolshevism, and he was a superb propagandist, creating thousands of poems, advertisements, posters, and slogans to sell Lenin and the Soviets to the masses.

Matching the age in which he lived, Mayakovsky was dramatic and demanding. His emotions—his love of women, his need for love, his need to belong, his loneliness—were, like his physical presence, larger than life.

> Time!
> You lame icon-painter,
> will you at least dab my countenance
> and frame it as a freak of this age!
> I am as lonely as the only eye
> of a man on his way to the blind! [2]

Vladimir Mayakovsky was born on July 19, 1893, in the Georgian village of Bagdadi, remote in the forest area, the youngest of three children and the only son. His father, Vladimir Konstantinovich, former Russian nobleman, was a forester. He died suddenly when Mayakovsky was thirteen. The family moved to Moscow where Mayakovsky's mother managed to secure a small pension on which to live and pay for her children's schooling.

> Marussia Burliuk (David Burliuk's wife):
> He used to wear a black velvet coat with a turned-down collar. At his neck was a black foulard scarf, a crumpled ribbon was visible, and [his] pockets were bulging with cigarette and match boxes.
> Mayakovsky was tall, his chest was a bit sunken, his arms long and big, his hands red from the cold. His youthful head was crowned with thick dark hair, which much later he began to cut short. His cheeks were yellow; his mouth was large, hungry for kisses, sweets, and tobacco. His lips were big too; the lower one twitched to the left when he was talking, which gave him the appearance of condescension and arrogance.[3]

At fourteen, Mayakovsky left school and went to work for the Social-Democratic Workers Party, distributing propaganda. On March 29, 1908, he was arrested in a raid on a printing press and placed under surveillance. He was arrested twice more, his third arrest landing him in solitary confinement for five months, during which time he read and wrote poetry. When he was released from prison a year later, he abandoned political activities and turned to painting, entering the Moscow Art School in 1911. There he met painter David Burliuk, ten years his senior, who encouraged Mayakovsky to pursue poetry and gave him fifty kopecs a day so he could eat.

> Today I wrote a poem. . . . I read the poem to Burliuk. I added: written by a friend. David stopped and looked at me. "You wrote it yourself!" he exclaimed. "You're a genius!". . . That evening, quite unexpectedly, I became a poet.[4]

Burliuk brought Mayakovsky into his circle of artists and writers, a group which was influenced by the Futurist movement begun in Italy with Marinetti. In a revolt against Russian literary tradition these Moscow Futurists composed their manifesto: "Slap to the Public's Taste: Pushkin, Dostoevsky, Tolstoy, etc., etc., must be thrown overboard from the steamer of the Present Time." Disassociating themselves from the other Futurist groups, they wanted to be recognized as the "world's only Futurists."

In October, 1913, they took to the streets of the city. Their faces painted, costumed in outlandish and gaudy garb, they paraded around and recited poetry. In the evening, crowds gathered to listen to them read. Mayakovsky, wearing a bright yellow tunic and top hat, roses painted on his cheeks, became the star of this street theater. In a deep loud voice he read verses intended to scandalize the audience, who in turn called him names and threw things at him.

> And if today I, the brutal Hun,
> won't clown for you—what will you do,
> if I laugh and spit with joy,
> spit in your face I will
> I—squanderer of priceless mines of words.[5]

In December, 1913, Mayakovsky wrote, produced, and acted in his first play at a Futurist theater festival in Petrograd. Essentially a one-man play, he called it *Vladimir Mayakovsky: A Tragedy*. The theater was obtained for four nights and all performances were sold out. Onstage, Mayakovsky, wearing a toga and laurel wreath, celebrated his poetic genius: as he ascended into heaven he was chanting his own name.

> Boris Pasternak:
> The art was called a tragedy. . . . The tragedy was called *Vladimir Mayakovsky*. The title contained the discovery (there was genius in its simplicity) that the poet is not the author but the object of lyric poetry, addressing the world in the first person. The title was not the author's name but the description of contents.[6]

War broke out on August 1, 1914. Although Mayakovsky volunteered to serve, he was rejected for "lack of political loyalty." He began writing articles and poems for the newspaper *Nov*, but the antiwar spirit of his verses lost him his job. He moved to Petrograd, where in order to eat he wrote poems for a popular literary magazine, *New Satyricon*, and recited poetry in The Stray Dog, a café frequented by artists and writers. Eventually, he was summoned by the Army and put to work as a draftsman in the Petrograd Automobile School.

> No gray hairs streak my soul,
> no grandfatherly fondness there!
> I shake the world with the might of my voice,
> and walk—handsome,
> twentytwoyearold.[7]

In the summer of 1915, Mayakovsky met Lili Brik, the woman who became the supreme love of his life and heroine of his poetry, as well as the source of personal anguish. She was red-haired and petite. Her large face was lit up by extraordinary hazel-brown eyes. Men were attracted to Lili and she reciprocated their affections. Although she was married to lawyer Osip Brik, the couple had an arrangement which allowed her to roam.

Osip was sincerely taken by the poet as well as by his verses. The three, Brik, Lili, and Mayakovsky, came together in an odd ménage à trois. Mayakovsky moved into the Palais Royal, close by the Briks' Petrograd apartment. He and Lili spent afternoons as lovers; in the evening the three gathered together for dinner, and to discuss poetry.

> If one suddenly tiptoed to the bedroom door
> and blessed the quilted cover above you,
> I know
> there would be a smell of scorching wool,
> and the devil's flesh would rise in sulphurous fumes.[8]

Greatly impressed by Mayakovsky's poems, Osip Brik provided

the money to have "The Cloud in Trousers" and "The Backbone Flute" published as books. The Brik apartment soon became the central gathering place for the Futurists, with Osip Brik becoming more and more active as a member of the group which included Boris Pasternak, David Burliuk, Victor Shklovsky, and Nicholas Asyeyev. Together, they founded a new Futurist periodical entitled *Seized*, to which they all contributed.

> Lili Brik:
> Volodya and I were always together: we went to the islands, took walks. . . . Volodya would put on a top hat, I a large black hat with feathers, and we would go to the Nevsky, for instance, to buy a pencil for Osya. We would enter a store and Volodya would address the salesgirl with a mysterious expression on his face: "Mademoiselle, will you please give us a pencil so strange it is red on one end and blue on the other!"
> Mademoiselle would jump, startled, to my great delight.[9]

The Revolution began in February, 1917, and culminated in October with Lenin and the Bolsheviks' seizure of power. Mayakovsky felt this was his revolution. It fit his needs like a glove: his revolt against literary tradition, his desire to depoetize poetry, his fascination with the city, the street, the people, language, and technology. It allowed him to get involved in something larger than his relationship with Lili. However, he found that his extremist philosophy, his championing of Futurism, was not necessarily acceptable to the new order. Mayakovsky maintained that an entirely new art—proletarian art—had to be created. All other art was worthless.

> To Lili Brik:
> Does love mean everything for me? Everything, but in a different way. Love is life, the essential life. It is the motor that moves the poetry, the work, all the rest. Love is at the heart of everything. If it stops, the rest will die, will be superfluous, unnecessary.[10]

At odds with Anatoly Lunacharsky, newly appointed People's Commissar of Education, Mayakovsky failed to find a relevant job in the new regime. In December, 1917, he went to Moscow, leaving Lili behind. There he and David Burliuk and other Futurists earned their bread by declaiming their verses in the evenings at the Poet's Café to an audience of bourgeois spectators looking for entertainment. The café was forced to close in April, 1918. By then, Mayakovsky had become involved in a film project, adapting Jack London's *Martin Eden* and starring in the film, which was entitled *Not Born for Money*.

Mayakovsky spent the summer of 1918 with Lili and Osip Brik in a hotel in the countryside near Petrograd writing his second play, *Mystery-Bouffe*, which he described as an "heroic epic, and satiric representation of our era." In the play the "Unclean" (the workers) overthrow the "Clean" (bourgeoisie) and inherit the earth. Mayakovsky completed the play in time for the first anniversary of the Revolution in October. Vsevolod Meyerhold agreed to direct, and the production was mounted but with a great deal of difficulty. The play was a failure.

> Who is he?
> Who is that free spirit?
> Who is he—
> that nameless one?
> Who is he,
> with no country of his own?
> Why did he come?
> What prophesies did he utter? [11]

Always apart from others, irrepressibly iconoclastic, Mayakovsky nevertheless wanted to belong to the Revolution. In 1918 he joined the Department for Visual Arts, formed by the People's Commissariat for Education. He wrote poems for their weekly paper. Still calling for the destruction of old traditions, he proclaimed Futurism as the new art of Communism, and was attacked for his adolescence and egocentricity.

> What we need is not a dead temple where dead works of art can fossilize but a live factory of human spirit. We need raw art, raw words, raw deeds. . . . Art ought to assemble not in

the lifeless temple-museums but everywhere—in the streets, in streetcars, factories, laboratories, and in workers' districts.[12]

Mayakovsky left the Department in 1919 and he and the Briks moved to Moscow where they shared tiny living quarters. For the next several years he worked industriously for ROSTA (Russian Telegraph Agency), drawing thousands of propaganda posters and composing texts and rhyming captions. Lili worked by his side, coloring in the posters.

He also functioned as a public poet, reciting before crowds and at public military meetings. During these years he wrote "150 Million," which got published despite Lenin's opinion that the poem was stupid and pretentious. It was a propaganda poem in which Mayakovsky claimed to be speaking for the population of Soviet Russia. Although its authorship was well known, in the spirit of the poem he had it published anonymously.

> Kornel Chukovsky (critic):
> Old writers had their readers, but Mayakovsky, when composing his poems, imagines himself standing before large, listening crowds. . . . He dreams of himself standing alone— like a wild, inspired giant—on a high platform, facing a raging or admiring crowd and carrying them away with his inspired cries.[13]

In December, 1922, a break occurred in Mayakovsky's love affair with Lili Brik; she wanted her sexual freedom. They agreed to a two-month separation during which time Mayakovsky, in torment, wrote the poem "About This," a love poem to Lili. Their relationship lost its intensity after this interlude, although they continued to be close.

The mid-1920s saw Mayakovsky at the pinnacle of his career as Russia's leading poet. Lenin's death on January 21, 1924, came as a crushing blow to him, and to the country. The artistic freedom experienced under Lenin would be gradually eclipsed under Stalin's rule. Mayakovsky spent nearly a year composing "Vladimir Ilyich Lenin," his ode to Lenin, which he read to a group of Communists and dedicated to the Russian Communist Party in October, 1924. The

Mayakovsky with Lili Brik

state publishing house, Gosizdat, planned to published his collected works in four volumes in 1925.

> Alexander Voronsky (writer):
> Mayakovsky is very lonely and remote from people. He does not like the masses, the collective. The tribune and orator of his poems is isolated from the crowd. He is an extreme individualist and an egocentric. He rightly calls himself a demon in American shoes: there lies on him the brand of rejection, exile, separation, and isolation.[14]

In the summer of 1925, Mayakovsky traveled to Mexico and on to the United States where he gave successful readings in New York, Philadelphia, and Chicago. The newspaper *Novy Mir* printed a collection of his poems entitled "To the Americans" which sold 10,000 copies. His friend David Burliuk, then living in New York, published two volumes of his poetry. Upon his return to Moscow, he began to tour provincial cities, calling himself a troubador. He continued these readings until his death, appearing in fifty cities in the Soviet Union in more than 200 appearances. To supplement the payments he received for public readings, Mayakovsky wrote newspaper articles.

> To Lili Brik:
> In my view, I have become a terribly proletarian poet: I have no money and do not write any poems.[15]

On December 27, 1925, Sergei Esenin, poet and rival, committed suicide in a hotel room in Leningrad. His last poem was printed by the papers. Mayakovsky, "prey to the same hotel rooms, the same pipes, and the same compulsory loneliness," wrote "To Sergei Esenin," a poem in which he attempts to neutralize the effect of Esenin's dramatic and compelling suicide.

> This epoch
>   resists the pen—
> but tell me,
>   you,
>   invalids and cripples,

who of the great ones,

       when,

           did choose

a smoother

    and lighter

       path?[16]

In 1927, Mayakovsky, in a new attempt to get a literary group established, brought out a new version of *LEF*, his Futurist periodical, which had folded in 1925. *New Lef*, headquartered in the Briks' apartment, declared itself dedicated to the continuation of the struggle for Communist culture. The periodical and editor Mayakovsky were strongly attacked in the press. The ideas, methods, and philosophy presented in *New Lef*, said the critics, were irrelevant, outmoded, and no longer valid for the Revolution. Mayakovsky stepped down as editor; the periodical soon ceased to exist.

Mayakovsky went to Paris in 1928 where he fell in love with eighteen-year-old Tatyana Yakoleva, a White Russian, as tall as he and beautiful. Mayakovsky wanted to marry her but Tatyana, who did not want to live in Russia, resisted. He would not accept her refusal as final and continued to court her. Commissioned to write political poems from Paris, he wrote a love poem instead—"Letter from Paris to Comrade Kostrov on the Nature of Love"—which angered the authorities.

Mayakovsky wrote his third play, a satire on Communist bureaucracy entitled *The Bedbug*, during 1928. Directed by Meyerhold, it opened in Moscow on February 13, 1929. The play was lighthearted enough to successfully avoid the ever-increasing censorship under Stalin. Immediately after it opened, Mayakovsky returned to Paris to continue his pursuit of Tatyana, but when his visa expired, he was forced to return to Moscow in March. Several months later, he learned that Tatyana had married a French count.

More and more often I think:
it might be far better for me
to punctuate my end with a bullet.
This very day,

just in case,
I'm staging my final performance.[17]

The Bathhouse, Mayakovsky's last play, was written during the summer of 1929. Dramatically more obvious in its ridicule and condemnation of Soviet bureaucracy, it was angrily attacked in the newspapers when it opened both in Leningrad and Moscow. The critics claimed that the workers would not understand it. As a result the play was a disaster, and Mayakovsky began to feel isolated, persecuted, and lonely.

> Comrades, I have been existing physically for thirty-five years, and for twenty years as a so-called creative writer. Through all this time I have defended my views with the strength of my lungs, with the force and vigor of my voice. And I am not afraid that what I am doing will be declared null and void. Lately an opinion has circulated that I was a widely recognized talent and I am glad that The Bathhouse is shattering this opinion. Leaving the theater I wipe the spittle from my massive forehead, metaphorically, of course.[18]

Mayakovsky's last "work" and a final monument to his egocentricity as well as a measure of his growing isolation was "Twenty Years of Work," an exhibition of his work which he organized in December, 1929, with Lili's help. When the exhibition opened at the Writers Union in Moscow, it was swarmed by young students, but Mayakovsky's peers and the official literary groups stayed away. Mayakovsky was exhausted, depressed, and suffering from severe hoarseness when he read his poem, "At the Top of My Voice."

In February, Lili and Osip Brik departed from Moscow for a trip to London leaving Mayakovsky alone in his room at 2 Lubyansky Passage. Although he continued to make public appearances, his emotional condition was unstable. At the time he was having an unsatisfactory affair with a young actress.

On the morning of April 14, 1930, immediately after quarreling with his new lover, Vladimir Mayakovsky fatally shot himself through the heart. His weapon was the pistol he had used twelve years before in the film, Not Born for Money. He left a suicide letter addressed

"To all." In it he wrote: "Lili—love me." He was thirty-six years old.

His body lay in state at the Club of the Writers Federation. More than 150,000 mourners came to view the poet's body. A wreath made of flywheel, hammer, and screws was placed at his coffin. It was inscribed: "To the iron poet—an iron wreath."

> Past one o'clock. You must have gone to bed.
> The Milky Way streams silver through the night.
> I'm in no hurry; with lightning telegrams
> I have no cause to wake or trouble you.
> And, as they say, the incident is closed.
> Love's boat has smashed against the daily grind.
> Now you and I are quits. Why bother then
> to balance mutual sorrows, pains, and hurts.
> Behold what quiet settles on the world.
> Night wraps the sky in tribute from the stars.
> In hours like these, one rises to address
> The ages, history, and all creation.[19]

Notes

1 Woroszylski, *The Life of Mayakovsky*, p. 360.
2 Mayakovsky, "I," *The Bedbug and Selected Poetry*, p. 59.
3 Woroszylski, op. cit., p. 33.
4 Ibid., p. 30.
5 Ibid., p. 63.
6 Ibid., p. 83.
7 Mayakovsky, "The Cloud in Trousers," *The Bedbug and Selected Poetry*, p. 61.
8 Mayakovsky, "The Backbone Flute," *The Bedbug and Selected Poetry*, p. 113.
9 Woroszylski, op. cit., p. 165.
10 Ibid., p. 302.
11 Mayakovsky, "Mystery-Bouffe," *The Complete Plays of Vladimir Mayakovsky*, p. 90.
12 Ibid., p. 246.
13 Ibid., p. 272.
14 Ibid., p. 356.
15 Ibid., p. 402.

16   Ibid., p. 397.
17   Mayakovsky, "The Backbone Flute," *The Bedbug and Selected Poetry*, p. 111.
18   Woroszylski, op. cit., p. 488.
19   Mayakovsky, "Past One O'Clock," *The Bedbug and Selected Poetry*, p. 237.

Sources

Mayakovsky, Vladimir. *The Complete Plays of Vladimir Mayakovsky.* Translated by Guy Daniels. New York: Simon & Schuster, 1968.
———. *The Bedbug and Selected Poetry*. Edited by Patricia Blake. Translated by Max Hayward and George Reavey. Bloomington: Indiana University Press, 1975.
Woroszylski, Wiktor. *The Life of Mayakovsky*. Translated by Boleslaw Taborski. New York: The Orion Press, 1970.

YUKIO MISHIMA
1925-1970

It was in death that I had discovered my real
"life's aim." [1]

YUKIO MISHIMA. Japanese writer, the author of forty novels, eighteen plays, twenty volumes of short stories, and numerous essays. Although he considered much of it hack writing for purely commercial purposes, his best works placed him in the forefront of the Japanese writers of his generation, a position he continues to hold today. Mishima's dominant theme and obsession was the Westernization of Japanese culture.

Mishima was a popular and flamboyant character. He was called the Japanese Hemingway, a Renaissance man. He indulged in weight lifting, sword play, and acting. He was a homosexual who was fascinated by physical beauty and violence. He was, finally, an Emperor worshiper, and death lover.

> In the average person, I imagine, the body precedes language. In my case, words came first of all; then—belatedly, with every appearance of extreme reluctance, and already clothed in concepts—came the flesh. It was already, as goes without saying, sadly wasted by words.[2]

He was born Kimitake Hirakoa on January 24, 1925, in Tokyo.

His father, Azuza, Deputy Director of the Bureau of Fisheries in the Agriculture Ministry, was a bureaucrat. His mother, Shizue, to whom he would become intimately attached, was the daughter of a school principal, an educated woman with an appreciation of literature. Mishima was the first of three children.

Shortly after his birth, he was taken from his mother's side by Natsu, his grandmother, who lived on the first floor of their house. She maintained that it was dangerous for a child to live on the second floor: he might fall. Natsu took possessive control of him for the first twelve years of his life. Raised in near isolation, overprotected, his every move watched, he grew up into a pale, bony, frail young boy.

> My bed was placed in my grandmother's sickroom, perpetually closed and stifling with odors and sickness and old age, and I was raised there beside her sickbed.[3]

Natsu sent the boy back to his parents when he was twelve. By now Mishima had become an avid reader and was beginning to fill notebooks with poetry. He was obviously brilliant and precocious. He was also very delicate, emotionally as well as physically. From this point on, his relationship to his mother, Shizue, was primary and would remain so even after his marriage. His mother was a major figure in his life: she was his confidante and protector, while his father remained largely unsympathetic to his firstborn son, even going so far as to confiscate and destroy his writings on a regular basis.[4]

> The period of childhood is a stage on which time and space become entangled. . . . I could not believe that the world was any more complicated than a structure of building blocks, nor that the so-called "social community," which I must presently enter, could be more dazzling than the world of fairy tales. Thus, without my being aware of it, one of the determinants of my life had come into operation. And because of my struggles against it, from the beginning my every fantasy was tinged with despair, strangely complete and in itself resembling passionate desire.[5]

He attended the aristocratic Peers School where, at fifteen, he became the youngest member of the literary club's editorial board. At sixteen, he was made the editor. That same year he was the first student ever invited to contribute to the literary magazine *Bungei-Bunka*. His short story "A Forest in Full Flower" was serialized in four issues and published under his newly chosen pen name: Yukio Mishima.

Mishima soon became the darling of a circle of literary men who identified themselves with the death-obsessed Japanese Romantic school that flourished during the war years. In his adolescent mind, death and eroticism became subtly interconnected.

> Although as a child I read every story I could lay my hands on, I never liked the princesses. I was fond only of the princes. I was all the fonder of princes murdered or princes fated for death. I was completely in love with any youth who was killed.[6]

After graduating with top honors from the Peers School, Mishima, obeying his father's wishes, entered law school at Tokyo Imperial University in the fall of 1944. His class was soon mobilized on account of the war but as a result of his frail health, Mishima was assigned to office or library jobs which enabled him to read and write without interruption.

In February, 1945, Mishima received his draft notice. He failed the medical exam and was rejected for service. A few months later, on August 15, 1945, Japan surrendered. The war was over.

> It was not the reality of defeat. Instead, for me—for me alone—it meant that fearful days were beginning. It meant that, whether I would or no, and despite everything that had deceived me into believing that such a day would never come, the very next day I must begin that "everyday life" of a member of human society. How the mere words made me tremble![7]

After graduating from law school, Mishima went to work for the Banking Bureau of the Ministry of Finance. Upon his return from the office each evening, he would write until dawn. This self-imposed schedule exhausted him dangerously. In September, 1948, with his father's reluctant permission, he quit his job at the bank to devote full time to writing.

> I had been handed what must be called a full menu of all the troubles in my life while still too young to read it. But all I had to do was spread my napkin and face the table. Even the fact that I would now be writing an odd book like this was precisely noted on the menu, where it must have been before my eyes from the beginning.[8]

Confessions of a Mask, Mishima's autobiographical novel, was published in 1949. In it he revealed himself to the public—his homosexuality, his erotic fascination with the well-tanned naked bodies of young men, and with blood and death; his adoration of Guido Reni's portrait of the death of St. Sebastian, the Christian martyr. Mishima's novel dazzled and disturbed the critics, who acclaimed it a work of genius.

> There, in my murder theater, young Roman gladiators offered up their lives for my amusement; and all the deaths that took place there not only had to overflow with blood but also had to be performed with all due ceremony. I delighted in all forms of capital punishment and all implements of execution.[9]

By the end of 1956, Mishima had published, among others, *Forbidden Colors*, a novel about homosexuality in Tokyo; *The Sound of Waves*, a love story which was a record-breaking best-seller; and *The Temple of the Golden Pavilion*, more popular even than *Waves* as well as being an important critical success. *Waves* was published that year in the United States by Alfred A. Knopf, and in the spring of 1957 *Five Modern Nō Plays* was published and well received.

> What I wanted was to die among strangers, untroubled, beneath a cloudless sky . . . What I wanted was some natural spontaneous suicide. I wanted a death like that of a fox, not yet well versed in cunning, that walks carelessly along a mountain path and is shot by a hunter because of its own stupidity.[10]

Mishima began traveling to the West, to San Francisco and New York, to Rio for Carnival, to London and Paris, and to Greece. The latter country wrought a change in him: "Greece cured my self-hatred and my loneliness and awoke in me a *will to health* in the Nietzschean sense."[11] He embarked upon a body-building program that he would continue until his death. Working with a coach at a gym in Tokyo, exercising and weight lifting, he gradually transformed his slight frame into a body that he could admire and show off, posing naked for photographers.

> Specifically, I cherished a romantic impulse toward death, yet at the same time I required a strictly classical body as its vehicle; a peculiar sense of destiny made me believe that the reason why my romantic impulse toward death remained unfulfilled in reality was the immensely simple fact that I lacked the necessary physical qualifications. A powerful, tragic frame and sculpturesque muscles were indispensable in a romantically noble death. Any confrontation between weak, flabby flesh and death seemed to me absurdly inappropriate.[12]

In 1958 Mishima married Yoko Sugiyama, the pretty nineteen-year-old daughter of a Japanese painter. The marriage was arranged according to Japanese custom, with Mishima interviewing several young women in formal meetings. Although Yoko never replaced Shizue or Mishima's desire for young male lovers, their relationship was respectful and affectionate and more Western than the traditional Japanese marriage. Soon after, Mishima built a house for his entire family with a private wing for his mother and father. The house was his own design, a mixture of Spanish, Italian, and colonial architecture. He called it an "anti-Zen house." There he and Yoko entertained flamboyantly.

> My ideal is to live in a house where I sit on a rococo chair wearing an aloha shirt and blue jeans.[13]

Mishima's next novel, *Kyoko's House*, was published in 1960. He called it a study of nihilism and considered it to be an important work. The critics, however, disagreed and branded the novel Mishi-

Mishima at a Tokyo gym

ma's first major failure. A political novel, *After the Banquet*, followed
in 1961 and regained him popular ground as did *The Sailor Who Fell
from Grace with the Sea*. But sales of his books were disappointing
on the whole and Mishima's place as an important and popular novelist appeared to be in question.

> Death began from the time when I set about acquiring an
> existence other than that of words.[14]

The political right wing in Japan had begun to reactivate in the
early 1960s. Mishima, until then politically unencumbered, published
"Patriotism," a short story in 1961 that graphically depicts the *seppuku*
(ritual suicide) of a lieutenant in the Imperial Guard who prefers
death to betraying his fellow officers. The story exalts the virtues of
patriotism and the right wing to which Mishima had become attracted.

A film version of the story was later made entitled *The Rites of
Love and Death*. Mishima both directed the film and played the role
of the lieutenant who commits *seppuku*. The film won second prize
at a film festival in Paris, and became a major box office hit in Japan.

From 1966 to 1970, Mishima was simultaneously involved in two
major enterprises. The first was the writing of *The Sea of Fertility*,
a tetralogy, and his most ambitious undertaking since *Kyoko's House*.
The second was the Shield Society, a private army founded by Mishima with a group of students. Nationalistic in spirit, the purpose of
the army was to defend the Emperor with their lives against any
enemy, from the political left or right. When Mishima announced the
formation of the Shield Society to the press, the reaction was one of
amusement. The literary establishment, on the other hand, did not
appreciate his Emperor-worship and ostracized him.

> Only through the group, I realized—through sharing the suf-
> fering of the group—could the body reach that height of ex-
> istence that the individual alone could never attain.[15]

Mishima's devoted aide in the operations of the Shield Society
was Masakatsu Morita, a young student, an orphan, who fervently
shared Mishima's right-wing political ideas. His job was to screen the
applicants to the Society after which Mishima would make the final

*Mishima with the four members of the Shield Society who took part
in hara-kiri (Morita is on far left)*

decision. By 1970, the Shield Society had grown into a rigorously trained and uniformed force of eighty young men. Early that year Mishima began plotting the event that would culminate in his death by hara-kiri. With four young members of the Society, including Morita, he secretly worked out details of the action that would take place on November 25—essentially what they planned was a coup d'etat against the Japanese Self-Defense Forces, the Jieitai (Japan's armed forces), in protest of what Mishima felt to be the gradual undermining of Japan's history and traditions through Westernization. Mishima wanted the Jieitai reinstated as the national army.

> Our fundamental values, as Japanese, are threatened. The Emperor is not being given his rightful place in Japan.
> We have waited in vain for the Jieitai to rebel. If no action is taken, the Western powers will control Japan for the next century! . . .
> Let us restore Nippon to its true state and let us die.[16]

Mishima, at the same time, continued to write the final volume of *The Sea of Fertility*, which was due at the publisher on the same day, November 25. His family suspected nothing; that summer, as usual, he spent several weeks at the beach with his wife and two young children.

> What he was about to perform was an act in his public capacity as a soldier, something he had never previously shown his wife. It called for a resolution equal to the courage to enter battle; it was a death of no less degree and quality than death in the front line. It was his conduct on the battlefield that he was now to display.[17]

On the morning of November 25, 1970, shortly after he placed the final section of *The Sea of Fertility* in an envelope for his publisher, Mishima was picked up by Morita and three others, dressed in their Shield Society uniforms. They drove to the Jieitai base in central Tokyo and were admitted into the office of the Commandant of the Eastern Army Headquarters. Mishima was wearing a long sword.

On signal, one of the group grabbed the general, who was gagged and bound. Then they barricaded themselves in the office. Mishima demanded that the soldiers of the Thirty-second Infantry Regiment be gathered outside, or the general would be killed. He had a speech to make. At noon, Mishima stepped out onto the balcony and began to appeal to the soldiers gathered below to rise up against the Constitution to protect the Emperor and to protect the traditions and values of Japan. His words were greeted by jeers and heckling.

> Resting the sword in its cloth wrapping on the mat before him, the lieutenant rose from his knees, resettled himself cross-legged, and unfastened the hooks of his uniform collar. . . . Slowly, one by one, he undid the flat brass buttons. The dusky brown chest was revealed, and then the stomach. He unclasped his belt and undid the buttons of his trousers. The pure whiteness of the thickly coiled loincloth showed itself.[18]

At the conclusion of his speech, most of which went unheard over the noise of the soldiers, Mishima stepped back inside the office. Facing the general and his four companions, he stripped to his loincloth and knelt on the floor; in his hand he held a short dagger. Morita took his place behind Mishima, holding the long sword above the head of his forty-five-year-old leader. Mishima lifted his arms and in a violent movement drove the short sword into his belly.

> He returned to consciousness. The blade had certainly pierced the wall of the stomach, he thought. His breathing was difficult, his chest thumped violently, and in some far deep region, which he could hardly believe was a part of himself, a fearful and excruciating pain came welling up as if the ground had split open to disgorge a boiling stream of molten rock.[19]

As Mishima's dagger entered his stomach, Morita brought the long sword down on the back of Mishima's neck, severing his head from his body. Morita immediately proceeded to kneel in the same position while another follower took his place behind him with the long sword. Within moments Morita's head lay on the floor next to Mishima's.

Dress my body in a Shield Society uniform, give me white

gloves and a soldier's sword in my hand, and then do me the favor of taking a photograph. . . . I want evidence that I died not as a literary man but as a warrior.[20]

Notes

1 Mishima, *Confessions of a Mask*, p. 183.
2 Mishima, *Sun and Steel*, p. 8.
3 Mishima, *Confessions*, pp. 5–6.
4 Nathan, *Mishima: A Biography*, p. 44.
5 Mishima, *Confessions*, p. 15.
6 Ibid., p. 20.
7 Ibid., p. 218.
8 Ibid., p. 15.
9 Ibid., pp. 92–93.
10 Ibid., p. 138.
11 Nathan, op. cit., p. 115.
12 Mishima, *Sun and Steel*, pp. 27–28.
13 Scott-Stokes, *The Life and Death of Yukio Mishima*, p. 151.
14 Mishima, *Sun and Steel*, p. 67.
15 Ibid., p. 87.
16 Scott-Stokes, op. cit., p. 43.
17 Mishima, "Patriotism," *Death in Midsummer and Other Stories*, p. 111.
18 Ibid., p. 112.
19 Ibid., p. 113.
20 Nathan, op. cit., p. 273.

Sources

Mishima, Yukio. *Confessions of a Mask*. Translated by Meredith Weatherby. New York: New Directions, 1958.
———. *Death in Midsummer and Other Stories*. New York: New Directions, 1966.
———. *The Decay of the Angel*. Translated by Edward G. Seidensticker. New York: Pocket Books, 1975.
———. *Forbidden Colors*. Translated by Alfred H. Marks. New York: Berkley Books, 1974.

———. *Runaway Horses.* Translated by Michael Gallagher. New York: Pocket Books, 1973.

———. *The Sound of Waves.* Translated by Meredith Weatherby. New York: Berkley, 1961.

———. *Spring Snow.* Translated by Michael Gallagher. New York: Pocket Books, 1973.

———. *Sun and Steel.* Translated by John Bester. New York: Grove Press, 1970.

———. *The Temple of Dawn.* Translated by E. Dale Saunders and Cecile Segawa Seigle. New York: Pocket Books, 1973.

———. *The Temple of the Golden Pavilion.* Translated by Ivan Morris. New York: Berkley, 1971.

Nathan, John. *Mishima: A Biography.* Boston: Little, Brown & Co., 1974.

Scott-Stokes, Henry. *The Life and Death of Yukio Mishima.* New York: Delta Books, 1975.

AMEDEO MODIGLIANI
1884-1920

I want to be a tuneswept fiddle string that feels
the master melody and snaps.[1]

AMEDEO MODIGLIANI. Italian painter and sculptor. Called the "Prince of Montparnasse" and "King of the Bohemians," his wild life-style—his drinking, drug-taking, and womanizing—made him a legendary figure in the artist quarters of Paris in the first decades of the twentieth century. It also served to obscure completely the importance of his art. Although acknowledged by his fellow artists, Modigliani received virtually no public recognition for his work during his lifetime: the magnificent portraits, the long-necked women with pupil-less eyes, the monumental nudes, which today are considered masterpieces.

> Life is a Gift: from the few to the many; from those who know and have to those who do not know and have not.[2]

Amedeo Clemente Modigliani was born on July 12, 1884, in Leghorn (Livorno), Italy, the fourth and last child of Flaminio Modigliani and Eugenia Garsin, both Sephardic Jews. His father had a prosperous coal and wood business that failed around the time of Modigliani's birth. Thereafter, Flaminio would be considered a nonentity in the family; the dominant personality became Eugenia.

Independent, resourceful, and headstrong, she came from a "mad" French family whose history was laced with suicides.

> Jeanne Modigliani (daughter):
> The [Garsin] family acknowledged his drug addiction because they too venerated Baudelaire and Verlaine, but they minimized his drinking because they themselves were light drinkers. And they instinctively converted his sacred madness into the frenzy of genius because it was present in practically all the Garsin, and thus something too close to home to be faced.[3]

Flaminio Modigliani's business failure forced the family to assume a more humble style of living. Eugenia, with the help of her sister, Laure, began a private day school at home to bring in money. Amedeo Garsin, Eugenia's favorite brother, also made contributions to the family. Although no longer rich, Eugenia maintained a sense of aristocratic superiority which she passed on to her youngest, and favorite, son.

At fourteen, Modigliani began to take drawing lessons. He was a bright, intellectually precocious child. (He was sexually precocious too: legend has him seducing the household maid at a young age.) His art lessons were interrupted when he contracted a nearly fatal case of typhoid fever. Once he was well enough to return to art school, his mother gave him permission to give up all other studies to devote himself to drawing and painting. Independently, he indulged his love for reading (he was fluent in both Italian and French) and immersed himself in Bergson, D'Annunzio, and Nietzsche (for which his friends nicknamed him "Superman"). His closest friend in art school was Oscar Ghilia, a painter, eight years his senior, and wise in the ways of the world.

> To Oscar Ghilia:
> I write to pour myself out to you and to affirm myself before myself.
> I am prey to the splintering and diffusion of tremendous energy.
> But I want my life to be like a richly abundant river that

spreads with joy over the land. . . . I am rich and fecund with germination, and need to work.

I have the excitation, but the excitation which precedes joy, and which follows the uninterrupted activity of the intelligence.[4]

In 1900, Modigliani fell seriously ill once again, with pleurisy. When he had recovered sufficiently, Eugenia took her sixteen-year-old son south for a cure. On the sojourn Modigliani first encountered the treasures of the museums of Naples, Rome, and Venice, and became fascinated by Greek and Roman sculptures. Modigliani now decided that sculpture was the medium through which he ultimately wanted to express himself.

To Oscar Ghilia:
We (excuse the we) have rights different from other people because we have different needs which place us . . . above the moral law. Your obligation is *not to consume yourself in the sacrifice.* Your obligation is to save your dream.[5]

Modigliani went to Florence in 1902 where he attended classes at the Scuola Libera di Nudo, and shared a studio with Oscar Ghilia. Art school bored Modigliani. The following year he went to the Institute of Fine Arts in Venice, his tuition costs borne by his uncle, Amedeo Garsin. Modigliani rarely attended classes but pursued his own interests—especially the fourteenth-century Sienese masters and the works of Carpaccio. He found his live models in the cafés and brothels of the city. In Venice, he was first introduced to the pleasures of hashish and the mysteries of the occult by a corpulent baron who called himself Cuccolu.

Modigliani's goal was to live in Paris, the art capital of the world. It was a city filled with young artists from all over the world, and the hub of the modern art movement. Fauvism was at its peak and Cubism was on the verge of being born. His dream was realized in 1906. With his mother's blessing and a small sum of money, enough to last for several months if he were prudent, Modigliani, twenty-one years old, took the train to Paris in January.

Pierre Sichel (biographer):

[Modigliani] wears an immaculate black suit with the lapels high, flat, and smartly notched. His vest crosses high on his chest, all six buttons buttoned; his trousers are tapered, his shoes pointed . . . his bowtie is black, wide, and jaunty; his pointed collar armor-plate stiff; and his starched shirt cuffs peep out from his sleeves an exact quarter-inch or so. He is the rich young aristocrat with his black cape, his spats, his gloves.[6]

He enrolled at the Académie Colarossi and, at first, lived in luxurious quarters on the Right Bank. By fall, having impetuously squandered his money, Modigliani moved to the *maquis* in Montmartre, a wasteland of handmade shacks inhabited by poor artists. Here, he lived in "wild disorder" in an iron-and-wood hut which he furnished with a crude bed, a couple of chairs, and a tin basin. His sketches covered the walls.

By now, he had abandoned his aristocratic clothes for a new style of dress. While most artists in the *maquis* wore plain work clothes, Modigliani sported bright-colored shirts; belted his brown corduroy trousers with a red sash; and tied a silk scarf at his neck. He wore a wide-brimmed black felt hat and, when it was cold, a cape.

My Italian eyes cannot get used to the light of Paris . . . such an all-embracing light . . . you cannot imagine what new themes I have thought up in violet, deep orange, and ochre. . . . There is no way of making them sing just now.[7]

During his early years in Paris, Modigliani developed a life-style that matched his bohemian clothes. At first shy and reticent, a boy who watered his wine and did not smoke, Modigliani soon began to indulge heavily in alcohol, hashish, and ether. The painter Maurice Utrillo, himself a mad alcoholic who would go to great lengths to get a drink, became Modigliani's frequent companion. It soon became an event to see Modigliani sober. When very drunk, he would begin to recite poetry from memory, Dante to Villon, and continue until exhausted. At other times, in a drunken frenzy, he would take off all his clothes; his friends were soon able to predict when Modigliani would begin to strip. And then there were his women, his models, a procession of them, whom he sketched and painted and slept with.

> Alcohol is for the middle class evil. It is a vice. It is the Devil's beckon. But for us artists it is necessary.[8]

Despite a regular small allowance from his mother, he was forever broke and owing rent money. He moved from room to room like a vagabond. Often, in his haste to depart he would leave behind his drawings. He preferred to spend his money on the pleasures of wine, hashish, or absinthe than on food or rent. If he needed a meal he would exchange a drawing for it. If he needed a few francs he would sketch a customer in a café and hope to sell it to the client.

> To Oscar Ghilia:
> Beauty herself makes painful demands; but these nevertheless bring forth the most supreme efforts of the soul.[9]

Modigliani's first years in Paris were artistically exciting and full of promise. He met Picasso and was invited to the gatherings of artists and writers at his studio in the Bateau-Lavoir. In 1907, five watercolors and two oil paintings of his were accepted for exhibition at the Salon d'Automne, an important credential for the young artist, as well as a hopeful sign of future success. That year Modigliani met Paul Alexandre, a young doctor who was the first person to become sufficiently interested in his work to buy it. Alexandre set up a colony for artists where Modigliani could work; he also shared the painter's interest in hashish, which they indulged in together. In 1908, Modigliani exhibited five oils and a drawing at the Salon des Indépendants. His work, showing the influence of Matisse and Fauvism, attracted critical attention.

> Max Jacob:
> Everything in [Modigliani] tended toward purity in art. His unsupportable pride, his black ingratitude, his haughtiness did not exclude familiarity. Yet all that was nothing but a need for crystalline purity, a trueness to himself in life as

in art. He was cutting, but as fragile as glass; also as inhuman as glass, so to say.[10]

In 1909, Modigliani moved to Montparnasse, the artist quarter on the Left Bank, where he continued his immoderate way of life. He was now putting his energies into sculpting, having discovered African sculpture, in particular the masks of the Ivory Coast. Alexandre had introduced him to Brancusi, the Rumanian sculptor, now his neighbor in the Cité Falquière, who encouraged him. He also met sculptor Jacques Lipchitz. Modigliani pursued his passion, begging for stone when he had no money to buy it. He continued painting as well, and in 1910 exhibited six canvases at the Salon des Indépendants. Noted by the critics, including Apollinaire, he proudly sent the articles to his mother. However, as before, nothing concrete resulted from this publicity. He approached many dealers but none was willing to handle his work. Modigliani's failure to make any progress as an artist, to experience any real rewards or success, soon began to have its effect.

> I do at least three pictures a day in my head. What's the use of spoiling canvas when nobody will buy.[11]

Modigliani publicly displayed the results of his efforts in sculpture at the Salon d'Automne in 1912, where he exhibited seven sculpted stone heads which show the influences of Cubism and African sculpture. Modigliani had conceived them as an ensemble, and arranged them in "step-wise fashion like the tubes of an organ to produce the special music he wanted."[12] It was extremely unusual for this Salon to accept an artist's work *en bloc,* and Modigliani took it as an encouraging sign. Once again, however, nothing happened. The dealers were even less inclined to represent his sculptures than they were his canvases.

> Anna Akhmatova (Russian poet):
> He seemed enclosed in a ring of solitude. Never mentioned the name of a friend, never joked. Never spoke of past love, never mundane things. He was nobly courteous. . . .
> He had a large black very old umbrella; we sat under it in

the Luxembourg in the warm summer rains of Paris. We recited Verlaine in chorus. He was that rarity, a painter who knew and loved poetry. . . . What did he seek? A friend came to Russia who had heard of him: "An alcoholic monster."[13]

Modigliani, at twenty-nine, was exhausted and ill from debauchery, and bitterly discouraged by his lack of success. In the winter of 1913 he suffered a complete breakdown and returned home to Leghorn. His childhood friends noticed a great alteration in his appearance. Once a fastidious dandy, his clothing was disheveled and his head shaved. He seemed to be addicted to absinthe. At Modigliani's insistence, his friends located an abandoned storeroom where he could work and supplied him with pieces of paving stone from the street in which to sculpt. They saw little of him during his stay in Leghorn. Before leaving, he inquired about storing the pieces of sculpture he had completed. His friends advised him to "throw them in a ditch."

Back in Paris, Modigliani resumed his debauched life-style. In need of money he went to work for Cheron, a picture dealer, who paid him twenty francs a day to paint. Cheron supplied him with painting materials, a bottle of cognac, and his maid who served as model, and locked him up in his cellar. When Modigliani had finished he would kick the door, and Cheron would let him out.

Jacques Lipchitz:
His own art was an art of personal feeling. He worked furiously, dashing off drawing after drawing, without stopping to correct or ponder. He worked, it seemed, entirely by instinct—which was, however, extremely fine and sensitive. . . . He could never forget his interest in people and he painted them . . . with abandon, urged on by the intensity of his feeling and vision.[14]

In July, 1914, Modigliani met Beatrice Hastings, a South African journalist and poet who was in Paris as correspondent for a London weekly. She was good-looking and rich. She was also wildly eccentric, occasionally carrying baskets of live ducks on her arms. She and

Modigliani lived together in her studio for two years and he painted her many times. Their relationship was stormy: Modigliani once threw her out a window.

> Jean Cocteau:
> Modigliani's portraits, even his self-portraits, are not the reflection of his external observation, but of his internal vision, of a vision as gracious, noble, acute, and deadly as the fabulous horn of the unicorn.[15]

Modigliani painted steadily throughout 1915, encouraged by Paul Guillaume, poet and art dealer, who purchased some of his work and rented a studio for him. By now, Modigliani had abandoned sculpting, leaving pieces unfinished.

In the summer of 1916, his relationship with Beatrice ended; he was close to another physical breakdown, his health nearly ruined by constant drinking and drug use. That year, several of his paintings on exhibition at an avant-garde show organized by Erik Satie were admired by Leopold Zborowski, a Polish poet. They met and Zborowski became Modigliani's dealer, as well as steadfast friend. Zborowski devoted himself to making Modigliani known as a painter, and to taking care of the dissolute artist. He gave him fifteen francs a day and provided him with a room in his apartment in which to work, and also supplied the models that he needed.

In the summer of 1917, Modigliani met Jeanne Hébuterne, a nineteen-year-old art student at the Académie Colarossi. Not pretty in a conventional way, she was small and pale, her long chestnut-colored hair usually worn in braids around her head. Modigliani would paint more portraits of Jeanne than any other woman. However, despite her devotion to him, she could do nothing to change the dissipated life-style of the thirty-three-year-old painter. She simply resigned herself to it.

That year Zborowski arranged for Modigliani's first (and only) one-man exhibition at the Berthe Weil Gallery. The exhibit caused a scandal, and the police were summoned to remove some of his more suggestive nudes from the walls.

> Jeanne Modigliani (daughter):
> Alcohol made it possible for him to maintain his creative

force at a high pitch. If the question as to why Modigliani drank is a purely psychological one, the question as to why he *had* to finish a picture at one sitting and why, after resting from it, he was unable to take it up again, is of fundamental importance. Perhaps to his knowledge that he had only a few years to live was added the anxiety of an artist tortured by conflicting aesthetic problems, and easily discouraged. He never ceased to long for the sculpture that he had abandoned, and it was his consuming regret . . . that undermined his mental stability and his own faith in himself.[16]

By 1918 Modigliani was desperately in need of a rest and Jeanne was pregnant. Zborowski and Mme Hébuterne arranged for them to spend the winter in Nice, where, on November 29, Jeanne gave birth to a daughter. Modigliani soon grew restless and bored in the south; he longed to return to Paris. He painted and often wrote to Zborowski asking for money. Although delighted with their child, he lived apart from Jeanne, who was living in a hotel with her mother.

Modigliani returned to Paris in May, 1919, and Jeanne, once again pregnant, joined him a month later, having left their daughter with a wet nurse. Somewhat restored to health, Modigliani quickly fell back into his debaucheries, alcohol and drugs. Zborowski, working hard in his behalf, arranged for Modigliani's paintings to be featured in a show in London in July, which resulted in critical acclaim for Modigliani.

Jacques Lipchitz:
One night during dinner I saw how ill he looked. He was eating in a strange way, almost covering his food with salt and pepper before even tasting it. But when I began to urge him to be less self-destructive and to put some kind of order into his life he became as angry as I had ever seen him.[17]

On January 18, 1920, Modigliani went to bed suffering from a kidney ailment. His illness worsened and soon he was spitting

"The Yellow Sweater," 1919. *Portrait of Jeanne Hébuterne.*

blood. On January 22, he was taken unconscious to the Hospital of Charity. Amedeo Modigliani died on the evening of January 24; he was thirty-five years old.

Hours later in the early dawn, Jeanne Hébuterne, nine months pregnant, leaped to her death from a window in her family's apartment.

> Jacques Lipchitz:
> He said to me time and again that he wanted a short but intense life—"Une vie brève mais intense." [18]

Notes

1 Fifield, *Modigliani*, p. 53.
2 Sichel, *Modigliani*, p. 72.
3 Fifield, op. cit., p. 9.
4 Ibid., p. 46.
5 Ibid., p. 48.
6 Sichel, op. cit., p. 79.
7 Modigliani, *Modigliani: Man and Myth*, p. 40.
8 Fifield, op. cit., p. 36.
9 Sichel, op. cit., p. 55.
10 Douglas, *Artist Quarter*, p. 113.
11 Sichel, op. cit., p. 181.
12 Lipchitz, *Amedeo Modigliani*, p. 39.
13 Fifield, op. cit., p. 16.
14 Lipchitz, op. cit., p. 7.
15 Ibid., p. 36.
16 Modigliani, op. cit., p. 82.
17 Lipchitz, op. cit., p. 10.
18 Ibid.

Sources

Douglas, Charles. *Artist Quarter*. London: Faber & Faber, 1941.
Fifield, William. *Modigliani*. New York: William Morrow & Co., 1976.

Lipchitz, Jacques. *Amedeo Modigliani.* New York: Harry Abrams, 1967.
Modigliani, Jeanne. *Modigliani: Man and Myth.* New York: The Orion Press, 1958.
Sichel, Pierre. *Modigliani.* New York: E. P. Dutton & Co., 1967.

MARILYN MONROE
1926-1962

People didn't take me seriously—or they only
took my body seriously.[1]

MARILYN MONROE. American film actress and sex symbol. Called the "Love Goddess of the Nuclear Age," or just "M. M.," she was the epitome of the sexy dumb blonde and, as such, one of the most famous stars to emerge from Hollywood in the 1950s. She played in thirty films in her thirteen-year career, some of them mediocre, most of them commercially successful because of her box office power. Her talent as an actress, however, especially as a comedienne, was never fully appreciated, her intelligence and creative skills held in question by the image of her easy voluptuousness.

Marilyn Monroe drank too much. She took pills. She could not sleep. While cooperating publicly with the requirements of her sex-symbol image, in private she was shy and insecure, she felt misunderstood, she was scared of being a loser. She feared the fading of her physical beauty; at the same time she yearned to be respected for her "own sake."

Norman Mailer:

So we think of Marilyn who was every man's love affair with America, Marilyn Monroe who was blonde and beautiful and had a sweet little rinky-dink of a voice and all the cleanliness of all the clean American backyards. She was our angel, the sweet angel of sex, and the sugar of sex came up from her like a resonance of sound in the clearest grain of a violin.[2]

She was born Norma Jean Baker on June 1, 1926, in Los Angeles General Hospital, the illegitimate child of Gladys Monroe Baker and C. Stanley Gifford, both employees at Consolidated Film Industries in Hollywood. She was raised in a series of foster homes, and while she struggled to grow up, her mother wrestled with her own demons in a California mental home.

> I daydreamed chiefly about beauty. I dreamed of myself becoming so beautiful that people would turn to look at me when I passed. And I dreamed of colors—scarlet, gold, green, white. I dreamed of myself walking proudly in beautiful clothes and being admired by everyone and overhearing words of praise.[3]

At the age of sixteen she married Jim Dougherty, a handsome twenty-two-year-old Irish boy. Dougherty joined the Merchant Marines in 1944, and she went to live with her in-laws and to work in a defense plant packing parachutes. She was spotted at the factory by a photographer from *Yank* magazine who asked her to pose for him. Thus began her career as a photographer's model. She signed up with the Blue Book Model Agency and learned how to walk and how to use makeup; she dyed her dirty-brown hair golden blonde.

> I paid no attention to the whistles and whoops. In fact, I didn't hear them. I was full of a strange feeling, as if I were two people. One of them was Norma Jean from the orphanage who belonged to nobody. The other was someone whose name I didn't know. But I knew where she belonged. She belonged to the ocean and the sky and the whole world.[4]

Her picture began to appear on the covers of magazines like *Peek, See, Laff, Pageant, U. S. Camera.* Her marriage to Dougherty ended in divorce. In 1946 she managed to get a screen test at Twentieth Century–Fox and a seventy-five-dollars-a-month contract. She took a new name: Marilyn Monroe, after President Monroe. Her first two films were *Scudda Hoo! Scudda Hay!* and *Dangerous Years* in which she had bit parts that eventually landed on the cutting-room floor. After a year Twentieth Century–Fox dropped their option: she was not photogenic enough, they explained.

> No sooner was I in the pew with the organ playing and every-body singing a hymn than the impulse would come to me to take off all my clothes. I wanted desperately to stand up naked for God and everyone else to see.[5]

Monroe went back to modeling to pay her rent but at the same time was busy making connections that would help her acting career. Joe Schenck, the seventy-year-old producer and cofounder of Twentieth Century–Fox, became infatuated with the sexy twenty-year-old girl, and used his influence to get her a contract with Columbia Pictures and a substantial part in *Ladies of the Chorus* in 1948. Even with his backing, however, her option was dropped after six months, no one at the studio seeing any promise in her performance. Unemployed once more, Monroe posed for pinup cal-endars; photographs taken by Tom Kelley of her stretched out on her side naked against a background of red velvet would later cause a sensation.

> But there was this secret in me—acting. It was like being in jail and looking at a door that said "This Way Out." [6]

Monroe got her first significant break in *Love Happy* with Groucho Marx. In a thirty-second bit, she played "Mae West, Theda Bara, and Bo Peep all rolled into one," and she was so good that United Artists sent her on the road to publicize the picture. Photo-graphed in a bathing suit, she was called "the hottest thing in pic-tures cooling off." Johnny Hyde, a successful Hollywood agent, saw the film and decided that Monroe had the makings of a star. He took over her career, and he persuaded her to have plastic surgery on her nose and jaw line: the alteration in her face was subtle but sensational.

Hyde got her minor but important parts in *The Asphalt Jungle,* directed by John Huston (MGM), and *All About Eve*, directed by Joseph L. Mankiewicz. Hyde had fallen in love with Monroe and wanted to marry her. He was rich, and he was also very ill. She refused to marry him. Shortly before his death, he negotiated a seven-year contract for her with Twentieth Century–Fox at $750 a week. Hyde's death was a shock to her; she had lost an important friend—a man who she felt respected her.

> I want to be an artist . . . not an erotic freak. I don't want to be sold to the public as a celluloid aphrodisical.[7]

From 1950 to 1952, Monroe appeared in minor parts in nearly a dozen films. In March, 1952, just before *Clash by Night*, her fourteenth film, was scheduled to be released, RKO learned about the existence of the nude calendar pinup of Monroe. Instead of trying to hide the model's identity, the studio planted a story in the gossip columns with Monroe's confession that she was "broke and did it for the money." As a result, when *Clash by Night* opened, Marilyn Monroe's name was in first place on the marquee and the public lined up to see her in the movie.

> I realized that just as I had once fought to get into the movies and become an actress, I would now have to fight to be able to become myself and to use my talents. If I didn't fight I would become a piece of merchandise to be sold off the movie pushcart.[8]

Next came *Gentlemen Prefer Blondes* with Jane Russell, directed by Howard Hawks, and *How to Marry a Millionaire* with Betty Grable and Lauren Bacall. Monroe's salary at this point was $1,200 a week. The movies were huge successes for the studios, grossing millions of dollars. Monroe asked for a new contract. She wanted a higher salary and the right to choose her scripts. The studio resisted and suspended her after her refusal to do *The Girl in Pink Tights* because she liked neither the part nor the script.

Howard Hawks:
    The two girls, Jane Russell and Marilyn Monroe, were so

good together that any time I had trouble figuring out any business, I simply had them walk back and forth, and the audiences adored it. I had a staircase built so that they could go up and down, and since they are well built. . . . This type of movie lets you sleep at night without a care in the world.[9]

In 1954 Monroe married Joe DiMaggio, the famous New York Yankee Clipper. They had been having an on-again, off-again relationship for two years. DiMaggio, conservative and traditional, wanted Monroe to give up her movie career to be a wife. They honeymooned in Japan and she entertained the troops in Korea in a final display before returning to DiMaggio's large home in San Francisco. As Mrs. Joe DiMaggio, she stayed at home and did not work in pictures for several months. She let herself get out of shape and drank too much. Their marriage was not working.

That was something I had never planned on or dreamed about—becoming the wife of a great man. Any more than Joe had ever thought about marrying a woman who seemed 80 percent publicity.[10]

Monroe went back to work in *There's No Business Like Show Business*, which was released later that year. The film did not flatter her; her dancing and singing were considered in bad taste, and the critics were not kind. *The Seven-Year Itch*, directed by Billy Wilder, followed immediately. When the movie came out in 1955, Monroe received some of her best reviews and, once again, her public lined up outside theaters to see her. In Times Square, her image decorated a billboard—in a white backless dress, standing over a subway grating, her skirt billowing high above her thighs. The success of this picture put Monroe back in favor with Hollywood and she now had the leverage to fight for her own way with the studios. In the meantime, she and DiMaggio had separated.

Monroe went to New York that year to study acting with Lee Strasberg, revered founder of the Actors' Studio, from whom she learned the secrets of the "Method." His wife, Paula Strasberg, became her personal acting coach for her future movies. Milton Greene, fashion photographer and friend, helped her with her business arrangements and encouraged her to form her own company. And she fell in love with Arthur Miller, highly respected American playwright, whom she had met several years before. As had happened with her relationship with DiMaggio, news about Monroe and Miller fascinated her eternally curious fans. Miller obtained a divorce from his current wife and Monroe began the process of converting to Judaism.

> There were times when I'd be with one of my husbands and I'd run into one of these Hollywood heels at a party and they'd paw me cheaply in front of everybody as if they were saying, *Oh, we had her.* I guess it's the classic situation of an ex-whore, though I was never a whore in that sense. I was never kept; I always kept myself.[11]

In March, 1956, she returned to Hollywood to star in *Bus Stop,* directed by Joshua Logan. This was one of her best and most interesting movies, one in which she displayed the acting talent she was struggling to develop, the talent that would, she hoped, earn her "respect."

Arthur Miller and Marilyn Monroe were married in June, and honeymooned in London on the set of *The Prince and the Showgirl.* Monroe was unhappy working on this film. Her relationship with director Laurence Olivier was unfriendly, and, despite the presence of Miller, her coach Paula Strasberg, and friend Milton Greene, she felt insecure and out of place. She began to deteriorate, taking too many sleeping pills, showing up late for work, or not showing up at all. The film, weeks late, was finally completed, and she returned to New York with her new husband.

> Nobody's really ever been able to tell me why I sleep so badly, but I know once I begin thinking, it's good-bye sleep. I used to think exercise helped—being in the country, fresh air, being with a man, sharing—but sometimes I can't sleep

whatever I'm doing, unless I take some pills. And then it's only a drugged sleep. It's not the same as really sleeping.[12]

They lived together first on a farm in Connecticut and then in a New York City apartment. Miller began to work on a screenplay for his wife, an adaptation of his short story "The Misfits." During this period Monroe tried unsuccessfully to get pregnant, and was taking a wide variety of sedatives to numb her depressions and her fears. Husband and wife were having a hard time making it work.

I'm going into the theater or character acting—or I'm just *going.* I'll never wait for them to say "so long." I've had fame, but maybe I can learn to live without it.[13]

Monroe was splendid as Sugar Kane in *Some Like It Hot* with Tony Curtis and Jack Lemmon. The actual making of the movie, however, was excruciatingly difficult for everyone because of her erratic behavior. She could not memorize her lines or follow Wilder's directions. Tony Curtis said that kissing her was like "kissing Hitler." Her next movie was *Let's Make Love* with Yves Montand. Although still married to Miller, Monroe pursued Montand and they were paired up as lovers in the gossip columns. The film was a failure.

Marilyn Monroe became a burden . . . an albatross. People expected so much of me, I sometimes hated them. It was too much of a strain. . . . Marilyn Monroe has to look a certain way—be *beautiful*—and act a certain way, be talented. I wondered if I could live up to their expectations.[14]

In 1960, shooting began in Reno, Nevada, on *The Misfits*, the last film Marilyn Monroe would complete. With Miller as screenwriter and John Huston as director, hopes were high that the film would be a classic, "the ultimate motion picture." As usual, however, due to her unsteady emotional state, the filming was frequently interrupted by delays and crises. In the midst of the shooting schedule, she was abruptly flown to Los Angeles to spend a week in a hospital resting. Filming was finally completed in November, way over budget.

On location while filming The Misfits, *1960 (Montgomery Clift, Eli Wallach, Arthur Miller, John Huston, Clark Gable, and Marilyn Monroe)*

Montgomery Clift:

I have the same problem as Marilyn. We attract people the way honey does bees, but they're generally the wrong kind of people. People who want something from us, if only our energy. We need a period of being alone to become ourselves. To be an actor, you can't afford defenses, a thick skin. You've got to be open, and people can hurt you easily.[15]

Monroe returned to New York. She announced her separation from Miller and in January flew to Mexico to get a divorce. Monroe spent several weeks in a New York hospital getting off pills and resting, and, after a lonely year in New York City, in the spring of 1962, she moved back to Los Angeles to Fifth Helena Drive in Brentwood to be close to her psychiatrist. She began a project of remodeling her house. She was suffering from chronic insomnia, and taking Librium, Nembutal, Sulfathallidine, or chloral hydrate to put her to sleep.

When my looks start to go, so will most of the fans. *So long, it's been nice knowing you.* But I won't care. I'll be ready. There's other kinds of beauty, other ways of impressing people, and getting over. I hope to go for it by sheer acting. I *do*.[16]

She began to work on a new picture, *Something's Got to Give*, directed by George Cukor. She caught a cold and, as a result, was often absent from the set. She had been spending time with Frank Sinatra and the "Rat Pack" and, in May, 1962, she flew to New York to sing "Happy Birthday" for President John F. Kennedy in Madison Square Garden. Peter Lawford announced her appearance onstage as "the *late* Marilyn Monroe." She returned to Hollywood and to work on the picture. On June 1, she was given a birthday party on the set: she was thirty-six. The following week she failed to show up for work for several days and was fired. Twentieth Century–Fox decided that they would also sue her for violating her contract.

Arthur M. Schlesinger, Jr.:

I do not think that I have seen anyone so beautiful; I

was enchanted by her wit, at once so masked, so ingenious and so penetrating. But one felt a terrible unreality about her—as if talking to someone under water.[17]

Marilyn Monroe died in her bedroom on the night of August 4, 1962. Her body was discovered by her psychiatrist, who was summoned by Monroe's housekeeper, Eunice Murray, after she found Monroe's door locked and the lights on. The Los Angeles County Coroner's report stated the cause of death as acute barbiturate poisoning.

Yes, there was something special about me, and I knew what it was. I was the kind of girl they found dead in a hall bedroom with an empty bottle of sleeping pills in her hand.[18]

Notes

1 Weatherby, *Conversations with Marilyn*, p. 146.
2 Mailer, *Marilyn: A Biography*, p. 15.
3 Monroe, *My Story*, p. 19.
4 Ibid., p. 25.
5 Ibid., p. 16.
6 Ibid., p. 39.
7 Ibid., p. 135.
8 Ibid., p. 135.
9 Andrew Sarris, *Interviews with Film Directors*, New York: Avon Books, 1967, p. 233.
10 Monroe, op. cit., pp. 139–40.
11 Weatherby, op. cit., p. 106.
12 Ibid., p. 145.
13 Ibid., p. 106.
14 Ibid., p. 108.
15 Ibid., p. 55.
16 Ibid., p. 115.
17 Arthur M. Schlesinger, Jr., *Robert Kennedy and His Times*, Boston: Houghton Mifflin Company, 1978, pp. 590–91.
18 Monroe, op. cit., p. 66.

Sources

Guiles, Fred Lawrence. *Norma Jean: The Life of Marilyn Monroe*. New York: McGraw-Hill Book Co., 1969.

Mailer, Norman. *Marilyn: A Biography*. New York: Warner Books, 1975.

Monroe, Marilyn. *My Story*. New York: Stein & Day, 1974.

Murray, Eunice, with Rose Shade. *Marilyn: The Last Months*. New York: Pyramid Books, 1975.

Weatherby, W. J. *Conversations with Marilyn*. New York: Ballantine Books, 1976.

VASLAV NIJINSKY
1888-1950

I can no longer dance as before, as all dances are
death. By death I do not mean only the state of
things when the body dies. The body dies, but
the soul lives. The soul is a dove, in God. I am
in God.[1]

VASLAV NIJINSKY. Russian ballet dancer, soloist of the Mariinsky Theater and lead dancer of the Ballets Russes. Called "Le Dieu de la Danse," he is considered the greatest male dancer of the twentieth century; as a choreographer he changed the patterns and forms of dance. Nijinsky began a revolution in ballet that would not be fully understood or appreciated for years to come. His career spanned but a single decade and ended abruptly in madness.

Romola Nijinsky (his wife):
Suddenly a slim, lithe, catlike Harlequin took the stage. Although his face was hidden by a painted mask, the expressions and beauty of his body made us all realize that we were in the presence of genius. . . . Intoxicated, entranced, gasping for breath, we followed this superhuman being, the very spirit of Harlequin incarnate; mischievous, lovable. The power, the featherweight lightness, the steel-like strength, the suppleness of his movements, the incredible gift of rising and remaining in the air and descending in twice as slow a time as it took to rise . . . the execution of the most difficult pirouettes and *tours en l'air* with an amazing nonchalance

and apparently no effort whatever, proved that this extraordinary phenomenon was the very soul of the dance.[2]

Vaslav Nijinsky was born on March 12, 1888, in Kiev, Ukraine, the second son of three children born to Thomas and Eleanora Nijinsky. His parents were well-known dancers; his father, famous for his leaps, had his own company. The family toured Russia together until Thomas Nijinsky took a mistress. Eleanora left him and took their three children to St. Petersburg. At the age of six, Stanislav, Nijinsky's older brother, fell out of a window and suffered brain damage. He would be confined to an institution. Nijinsky's sister, Bronia, would become a ballet dancer. Nijinsky saw his father again only twice.

> When I was a boy and my father wanted to teach me to swim
> he threw me into the water; I fell and sank to the bottom. I
> could not swim, and felt that I could not breathe. I kept the
> little air that I had, shutting my mouth, thinking that if God
> wishes, I shall be saved. . . . I saw no sky above me, only
> water. Suddenly I felt a physical strength in me and jumped,
> saw a cord, grasped it, and was saved.[3]

When Nijinsky was ten, his mother took him to audition for the Imperial School of ballet in St. Petersburg. The instructors noticed him immediately: he had unusually strong legs and could leap higher than any of the other boys. He was accepted into the class of 1898. Because he was odd-looking with almost oriental features, and very inarticulate and shy, the other students laughed at him and teased him, calling him "the little Japanese." Nijinsky had no friends for the next eight years at school and was involved in numerous fistfights in self-defense.[4]

Upon his graduation in 1907, Nijinsky was admitted to the Mariinsky Theater. He had already danced as a member of their *corps de ballet* and had performed for the Tsar at Tsarskoe-Selo. For the next four years Nijinsky danced the lead parts at the Mariinsky Theater in ballets such as *Swan Lake*, *Ivanotska*, and *Sleeping Beauty*, as well as appearing at the Bolshoi Theater in Moscow. He was considered a phenomenon, his spectacular performances highly acclaimed.

Nijinsky gave most of his salary—sixty-five roubles a month—to his mother to help with Stanislav's care as well as for the upkeep of their apartment. He was asked to give ballet lessons, which added to their income. The family's financial situation was strained, nevertheless.

> I finished school at eighteen and graduated. I did not know how to dress—I had been used to uniforms. I did not like civil clothes and therefore did not know how to wear them. I thought that shoes with very big soles were the best looking and therefore bought a pair with enormous soles. As I graduated I felt freedom, but this freedom frightened me.[5]

In 1908, Serge Pavlovitch Diaghilev entered Nijinsky's life. Diaghilev was an entrepreneur and businessman who had been commissioned to form a ballet company: he was interested in a renaissance of Russian culture and in bringing Russian ballet to the West. Diaghilev was homosexual and quickly fell in love with Nijinsky. In both roles, those of personal manager and lover, this man who was sixteen years his senior would play a critical part in the dancer's life, instrumental in his rise to international fame, as well as his fall.

> Ivor introduced me to Diaghilev, who asked me to come to the Hotel Europe, where he lived. I disliked him for his too self-assured voice, but went to seek my luck. I found my luck. At once I allowed him to make love to me. I trembled like a leaf. I hated him, but pretended. . . . I understood Diaghilev from the first moment and pretended to agree with him at once.[6]

The mustached and monocled impresario picked his company, including young Nijinsky, from members of the Mariinsky and Bolshoi theaters, borrowing them during their vacations. Alexandre Benois and Leon Bakst were responsible for theatrical design. Michel Fokine, a young and brilliant choreographer, created the dances. The collaboration was successful. On May 18, 1909, the Ballet Russe opened at the Théâtre du Châtelet in Paris.

> Richard Buckle (biographer):
> Nijinsky had arrived at the Châtelet between half-past six and seven. He changed into practice clothes and went through a class by himself at the back of the stage. Then he washed and put on his makeup, which took him half an hour. Order ruled the dressing room, where costumes were hung just so, and the sticks of makeup were lined up on the dressing room table with military precision. . . . To *le tout Paris*, seething with expectancy on the other side of the red curtain, Nijinsky gave no thought.[7]

What the select Parisian audience witnessed that evening was unlike anything seen on the ballet stage before. For the next three years, Diaghilev brought his company back to Europe—Paris, London, Rome, Monte Carlo—with new astonishments, each season more successful than the last, and Nijinsky's fame was assured as he created some of his most famous roles in the ballets of Fokine: as Harlequin in *Carnaval*, as a rose in *Le Spectre de la Rose*, as Petrushka in *Petrushka*. He was the undisputed star of Diaghilev's ballet, the dancer the audiences came to see.

> Romola Nijinsky:
> In each part . . . he had the chance to give a complete and separate impersonation. He was so different in each part that he was almost unrecognizable. Where the essential Nijinsky existed was a constant mystery. His face, his skin, even his height, seemed to change in each ballet. There was only constant his one unmistakable signature, his genius.[8]

Offstage, Nijinsky lived with Diaghilev. In 1911, he was dismissed from the Mariinsky Theater for appearing in *Giselle* in a costume that was considered too revealing. Henceforth, he worked exclusively for Diaghilev and the Russian Ballet; in a sense, he was Diaghilev's possession and the relationship was uncomfortable for him.

Diaghilev wants to be called "a patron of art," he wants to get into history. Diaghilev cheats people, and thinks that no one sees through him. He dyes his hair in order to look young. Diaghilev's hair is white. He buys black dyes and rubs them in. . . . Diaghilev has two false front teeth. When he is nervous he passes his tongue over them.[9]

L'Après-Midi d'un Faune, the first ballet choreographed by Nijinsky, premiered at the Châtelet on May 29, 1912. The dance was twelve minutes long. The reaction of the audience was a mixture of applause and cat calls. After the performance Diaghilev announced that the ballet would be repeated (after champagne and caviar were served in the foyer) and it was. The following day, the French newspapers were alive with controversy. The critics were divided: the "anti-Faunists" called the ballet obscene and demanded that the police close it down; the "Faunists" announced Nijinsky's choreographic revolution.

Richard Buckle:
The Faun holds up the veil, nuzzles in it, then stretching it out on the ground, lowers himself on it, head tucked under, and finally, as muted horns and harp harmonies over a quiet flute chord conclude the choreographic poem, consummates his union with it, taut on the ground by a convulsive jerk.[10]

Precisely one year later, on May 29, 1913, Nijinsky's second ballet, *Le Sacre du Printemps,* premiered at the Théâtre des Champs Elysées in Paris. Critics called it *"Le Massacre du Printemps."*

Romola Nijinsky:
People whistled, insulted the performers and the composer, shouted, laughed . . . the fights and controversy did not remain in the domain of sound, but actually culminated in bodily conflicts. One beautifully dressed lady in an orchestra box stood up and slapped the face of a young man who was hissing in the next box. . . . Another society lady spat in the face of one of the demonstrators. . . . [Nijinsky] was in practice costume. His face was as white as his *crêpe de*

Nijinsky in Schéhérazade, 1911

Chine dancing shirt. He was beating the rhythm with both fists shouting "*Ras, dwa, tri,*" to the artists. The music could not be heard even on the stage, and the only thing which guided the dancers was Nijinsky's conducting from the wings.[11]

The ballet was performed four times in Paris, and three times in London. Considered a critical failure, the dance today is held by many to be the pinnacle of Nijinsky's career and an important mile-stone in the history of ballet.

I realized that people love art, but are afraid to say to themselves: "I don't understand art." People are cowards because the critics frighten them. They frighten people to make them ask their opinion. The critics believe that the public is stupid. . . . I know what criticism means—it is death.[12]

On August 15, 1913, the S.S. *Avon* sailed from Southampton, England, with certain members of the ballet company bound for engagements in South America. Nijinsky was on board, without Diaghilev at his side for the first time in several years. Also on board was Romola de Pulszky, a twenty-four-year-old Hungarian, and new member of the company. She was infatuated with Nijinsky and pursued the dancer with stubborn determination. The pretty blue-eyed young woman succeeded in winning him. When the boat landed in Buenos Aires, Romola and Nijinsky were engaged to be married despite the fact that they did not speak the same language and com-municated with few common words in French. Although the com-pany was genuinely surprised, even shocked, the marriage ceremony took place almost immediately, on September 10, 1913.

Nijinsky wrote to Diaghilev telling him the good news. By the conclusion of their South American tour Romola was pregnant. Soon after, while visiting Romola's family in Budapest, Nijinsky learned that he had been fired by a jealous, angry Diaghilev.

To Igor Stravinsky:
I went with my wife to her parents' home in Budapest

and there I immediately sent a telegram to Serge asking him when we could see each other. The answer . . . was a letter . . . informing me that I shall not be asked to stage my ballets this season, and that I am not needed as an artist. Please write to me whether this is true. I do not believe that Serge can act so meanly to me. Serge owes me a lot of money. I have received nothing for two years. . . . If it is true that Serge does not want to work with me, then I have lost everything.[13]

Severed from the Russian Ballet, Nijinsky attempted to assemble his own company, without success. In part, the reason was his own underlying desire to work again with the Diaghilev ballet. In Budapest, after the birth of their daughter Kyra, Romola and Nijinsky were arrested and detained as prisoners of war, for Hungary was now at war with Russia.

They remained in Romola's mother's house during this period while in New York, Otto Kahn of the Metropolitan Opera House was arranging to bring Diaghilev's company to America with the stipulation that Nijinsky be included. After a long delay, Nijinsky (and Romola) finally arrived in New York in April, 1916, in time for the company's second season at the Opera House. He remained until October when *Till Eulenspiegel*, his last new ballet, was performed. Then the Diaghilev ballet set off on an exhausting tour of the United States which lasted for five months.

Till had great success, but it was produced too quickly. It was "taken out of the oven" too soon, and therefore was raw. The American public liked my "raw" ballet. It tasted good, as I cooked it very well. I did not like this ballet but said, "It is good." [14]

In June, 1917, the company gathered in Madrid to begin a new season of performances. The relationship between Nijinsky and Diaghilev (who now had a new protégé, Massine, by his side) eased a bit until Nijinsky, at Romola's urging, decided not to go with the company to South America where they were next scheduled to perform. Diaghilev, however, trapped Nijinsky into going by using a legal technicality that would put him in jail in Spain if he broke the contract. Nijinsky performed with the company under very strained emotional conditions, his relationship with Diaghilev irrevocably broken. In September, 1917, he quit the Russian Ballet for good, retreating with Romola to Switzerland to a villa in the mountains. At this point Nijinsky declared that he would not dance in public again until the end of the war.

> Finally I disentangled myself from the bushes but did not fall. God said to me: *"Go home and tell your wife that you are insane."* [15]

Unwilling to dance, Nijinsky was at a loss. He tried other forms of self-expression. He invented a windscreen wiper and an eversharp pencil. He worked on a system of dance notation. He wrote a diary. He drew pictures. He ran. One day, Nijinsky pushed his wife and child down the stairs; they were unharmed. Another day he appeared in the village wearing a large gold cross and commanding people to go to church. His behavior contained the signs of his encroaching madness.

> Once I went for a walk and it seemed to me that I saw blood on the snow. I followed the traces of the blood and sensed that somebody *who was still alive* had been killed.[16]

On January 19, 1919, two hundred people attended a dance recital given by Nijinsky for the benefit of the Red Cross. In the carriage on the way to hotel ballroom, Nijinsky told his wife that this was the day of his "marriage with God."

> The public came to be amused and thought I danced for their amusement. My dances were frightening. They were afraid of me, thinking I wanted to kill them. I did not. I loved everybody but nobody loved me and I became nervous and excited; the audience caught my mood . . . they wanted to go away. Then I started to do a joyful, merry dance and they began to enjoy themselves. . . . The audience began to

Nijinsky with Romola and Kyra

laugh when I did. I was laughing in my dance. The audience laughed.

I danced badly; I fell when I should not have. The audience did not care because my dancing was beautiful. They felt my mood and enjoyed themselves. I wanted to go on dancing but God said to me "Enough." I stopped.[17]

Several weeks later, a psychiatrist in Zurich informed Romola that her husband was a schizophrenic and incurably insane. Nijinsky, thirty-one years old, would never dance again. He lived for another thirty years, mostly silent, under the devoted care of his wife, and died in London on April 7, 1950, of kidney failure.

My little girl is singing: Ah, ah, ah, ah! I do not understand its meaning, but I feel what she wants to say. She wants to say that everything—Ah! Ah!—is not horror, but joy.[18]

Notes

1   Romola Nijinsky, *The Diary of Vaslav Nijinsky*, p. 75.
2   Romola Nijinsky, *Nijinsky*, p. 5.
3   R. Nijinsky, *Diary*, pp. 42–43.
4   Buckle, *Nijinsky*, p. 13.
5   R. Nijinsky, *Diary*, p. 64.
6   Ibid., p. 49.
7   Buckle, op. cit., p. 81.
8   R. Nijinsky, *Nijinsky*, p. 93.
9   R. Nijinsky, *Diary*, p. 53.
10 Buckle, *Nijinsky*, p. 240.
11 R. Nijinsky, *Nijinsky*, pp. 172–73.
12 R. Nijinsky, *Diary*, p. 135.
13 Buckle, *Nijinsky*, p. 333.
14 R. Nijinsky, *Diary*, p. 103.
15 Ibid., p. 169.
16 Ibid., p. 168.
17 Ibid., pp. 161–62.
18 Ibid., p. 184.

Sources

Buckle, Richard. *Nijinsky*. New York: Avon Books, 1975.
Nijinsky, Romola. *Nijinsky*. New York: Pocket Books, 1972.
———, ed. *The Diary of Vaslav Nijinsky*. Berkeley, Ca.: The University
of California Press, 1968.

SYLVIA PLATH
1932-1963

Dying
Is an art, like everything else.
I do it exceptionally well.

I do it so it feels like hell.
I do it so it feels real.
I guess you could say I've a call.[1]

SYLVIA PLATH. American poet. She was a pretty, all-American girl with bright red lips and a page-boy haircut. After her suicide, a manuscript of poems was discovered and published. Critics called the book, *Ariel*, terrifying, visionary, terrible, and strange. Sylvia Plath attained cult status. She became a priestess of poetry, a category unto herself.

> I saw that my body had all sorts of little tricks, such as making my hands go limp at the crucial second, which would save it, time and again, whereas if I had the whole say, I would be dead in a flash.
>
> I would simply have to ambush it with whatever sense I had left or it would trap me in its stupid cage for fifty years without any sense at all.[2]

Sylvia Plath was born in Boston, Massachusetts, on October 27, 1932. Her father, Otto Emil Plath, was a German emigré and professor of entomology at Boston University; his specialty was bumblebees. He was twenty-one years older than Plath's mother, Aurelia Schober, a woman of Austrian parentage whom he met in one of his German classes. Sylvia was their first child. Her brother, Warren, was born exactly two and a half years later. When Plath was eight years old her father died.

> Daddy, I have had to kill you.
> You died before I had time—
> Marble-heavy, a bag full of God,
> Ghastly statue with one grey toe
> Big as a Frisco seal
>
> And a head in the freakish Atlantic
> Where it pours bean green over blue
> In the waters off beautiful Nauset.
> I used to pray to recover you.
> Ach, du.[3]

Aurelia Plath went to work teaching secretarial skills at Boston University. The children were left in the care of her parents, who moved into their home in Winthrop. Soon after, the entire family moved to Wellesley, an upper-middle-class college town with good schools for the children.

Aurelia made a "tireless effort to see that her children had all the advantages given their much-better-off contemporaries. These included summer camps, Scouting, sailing, piano and viola lessons, dance 'assemblies,' painting and watercolor lessons, and numerous other, frequently expensive, extracurricular activities."[4]

> Mother, you sent me to piano lessons
> And praised my arabesques and trills
> Although each teacher found my touch
> Oddly wooden in spite of scales
> And the hours of practicing, my ear
> Tone-deaf and yes, unteachable.
> I learned, I learned, I learned elsewhere,
> From muses unhired by you, dear mother.[5]

A model student with a "genius" IQ, Plath's high school years were highlighted by rows of straight A's, honor roll, special awards and achievement certificates (even one for punctuality). She had a story published in *Seventeen* magazine and a poem in the *Christian Science Monitor*. She was editor of the yearbook in her senior year and wrote a column for the town paper. She was also growing up tall and slender, with long brown hair, and a lovely smile.

> To Aurelia Plath:
>
> It was one of those cartoon and personality write-ups titled "Teen Triumphs." There was a sketch of a girl s'posed to be me—writing, also a cow. It said, and I quote: "BORN TO WRITE! Sylvia Plath, seventeen, really works at writing. To get atmosphere for a story about a farm she took a job as a farmhand. Now she's working on a sea story." Then there's another sketch of me saying, "and I get a job on a boat." Not only that. "A national magazine had published two of her brain children, the real test of being a writer." [6]

At Smith College, where Plath had a partial scholarship, she continued to excel. In her sophomore year she won a $1,500 *Mademoiselle* prize for college fiction. In her junior year she won a guest editorship to the same magazine, and headed for New York City.

> I knew something was wrong with me that summer, because all I could think about was the Rosenbergs and how stupid I'd been to buy all those uncomfortable, expensive clothes, hanging limp as a fish in my closet, and how all the little successes I'd totted up so happily fizzled to nothing outside the slick marble and plate-glass fronts along Madison Avenue.
>
> I felt very still and very empty, the way the eye of a tornado must feel, moving dully along in the middle of the surrounding hullabaloo. [7]

Plath returned to Wellesley after her month in New York to learn that she had not been accepted for Frank O'Connor's summer writing course at Harvard. She had been counting on the class to occupy her during the long summer and had no alternative plans. Suddenly, she was at loose ends. She became insomniac and was unable even to read. Obviously disturbed, Plath saw a psychiatrist and was given shock treatments. She refused to return to him. On

August 24, her mother found a note from her daughter: "Have gone for a long walk. Will be home tomorrow." [8] She was discovered three days later lying in a crawlspace under the house—her brother had heard her faint cries.

> The second time I meant
> To last it out and not come back at all.
> I rocked shut
>
> As a sea shell.
> They had to call and call
> And pick the worms off me like sticky pearls. [9]

Plath spent six months at McLean Hospital in Belmont, Massachusetts, an expensive psychiatric institution, where she underwent insulin therapy and shock treatments. She was pronounced "cured" in time to return to Smith for the second semester. She bleached her hair blond and pursued a social life with her old determination to succeed, seeing many different men and experimenting with sex. She began to write poetry again, and won a scholarship for her final year at Smith.

> Gordon Lamayer (friend):
> Life was always full to the brim for Sylvia at Smith in those days and cresting over the brim, "overflowing." If she had been a Marlovian heroine, she would have been an "over-reacher," because she could not stick by the golden mean, nothing too much, but was always anxious to experiment *in extremis*, with Blake, to find out what "enough" was by indulging herself "too much." Her letters were filled with purple passages. In retrospect, I would say that at times she was whistling Dixie, telling herself she was extremely happy in an effort to mask her anxiety. [10]

In 1955, her last year at Smith, she dyed her hair back to its natural brown, and deliberately subdued her "healthy bohemianism" to concentrate on her studies, her writing, and the ever-present question of her future. Ever striving, she made a clean sweep of the poetry prizes, graduated summa cum laude, and won a Fulbright scholarship to study at Cambridge.

> If only England would by some miracle come through, I would be forced shivering into a new, unfamiliar world, where I had to forge anew friends and a home for myself, and although such experiences are painful and awkward at first, I know, intellectually, that they are the best things to make one grow—always biting off just a slight bit more than you chewed before.[11]

At Cambridge, Plath continued to succeed, both academically and socially. In March she met Ted Hughes at a party and fell in love with the "brilliant ex-Cambridge poet . . . the only man I've met yet here who'd be strong enough to be equal with."[12] Hughes was a tall, lanky, handsome man, the son of a Yorkshire carpenter, a "large, hulking, healthy Adam."[13] Most important, Hughes was a serious and dedicated poet. Since it was against the rules for Plath to be married while a student at Cambridge, she and Ted were married secretly in London in June, her mother in attendance.

> The last thing I wanted was infinite security and to be the place an arrow shoots off from. I wanted change and excitement and to shoot off in all directions myself, like the coloured arrows from a Fourth of July rocket.[14]

Plath and Ted spent the summer in a rented house in Spain, rising at seven each morning to write. Besides doing her own work, she typed Ted's poems for submission to magazines. To her mother, she described her newly wedded life with Ted in ecstatic, glowing terms. Her life was now perfect and it had a purpose. She could not remember what her life had been like without Ted.

> I felt myself melting into the shadows like the negative of a person I'd never seen before in my life.[15]

Back in Cambridge in the fall, Plath went back to her studies while she and Ted continued writing and submitting poems and stories. They received many rejections, but also some acceptances. In February, 1957, Ted's volume of poems entitled *Hawk in the Rain* won the Poetry Center First Publication Award and was accepted for publication by Harper's in the U. S. and Faber in England.

> I'm so happy *his* book is accepted *first*. It will make it so much easier for me when mine is accepted—if not by the Yale Series, then by some other place. I can rejoice then, much more, knowing Ted is ahead of me. There is no question of rivalry, but only mutual joy and a sense of us doubling our prize-winning and creative output.[16]

In the summer of 1957, she and Ted returned to the United States and rented an apartment in Northampton: Plath had a job teaching English at Smith. She soon discovered, however, that the amount of labor involved in teaching was "death to writing." She was frustrated and unhappy in the airless campus life. After the first year, she quit and they moved again, this time to an apartment on the "slummy side" of Beacon Hill, and she worked part-time for Massachusetts General Hospital. During this period, she met poet Anne Sexton in Robert Lowell's poetry course.

> Anne Sexton:
> Often, very often, Sylvia and I would talk at length about our first suicides, at length, in detail, in depth. . . . Suicide is, after all, the opposite of the poem.[17]

By October, 1959, she was pregnant. She and Ted decided to return to London to live. They moved into a small, inexpensive flat in Chalcot Square. In February, Plath signed a contract with Heinemann's to publish her first book of poems, *The Colossus*, some of which had been written during the previous fall at Yaddo, an artists' colony in Saratoga, New York. The dedication read: "For Ted." In March, a daughter, Frieda Rebecca, was born at home.

> I also remembered Buddy Willard saying in a sinister, knowing way that after I had children I would feel differently, I wouldn't want to write poems any more. So I began to

think maybe it was true that when you were married and had children it was like being brainwashed, and afterwards you went about numb as a slave in some private, totalitarian state.[18]

In January, 1961, Plath became pregnant again; she miscarried a month later. The *New Yorker* offered her a "first reading" contract in March which she accepted. In May, Alfred Knopf announced it would publish an American edition of her book of poetry entitled *The Colossus.* In September, pregnant once more, she moved into a cottage in Devon with Ted and Frieda. Nicholas, a son, was born in the new year.

> I do not stir.
> The frost makes a flower,
> The dew makes a star,
> The dead bell,
> The dead bell.

> Somebody's done for.[19]

The bubble burst: the world of the tall handsome "writing Hugheses" with their two beautiful babies in their cottage in Devon ended when Ted Hughes became seriously involved with another woman. Plath was stunned, heartbroken, and finally outraged. By August, 1962, Ted had departed. Plath tried to manage in the country but it was difficult, and, above all, isolated.

> Everything is breaking—my dinner set cracking in half, the health inspector says the cottage should be demolished—there is no hope for it. . . . Even my beloved bees set upon me today when I numbly knocked aside their sugar feeder, and I am all over stings.[20]

Plath moved herself and the children back to London, to a flat in "Yeats's house!" arriving just in time for one of the worst winters in the city's history. Severe bouts with flu for her and the babies, blackouts, frozen pipes, the inescapable cold, and no outside help

Sylvia Plath, 1959

contributed to her emotional and physical exhaustion. At first she managed to sustain herself, writing poem after poem each morning in the dawn hours before the children awoke and needed her.

> If I've killed one man, I've killed two—
> The vampire who said he was you
> And drank my blood for a year,
> Seven years, if you want to know.
> Daddy, you can lie back now.[21]

On a cold Monday morning, February 11, 1963, Sylvia Plath, her two children asleep, went downstairs to the kitchen, turned on the gas jets, and put her head in the oven. Her body was discovered several hours later by a nurse who had been sent over by her physician to help out with the children. Plath was thirty years old.

> The woman is perfected.
> Her dead
>
> Body wears the smile of accomplishment,
> The illusion of a Greek necessity
>
> Flows in the scrolls of her toga,
> Her bare
>
> Feet seem to be saying:
> We have come so far, it is over.[22]

Notes

1 Plath, "Lady Lazarus," *Ariel*, p. 7.
2 Plath, *The Bell Jar*, p. 168.
3 Plath, "Daddy," *Ariel*, p. 49.
4 Butscher, *Sylvia Plath: Method and Madness*, p. 21.
5 Plath, "The Disquieting Muses," *The Colossus*, p. 59.
6 Aurelia Schober Plath, *Letters Home*, p. 65.
7 Plath, *The Bell Jar*, pp. 2–3.

8   Aurelia Schober Plath, *Letters Home*, p. 135.
9   Plath, "Lady Lazarus," *Ariel*, p. 7.
10 Butscher, *Sylvia Plath: The Woman and the Work*, p. 39.
11 Aurelia Schober Plath, *Letters Home*, p. 155.
12 Ibid., p. 247.
13 Ibid., p. 263.
14 Plath, *The Bell Jar*, p. 87.
15 Ibid., p. 10.
16 Aurelia Schober Plath, *Letters Home*, p. 340.
17 Anne Sexton, *A Self-Portrait in Letters*, Boston: Houghton Mifflin, 1978, p. 273.
18 Plath, *The Bell Jar*, p. 89.
19 Plath, "Death & Co.," *Ariel*, pp. 28–29.
20 Aurelia Schober Plath, *Letters Home*, p. 549.
21 Plath, "Daddy," *Ariel*, p. 51.
22 Plath, "Edge," *Ariel*, p. 84.

Sources

Aird, Eileen. *Sylvia Plath: Her Life and Work*. New York: Perennial Library, 1975.

Butscher, Edward. *Sylvia Plath: Method and Madness*. New York: Pocket Books, 1977.

———. *Sylvia Plath: The Woman and the Work*. New York: Dodd, Mead & Co., 1977.

Plath, Aurelia Schober, ed. *Letters Home by Sylvia Plath, 1950–63*. New York: Bantam Books, 1977.

Plath, Sylvia. *Ariel*. New York: Harper & Row, 1966.

———. *The Bell Jar*. London: Faber & Faber, 1963.

———. *The Colossus*. New York: Vintage Books, 1968.

EDGAR ALLAN POE
1809-1849

Thank Heaven! the crisis—
 The danger is past,
And the lingering illness
 Is over at last—
And the fever called "Living"
 Is conquered at last.[1]

EDGAR ALLAN POE. American poet, short story writer, and critic. Considered one of the most original and brilliant writers in American literature, he invented the detective story. Influenced by Byron, his childhood hero, an avid reader and imitator of Shelley, Keats, and Coleridge, from whom he borrowed his own philosophy of poetry, Poe, in turn, influenced a wide spectrum of writers from the French Symbolists to Artaud to Dostoevsky to Dreiser and Nabokov.

Poe was a brilliant editor of literary magazines and earned a reputation as a virulent critic. Poe was also a tortured artist; he was an alcoholic and a laudanum addict. This opiate substance liberated the darkest regions of his mind from which spilled fantasies and horror tales, death romances, and tales of murder and mystery, poetry of haunting sounds and primitive rhythms. He has been analyzed as a necrophiliac, a madman, a dipsomaniac, an impotent lover, a man in terror of his own suffocation, and one obsessed with death.

> I am come of a race noted for vigor of fancy and ardor of passion. Men have called me mad; but the question is not yet settled, whether madness is or is not the loftiest intelligence—whether much that is glorious—whether all that is profound

—does not spring from disease of thought—from *moods* of mind exalted at the expense of general intellect.[2]

Edgar Poe was born on January 19, 1809, in Boston, Massachusetts, the second son of Elizabeth Arnold Poe, a beautiful, talented English actress, and David Poe, Jr., an actor of much less talent, and alcoholic. His brother, William Henry Poe, had been left with Poe's grandparents in Baltimore while the couple was touring with a stage company. After Poe's birth a third child was soon on the way and David Poe suddenly disappeared, never to be heard from again. On December 8, 1811, while on tour in Richmond, Virginia, Edgar Poe's mother died of tuberculosis, leaving Poe and his baby sister Rosalie orphans. Poe was rescued by Frances Allan, childless wife of John Allan, a Richmond merchant. Rosalie, who was later found to be mentally defective, was adopted by the McKenzie family of Richmond.

> I am the descendent of a race whose imaginative and easily excitable temperament has at all times rendered them remarkable; and, in my earliest infancy, I gave evidence of having fully inherited the family character. As I advanced in years it was more strongly developed; becoming, for many reasons, a cause of serious disquietude to my friends and of positive injury to myself. I grew self-willed, addicted to the wildest caprices, and a prey to the most ungovernable passions.[3]

Although Frances Allan was a devoted mother to the boy, John Allan vacillated in his attitude toward his foster child, whom he never legally adopted. Sometimes friendly, more often cold, his foster father was the source of great frustration, suffering, and disappointment to Poe, who hardly dared call him "Pa."

Poe, as "Master Allan," was expensively schooled abroad in Scotland and England from the age of six to eleven when business failures at home forced the Allans back to Richmond and less than affluent circumstances. Poe began to write poetry when he was fourteen. He was growing into a romantic, arrogant, rebellious, and ambitious boy who fashioned himself after Byron and felt every inch a Southern aristocrat. Poe was especially attracted to beautiful women with a touch of the tomb about them. His first infatuation was with the mother of one of his classmates, Jane Stanard, who was a sympathetic listener for the liquid-eyed Poe. She died at an early age of a brain tumor and Poe grieved heavily at her gravestone.

> I could not love except where Death
> Was mingling his with Beauty's breath—
> Or Hymen, Time, and Destiny
> Were stalking between her and me.[4]

In 1824, John Allan inherited a fortune from his uncle which permanently saved him from his downward financial slide. The family moved into a spacious house on Main Street in Richmond, and Poe was given his own room where he could read and write to his heart's content. That year Poe fell in love with fifteen-year-old Elmira Royster with whom he exchanged passionate love letters and became secretly engaged. In February, 1826, he entered the University of Virginia to study law at the behest of his foster father, and to become a Virginia gentleman. There he suffered the first of many humiliations as a result of his foster father's callousness. He discovered immediately that he had not been given enough money to cover expenses at the University. As a result, he borrowed and went into debt. When his expenses increased he gambled unsuccessfully to try to meet them. At the same time, he began to indulge in "peach and honey," an alcoholic drink that quickly made him drunk. His "secret" engagement to Elmira Royster was broken by her parents with John Allan's full cooperation.

> To John Allan:
> You will remember that in a week after my arrival I wrote to you for some more money, and for books. You replied in terms of the utmost abuse—if I had been the vilest wretch on earth you could not have been more abusive than you were because I would not continue to pay $150 with $110.[5]

Edgar Poe was $2,000 in debt at the end of his first year at the University. John Allan, furious, refused to honor his debts and pulled Poe out of school. Poe quarreled violently with his foster father and, in March, 1827, left home with a few articles of clothing and a small sum of money slipped to him in secret by Frances Allan. He sailed to Boston.

> Thomas Tucker (friend):
> He would always seize the tempting glass . . . and without the least apparent pleasure, swallow the contents, never pausing until the last drop had passed his lips. One glass at a time was all he could take; but this was sufficient to rouse his whole nervous nature into a state of strongest excitement, which found vent in a continuous flow of wild, fascinating talk that irresistingly enchanted every listener with sirenlike power.[6]

On May 26, 1827, after several hungry weeks in Boston, Poe, declaring his age as twenty-two and using the alias "Edgar A. Perry," enlisted in the Army. He was sent to Fort Independence in Boston Harbor with the First Artillery. In the meantime, he had persuaded a Boston printer to issue a forty-page volume of his poetry, *Tamerlane and Other Poems*. If the book ever went on sale, it quickly disappeared.

> Kind solace in a dying hour!
>   Such, father, is not (now) my theme—
> I will not madly deem that power
>   Of Earth may shrive me of the sin
>   Unearthly pride hath revell'd in—
>   I have no time to dote or dream:
> You call it hope—that fire of fire!
> It is but agony of desire.[7]

Poe succeeded in the Army and moved up through the ranks. He also found time to read widely and write poetry; "Al Aaraaf" was among the poems penned in his leisure time. By January, 1829, "Edgar Perry" had been promoted to Sergeant Major. Soon after, he learned of his foster mother's impending death and was granted a ten-day leave to return home. Before he arrived, Frances Allan was dead and buried. John Allan, temporarily softened by his wife's death, agreed to help Edgar get discharged from the Army and apply to West Point, which he entered on July 1, 1830. In the meantime his second volume of poems, *Al Aaraaf, Tamerlane and Minor Poems*, had been printed by Hatch and Dunning in Baltimore. Unlike his first book, this one was reviewed in several places. In the *Ladies Magazine* the reviewer compared the young poet with Shelley. This minor recognition was enough to fire Poe's spirit.

> To John Allan:
> If she had not have died while I was away there would have been nothing for me to regret. Your love I never valued —but she I believe loved me as her own child. You promised me to forget all—but you soon forgot your promise. You sent me to W. Point like a beggar.[8]

At West Point, Poe once again found himself suffering the humiliation of not having enough money to afford necessary items. His father would not help him—he was now a busy widower in search of a new wife. Poe rebelled quietly and earned a reputation at the military academy as a brandy drinker. And, late into the night, he escaped into his reading and poetry.

John Allan remarried and completely disinherited Poe. In January, 1831, after deliberately neglecting his duties, Poe was court-martialed and expelled. Penniless, he went to New York, where his third book, *Poems*, was published in 1831, including "To Helen" and "Israfel." Otherwise, the city was cold and inhospitable.

> To John Allan:
> I have no more to say—except that my future life (which thank God will not endure long) must be passed in indigence and sickness. I have no energy left, nor health.[9]

Poe sought refuge in Baltimore among blood relatives. There his widowed Aunt Clemm cared for Grandmother Poe, a crippled old woman on whose pension they lived, and her own nine-year-old daughter Virginia. Also living in the house was Poe's brother Henry, who lay dying of alcoholism and consumption. Poe set about looking for ways to earn money to contribute to the poor household. In response to a short story contest held by the *Philadelphia Saturday Courier* with a $100 first prize, Poe wrote his first prose, five stories which formed the basis of his "Tales of the Folio Club." The tales were intended to be satires, or burlesques. "Metzengerstein," Poe's imitation of the Gothic horror tale popular at the time, achieved the effect of genuine horror and marked the beginning of his pursuit of this form of *bizarrerie*.

Poe did not win the contest. However, the *Courier* published all five of his tales in 1832, for which he was not paid a cent. That winter as Poe labored over his tales, he first began to use laudanum, a drug prescribed for upset stomach. This opium preparation, along with alcohol, began to affect his behavior and his work.

> His action was alternately vivacious and sullen. His voice varied rapidly from a tremulous indecision . . . to that species of energetic concision—that abrupt, weighty, unhurried, and hollow-sounding enunciation—that leaden, self-balanced and perfectly modulated guttural utterance, which may be observed in the lost drunkard, or the irreclaimable eater of opium, during the periods of his most intense excitement.[10]

In 1833 Poe won a fifty-dollar first prize with *Ms. Found in a Bottle* in a contest sponsored by the *Baltimore Sunday Visitor*. The judges declared his stories to be "eminently distinguished by a wild, vigorous, and poetical imagination, a rich style, a fertile invention, and varied curious learning." John Kennedy, one of the lawyer-judges, as well as novelist, became an important mentor to the twenty-four-year-old Poe, whose foster father had just died, leaving Poe not a penny, his final humiliation at the hands of John Allan. On Kennedy's recommendation, in August, 1835, Poe went to Richmond to begin a job as assistant editor on the new *Southern Literary Messenger*. His salary was a meager ten dollars a week, but the job was an important step for Poe's career as editor and critic.

> J. H. B. Latrobe (contest judge):
> [Poe] was dressed in black, and his frock coat was buttoned to the throat, where it met the black stock. . . . Not a particle of white was visible. Coat, hat, books, and gloves had

evidently seen their best days, but . . . everything had been done apparently, to make them presentable. . . . Gentleman was written all over him. His manner was easy and quiet. . . . His forehead was high, and remarkable for the great development at the temple. . . . The expression on his face was grave, almost sad, except when he became engaged in conversation, when it became animated and changeable.[11]

Poe's life in Richmond was pressured and hectic. The demands of his job at the *Messenger* were great; its social pressures made him vulnerable to the alcoholic drinks freely offered at all occasions. Poe was also subject to pressures from Baltimore and Mrs. Clemm, who wrote him anxious letters about her financial state (which had worsened since the death of Grandmother Poe and the loss of her pension) and Virginia's future. Soon Poe was drinking before breakfast and incurring the disapproval of his employer.

To John Kennedy:
I am suffering under a depression of spirits such as I have never felt before. . . . I am wretched and know not why. Console me—for you can. But let it be quickly—or it will be too late. . . . Convince me that it is worth one's while, that it is necessary to live. . . . Persuade me to do what is right. . . . You will not fail to see that I am suffering under a depression of spirits which will ruin me should it be long continued.[12]

After a trial month at the *Messenger*, Poe abruptly departed for Baltimore. When he returned to the *Messenger*, he brought his Aunt Clemm and Cousin Virginia, thirteen years old, whom he had secretly married in Baltimore. Poe and Virginia were married publicly in May, 1836, her age listed as twenty-one. Like the women that haunt his stories, Virginia had raven tresses, unusually large eyes, a pale white complexion, and an aura of frailty about her. It is believed that their marriage was never consummated, as Poe had been made impotent by alcohol and opiates.

She whom I loved in youth, and of whom I now pen calmly

Virginia Clemm

and distinctly these remembrances, was the sole daughter of
the only sister of my mother long departed. Eleonora was
the name of my cousin. We had always dwelled together, be-
neath a tropical sun, in the Valley of the Many-Colored
Grass . . . we lived all alone, knowing nothing of the world
without the valley—I, and my cousin, and her mother.[13]

Poe remained with the *Messenger* for a year and a half earning
a reputation as a biting critic in his reviews, and increasing the
circulation of the magazine severalfold. He was fired for drinking.
Sometimes he was so sick from drink that he had to stay in bed to
be nursed by his Aunt Clemm, his "Muddy." Poe took his aunt and
wife to New York and then on to Philadelphia in the summer of
1838. Poe's years in this city, the publishing capital of the nation,
were to be his most prosperous and successful. At first, however,
their lives were hard and money scarce, Poe writing stories and
poems and doing hack work when he could get it. Among the stories
he wrote at this time was "The Fall of the House of Usher."

The character of his face had been at all times remarkable.
A cadaverousness of complexion; an eye large, liquid, and
luminous beyond comparison; lips somewhat thin and very
pallid, but of a surpassingly beautiful curve; a nose of delicate
Hebrew model, but with a breadth of nostril unusual in similar formations; a finely moulded chin, speaking, in its want
of prominence, of a want of moral energy; hair of a more than
weblike softness and tenuity—these features, with an inordi-
nate expansion above the regions of the temple, made up
altogether a countenance not easily to be forgotten.[14]

In July, 1839, Poe was hired as coeditor of William Burton's
Gentleman's Magazine in which he published many of his own
stories ("William Wilson" and "House of Usher") as well as essays
and reviews. His sixth book, a volume of stories entitled *Tales of the
Grotesque and Arabesque*, was published by Lea and Blanchard in
two volumes—his only payment a few free copies. The book was not
a publishing success. In October, 1840, Poe, once again fired for
drinking, was hired by *Graham's Magazine* as coeditor. His salary

was $800 a year, not by any means adequate, but more than he had ever earned. In the meantime Poe was intent on starting his own literary magazine, a dream he would pursue for the rest of his life. His job with *Graham's*, however, scotched this project for the time being.

> Prospectus of *The Penn Magazine*:
> It shall be the first and chief purpose of the Magazine now proposed to become known as one where may be found at all times, and upon all subjects, an honest and a fearless opinion. It shall be a leading object to assert in precept, and to maintain in practice, the rights, while in effect it demonstrates the advantages, of an absolutely independent criticism; a criticism self-sustained; guiding itself only by the purest rules of Art; . . . holding itself aloof from all personal bias; acknowledging no fear save that of outraging the right; yielding no point either to the vanity of the author, or to the assumptions of critical prejudice, or those organized cliques which, hanging like nightmares upon American literature, manufacture, at the nod of our principal booksellers, a pseudo-public opinion by wholesale.[15]

Poe, his wife, and aunt were living in relative comfort and security in Philadelphia when in January, 1842, Virginia, while singing, coughed violently, and suddenly blood spilled from her mouth. The hemorrhage was a sure sign of tuberculosis, the disease that had killed Poe's mother and brother. Her illness was traumatic for Poe, who had already foretold of it in "Eleonora": the "finger of Death was upon her bosom."

> Joseph Wood Krutch (biographer):
> Poe invented the detective story in order that he might not go mad.[16]

Poe's pioneer detective story, "The Murders in the Rue Morgue," had been published in *Graham's Magazine* in 1841. Poe continued writing tales of deductive reasoning from which the modern detective story derived, such as "The Mystery of Marie Roget" and "The

Purloined Letter," whose hero was detective Monsieur C. Auguste Dupin, the cool analyst with brilliant powers of deduction. Poe also penned more tales of horror, "The Black Cat" and "The Masque of the Red Death," among others. In April, 1842, he quit his job at *Graham's Magazine*, which had become very successful under his guidance. Frequently ill now, sick with too much drink or exhausted from opium, Poe watched his young wife go through stages of fading and recovery in her struggle with consumption. Until April, 1844, he continued to contribute stories to *Graham's Magazine*. In June, 1843, "The Gold Bug," submitted to the *Dollar Newspaper*, won a $100 contest. It was the first Poe story to be widely read.

In April, 1844, Poe moved his sick wife to a farm on Bloomingdale Road in New York City (the spot is now Eighty-fourth Street and Broadway) where they were cared for by Aunt Clemm. The isolation and clean country air (as well as the cheap rent) seemed to benefit Poe and his wife. He completed "The Raven" while on the farm. At the end of the summer, however, with finances dangerously low, Poe went down into the city to look for work. He was hired by the *New York Evening Mirror*, which he left in December to work for the *Broadway Journal*, a paper he would eventually own. Living alone in the city, Poe began to drink heavily.

> To George Eveleth (admirer):
> [Virginia's] life was despaired of. I took leave of her forever, and underwent all the agonies of her death. She recovered partially, and I again hoped. At the end of a year, the vessel broke again. . . . Then again—again—again—and ever once again. . . . Each time I felt the agonies of her death. . . . But I am constitutionally sensitive—nervous in a very unusual degree, I became insane, with long intervals of horrible sanity. During those fits of absolute unconsciousness I drank—God knows how often or how much.[17]

In January, 1845, the *Mirror* published "The Raven"; in February, the poem was published in the *American Review*, among other papers. "The Raven" attracted more attention than any of Poe's previous work and created a sensation. The poet became a much-sought-after lecturer. People asked him for his autograph, literary ladies flocked around him in platonic adoration, and for a brief time he was the star of New York literary society. Ironically, his fame did nothing for his financial situation. He made no money from "The Raven," which was reprinted countless times as the result of insufficient copyright laws. His *Tales*, published that year by Wiley and Putnam's, sold well, although Poe only received eight cents per copy.

> To George Eveleth:
> The causes which maddened me to the drinking point are no more, and I am done with drinking for ever.[18]

The last four years of Poe's life saw him steadily decline. He moved Virginia to a cottage in Fordham, New York, where she finally died on January 30, 1847. He had done little writing, and was ill himself, with drink, and possibly suffering from a brain lesion. After her death he began to write *Eureka*, a book which set forth his eccentric theories of the universe; he also wrote "Ulalume," "The Bells," and "Annabel Lee," three of his most famous poems. He became romantically entangled with two women at the same time: he proposed marriage to Mrs. Helen Whitman, a middle-aged poetess and widow, and while awaiting her reply he ardently pursued Annie Richmond, a young married woman, who refused to leave her husband. Poe, in love with Annie, tried to commit suicide by taking an overdose of laudanum which only made him sick to his stomach. Although Mrs. Whitman agreed to marry Poe, she soon broke the engagement; she was frightened off by his unstable behavior. Poe then returned to Fordham and shunned what he described as "the pestilential society of literary women."

In 1849, his ambition to found his own magazine was suddenly revived with the offer of financial backing from a wealthy benefactor. Poe eagerly conceived of a plan to tour the United States to get advance subscriptions, and requested fifty dollars in advance from his backer to pay for the first leg of his journey—to Richmond. This trip was interrupted by a drunken spell in Philadelphia.

> To Aunt Clemm:
> My *dear, dear* Mother—I have been *so* ill—have had the

cholera, or spasms quite as bad, and can now hardly hold the pen.

The very instant you get this, *come* to me. The joy of seeing you will almost compensate for our sorrows. We can but die together. It is no use to reason with *me* now; I must die. I have no desire to live since I have done *Eureka*. I could accomplish nothing more. For your sake it would be sweet to live, but we must die together. You have been all in all to me, darling, ever beloved mother, and dearest, truest friend.

I was never really insane, except on occasions where my heart was touched.[19]

Poe finally arrived in Richmond on Friday the 13th of July. For the next few months, alternately drunk and cold sober, he let his magazine project take second place to his pursuit of an old love. Elvira Royster Shelton, now a widow, eventually agreed to marry Poe if he would remain sober. The wedding date was set for October 13.

Shortly before the wedding was to take place, on September 27, Poe took a boat to Baltimore on his way to Philadelphia to edit some poems for the very handsome fee of $100. He never reached Philadelphia. Disembarking in Baltimore, he disappeared into the city, finally to be discovered seriously ill and miserably disheveled in a tavern by a Dr. Snodgrass who had him transported to Washington Hospital. Poe lingered for four days in a state of delirium, incoherent and hallucinating. On October 7, 1849, Edgar Allan Poe died. He was forty years old.

Lord help my poor soul.[20]

Notes

1 Poe, "For Annie," *The Portable Poe*, p. 628.
2 Poe, "Eleonora," *The Portable Poe*, p. 95.
3 Poe, "William Wilson," *The Portable Poe*, p. 58.
4 Poe, "Romance (Introduction)," *The Selected Poetry and Prose of Edgar Allan Poe*, p. 17.
5 Poe, *The Portable Poe*, p. 5.
6 Mankowitz, *The Extraordinary Mr. Poe*, p. 37.

7 Poe, "Tamerlane," *The Selected Poetry and Prose of Edgar Allan Poe*, p. 3.
8 Poe, *The Portable Poe*, p. 7.
9 Ibid.
10 Poe, "The Fall of the House of Usher," *The Portable Poe*, p. 250.
11 Mankowitz, op. cit., p. 94.
12 Ibid., p. 107.
13 Poe, "Eleonora," *The Portable Poe*, p. 96.
14 Poe, "The Fall of the House of Usher," *The Portable Poe*, p. 250.
15 Mankowitz, op. cit., p. 132.
16 Joseph Wood Krutch, *The Portable Poe*, p. 330.
17 Poe, *The Portable Poe*, p. 29.
18 Ibid., p. 30.
19 Ibid., p. 48.
20 Mankowitz, op. cit., p. 242.

Sources

Bittner, William. *Poe, A Biography*. Boston: Atlantic-Little, Brown, 1962.

Carlson, Eric W., ed. *The Recognition of Edgar Allan Poe*. Ann Arbor: University of Michigan Press, 1970.

Hoffman, Daniel. *Poe Poe Poe Poe Poe Poe Poe*. New York: Avon Books, 1972.

Mankowitz, Wolf. *The Extraordinary Mr. Poe*. New York: Summit Books, 1978.

Moss, Sidney P. *Poe's Literary Battles*. Carbondale: Southern Illinois University Press, 1963.

Poe, Edgar Allan. *The Portable Poe*. Edited by Philip Van Doren Stern. London: Penguin Books, 1945.

———. *The Selected Poetry and Prose of Edgar Allan Poe*. Edited by T. O. Mabbott. New York: Random House, 1951.

ELVIS PRESLEY
1935-1977

Red West (Presley's cousin):

He believes there was a master plan by God in singling him out for his fantastic success. . . . I mean, how does it happen that a skinny little kid from a dirt-poor family in Tupelo, Mississippi, suddenly becomes the best-known name in the world? How is it that he commands all these fortunes and has all these millions of people who love him?[1]

ELVIS PRESLEY. American singer. "Elvis the Pelvis." The "King" of rock 'n' roll, who at the age of thirty was the highest-paid performer in the history of the music business, and whose hundreds of thousands of fans continued to sell out his concerts until his death. Presley was to the fifties what Frank Sinatra was to the forties, and Presley, both as a business and a cultural phenomenon, paved the way for the Beatles in the sixties. Throughout the Beatles era and after the peak of their popularity Presley endured.

> Jerry Hopkins (biographer):
> If one of Elvis's fans bought one of everything, she could, upon arising in the morning, pull on some Elvis Presley bobby socks, Elvis Presley shoes, an Elvis Presley skirt and Elvis Presley blouse, an Elvis Presley sweater, hang an Elvis Presley charm bracelet from one wrist, put an Elvis Presley handkerchief in her Elvis Presley purse, and head for school, where she might swap some Elvis Presley bubble gum cards before class, where she would take notes with an Elvis Presley pencil.[2]

Elvis Aron Presley, an identical twin, was born in a two-room house in Tupelo, Mississippi, on January 8, 1935. Jesse, his brother, was stillborn. Presley would be the only child of Vernon Presley, a farm worker, and Gladys Smith Presley, a sewing machine operator. He was the shining light of their life. Gladys Presley's relationship with her son was primary. Later it would be observed that he fully reciprocated this strong attachment.

Few clues to Presley's future can be found in his childhood. At the age of ten he won a five-dollar second prize in a talent contest at the Mississippi-Alabama Fair singing "Old Shep." At twelve his father gave him a guitar because he couldn't afford to buy him the bicycle he wanted. Presley taught himself to play it, and carried it around with him. He loved to sing the gospel songs which he learned in church and from his mother. In 1948, the family moved to Memphis in search of better jobs and a better life. They lived in a housing project and he attended L. C. Hume High School where he is remembered as a shy boy who distinguished himself by his appearance: while most teenage boys had crew cuts, Presley sported long hair and sideburns which he elaborately combed and arranged in a pompadour.

> Bill Hamilton (fellow student):
> There was a place on Beale Street that catered to country music men. They carried white, yellow, pink, blue suits and fancy shirts. When Elvis had money he started buying his clothes there. His preference was a pink jacket with black pants.[3]

In 1953, fresh out of high school, Presley went to work, first with the Precision Tool Company and then the Crown Electric Company as a truckdriver. That year he made a four-dollar record as a present for his mother at the Memphis Recording Service. He sang "My Happiness" and "That's When Your Heartaches Begin." Marion Keisker, who was managing the office that day for owner Sam Phillips of Sun Records, took special note of Presley because of his unusual sound. Presley returned to make another four-dollar record in January, 1954. Sam Phillips was the engineer that day and, prompted by Keisker, made note of the teenager's "Negro sound." Several months later he called Elvis Presley in to make a record. Although his first attempts were rough, practice with guitar player Scotty Morrow resulted in Presley's first legitimate record, a forty-five RPM, "That's All Right (Mama)," a black blues song written by Arthur (Big Boy) Crudup, and a white bluegrass standard, "Blue Moon of Kentucky." The record was played on a Memphis radio station and suddenly Sun Records was deluged with 5,000 orders. Presley's first professional record became a regional hit.

> Marion Keisker (Sun Records):
> He never had anything prepared, and the sessions always went on and on. . . . Elvis was different from the other Sun artists who came later. He did not write his own songs. We had to create them on the spot or take somebody else's song from our stable of writers. And he'd never rehearse. . . . Elvis never had anything ready.[4]

His star quickly rose. By the summer of 1955, twenty-year-old Presley had a record ("Baby, Let's Play House") on the national best-seller chart. He was a regular member of the country music radio show "Louisiana Hayride," and when he sang at live shows he had begun to get the wild reaction from the female members of the audience that became characteristic of his fans.

> Red West:
> He dated from time to time . . . but he wasn't girl crazy. He was more likely to have one steady girl friend. He had one little local dark-haired beauty in the early days and if I remember rightly, she jilted him. . . .
> Apart from his wild drape coats, most of his money went to the one woman in his life that mattered more to him than anything—his mother.[5]

In 1955 RCA Records bought Presley's contract from Sam Phillips and Sun Records for $35,000, a very substantial sum of money. Part of the deal included a $5,000 bonus for Presley. He used it to buy his first Cadillac—it was pink, and he gave it to his mother.

"Colonel" Tom Parker, former carnival barker turned personal manager (Eddy Arnold, Gene Austin, Hank Snow), became Presley's manager that year. The union of Presley with Parker was a critical factor in Presley's career, for the Colonel would be the mastermind behind the packaging and selling of the singer. Without Parker, it is doubtful that Presley would have become the phenomenon that he did.

Colonel Parker:

I discovered the big secret that would send Elvis to the pinnacle of success. Female entertainers have been using it for years to turn audiences on. I just had Elvis do it in reverse.[6]

The year 1956 was a turning point for Presley. In January, just twenty-one years old, he went to Nashville for his first recording session. Working in the studio with a group of musicians and a gospel/country recording group, the Jordanaires, Presley recorded three songs: "Heartbreak Hotel," "I Want You, I Need You, I Love You," and "I Was the One." On January 28, Presley went to New York for the first of six television appearances arranged for him by Colonel Parker on Tommy and Jimmy Dorsey's "Stage Show." His hair slicked back and his sideburns slicked down, Presley sang "Heartbreak Hotel" and performed the gyrations that earned him the nickname "Elvis the Pelvis." Soon afterward the record climbed the national charts to number one and Presley was getting 10,000 letters a week.

They all think I'm a sex maniac. They're just frustrated old types, anyway. I'm just natural.[7]

Colonel Parker continued to use television to promote Elvis Presley. After the Dorsey shows, he appeared on the Milton Berle show in April, 1956. By now both the single "Heartbreak Hotel" and his first album *Elvis Presley* were number one on the charts. That year, Presley earned his first million. With his new wealth he bought a ranch house in Memphis into which he moved his parents and grandmother. A brick wall was built around the house in a futile attempt to keep out his eager young fans.

On September 9, 1956, Elvis Presley was seen by fifty-four million Americans on Ed Sullivan's "Toast of the Town"—but from the waist up only. His leg-snapping and enthusiastic pelvic motions were considered suggestive and improper. He sang "Hound Dog" and "Love Me Tender," the title song from his first movie, then in production in Hollywood at Twentieth Century–Fox. Elvis Presley and rock 'n' roll were becoming controversial. Some critics considered him dangerous fare for the innocent minds of the young television audience. This reaction, of course, had little effect on his success. If anything, the controversy was good for his image. Presley's next three singles were number one hits, and when the movie *Love Me Tender* was released in November, 1956, it, too, was a box office smash despite some very bad reviews.

> *Time* magazine:
> Suddenly the figure comes to life. The lips part, the eyes half close, the clutched guitar begins to undulate back and forth in an uncomfortably suggestive manner. And wham! The midsection of the body jolts forward to bump and grind and beat out a lowdown rhythm that takes its pace from boogie and hillbilly, rock 'n' roll and something known only to Elvis and his Pelvis. As the belly dance gets wilder, a peculiar sound emerges. A rusty foghorn? A voice? . . . words occasionally can be made out, like raisins in cornmeal mush. . . . And then all at once everything stops, and a big trembling tender half smile, half sneer smears slowly across the Cinemascope screen. The message that millions of U. S. teenage girls love to receive has just been delivered.[8]

From 1956 to 1970 Presley would make thirty-two movies, all of which would make money. However, except for one or two (*Jailhouse Rock, King Creole*), none would receive any critical praise, and for good reason. The movies were formula fare, made quickly and cheaply for the sole purpose of capitalizing on Elvis Presley's box office draw. It was apparent very early on that Presley's fans would pay to see him in anything: just to see Elvis was enough.

Red West:

> He would sometimes see himself in a movie and he would get disgusted. He would say "Who's that fast-talking hillbilly sonofabitch that nobody can understand? One day he is singing to a dog, then to a car, then to a cow. They are all the damned same movies with that Southerner just singing to something different." [9]

By late 1957 Presley had completed two more movies: *Lovin' You*, directed by Hal Wallis for Paramount, and *Jailhouse Rock*, one of his most popular, for MGM; at the same time he was working on his fourth, *King Creole* (also directed by Wallis). He had moved his parents and grandmother into Graceland, a twenty-three-room converted church on thirteen acres in a Memphis suburb. Outside the high walls and the front gates, his fans constantly hovered. If Presley wanted to go out now, it had to be a well-planned maneuver. His forays into the outside world all took place at night while the rest of the world was asleep: he would rent a movie theater and watch movies all night, or he would take over the local skating rink and roller skate all night. Isolated, his personal freedom severely curtailed by his fame, Presley had surrounded himself with a personal male entourage that became known as the "Memphis Mafia." Their job was to take care of Presley, wait on him, run his errands, protect him, and entertain him.

> This is my corporation which travels with me at all times. More than that, all these members of my corporation are my friends. [10]

Gladys Presley died at the age of forty-six on August 14, 1958, six months after Presley had been drafted into the Army. Her health had been deteriorating over the last few years. The cause of death was listed as hepatitis and heart failure. Rumors, however, had her addicted to diet pills and alcohol and uncomfortable with the pressures of her son's fame. Presley, deeply attached to his mother, was heartbroken.

I was an only child. She was very close, more than a mother. She was a friend who let me talk to her any hour of the day or night if I had a problem. I would get mad sometimes when she wouldn't let me do something. But I found out she was right about almost everything.[11]

During his two years in the Army, Presley (and Parker) insisted that he be treated just like any other draftee, refusing any special treatment, and refusing to work as a performer for the Army. He spent eighteen months of his Army life in Friedberg, Germany, where he lived off base in a rented house with his father and grandmother. It is reported that Presley first began to use Dexedrine in Germany, as well as develop an interest in karate that later developed into an obsession.

Presley returned to civilian life in March, 1960, and soon afterward he appeared on television in a Frank Sinatra special, "Welcome Back, Elvis." The deal that the Colonel made guaranteed Presley $125,000 for a six-minute appearance. His absence had not hurt his career; but his public image had changed. After the Army he abandoned the sexy rock-'n'-roller image for that of wholesome, all-American boy. Even his sideburns had been cut short, and he began to dress more conservatively. Honey had replaced the blood in his veins, according to *New York Times* movie critic Bosley Crowther. The records he now cut were often ballads, spirituals, and religious songs.

Elvis Presley went back to making movies at the rate of three a year, and he continued to record, but from 1961 to 1968 Presley made no personal appearances at all. When he wasn't in Hollywood, he lived behind the walls at Graceland with his crew of hired men. Also added to the entourage was Vernon Presley's new wife and Priscilla Beaulieu, the fifteen-year-old daughter of an Army officer Presley had met in Germany. She had come to Graceland to stay and Presley sent her to Catholic school and finishing school. During this time he dated many different women.

Sonny West:
    He got what he wanted, put it away in storage, and went

on to something else. Priscilla could have anything she wanted but the thing she wanted most was Elvis.[12]

In May, 1967, Presley married Priscilla, now twenty-one years old. Daughter Lisa Marie was born nine months later. Their marriage was difficult from the start. Her presence caused a shifting of the place occupied in Presley's life by the Memphis Mafia, and, as a result, some of the members soon departed.

In 1969, his reentry deftly managed by Colonel Parker, Presley returned to public life. He had not had any hit records for several years, although his records always sold well, and his movies were losing popularity. Parker decided it was time for the thirty-five-year-old Presley to make a comeback.

Red West:
He takes pills to go to sleep. He takes pills to get up. He takes pills to go to the john, and he takes pills to stop him from going to the john. . . . His system doesn't work anymore like a normal human being's. The pills do all the work for him.[13]

Parker chose Las Vegas for the comeback. He booked Presley into the International Hotel, newly built, the largest in the city with a 2,000-seat show room. The contract called for two shows a night, seven days a week, for a month. Presley got himself in shape. His appearances were booked solid; his "resurrection" was enthusiastically affirmed by adoring audiences and the critics. Presley was superb in live performance.

International Hotel spokesman:
Elvis has changed the whole economy of Las Vegas. Business was way off, and when Elvis Presley is posted on the marquee, it's instant S. R. O.! People from all over the world come and fight for admittance during his engagement. Chartered planes bring his fans from as far as France, Japan, and Australia. . . . Elvis is a phenomenon.[14]

Once again, Elvis Presley was King. He returned to Las Vegas five months later in January, 1970, for another month of full-house performances, and then went on to play the largest arenas in the country. He performed at the Houston Astrodome and broke box office records as well as earning over a million-dollar fee for six shows. That year he appeared in a documentary made for television called *Elvis: That's the Way It Is*, filmed in concert in Las Vegas. In 1972, Presley made four concert appearances at Madison Square Garden and became the first performer to sell out the Garden.

But behind the glitter of the white, tight-fitting costumes, Presley was in trouble. In 1973, his strained marriage to Priscilla Beaulieu ended in divorce. Presley's emotional and physical health were unstable. Since the early 1960's, he had been relying on a wide variety of medications, prescribed by a private physician, in order to function. He lived at night, often playing racket ball until morning, and slept during the day, a sleep that had to be induced by pills. He suffered from hypertension, constipation, and weight problems which he treated with medications. His eyes were troubling him and he reportedly had glaucoma.

His behavior was eccentric: he shot bullet holes in television screens; he flew to a Denver hotel to satisfy a craving for a peanut butter and jelly sandwich. His weight fluctuated dramatically: he would eat ravenously and then starve himself in order to get in shape for a concert. A nurse lived at Graceland whose job was to administer his medicines when he wanted them, and when he went on tour, a doctor was in attendance. Sudden mysterious illnesses began to force him to cancel concert appearances. Presley would collapse without warning and need oxygen to revive.[15]

The money continued to roll in, however, under the watchful management of Colonel Parker. Elvis Presley was the highest-paid performer in history. He paid his taxes, and spent his millions on cars, guns, extravagant gifts to friends and charities, and drugs.

> Dave Hebler:
> It seems he is bent on death. . . . The thing about him is that Elvis doesn't care. He doesn't give a fuck. . . . He is a composite of contradictions. He is like a ping-pong ball go-

Presley performing in Lincoln, Nebraska, 1977

ing down the hallway. You never know from one minute to the next whether he is going to point a gun at somebody, or he is going to kiss them.[16]

Presley was found unconscious on the floor of his large bathroom at Graceland on August 16, 1977. He was rushed to the hospital, but he never regained consciousness and was pronounced dead at 3.30 P.M. A careful analysis of his blood later revealed that ten different drugs were present in the singer's blood stream; their interaction had caused his heart to fail.

Elvis Presley was forty-two years old.

Johnny Rivers:
He had created his own world. He had to. There was nothing else for him to do.[17]

Notes

1 West et al., *Elvis: What Happened?*, p. 157.
2 Hopkins, *Elvis*, p. 147.
3 Mann, *The Private Elvis*, p. 21.
4 Hopkins, op. cit., p. 75.
5 West et al., op. cit., p. 99.
6 Mann, op. cit., p. 27.
7 Ibid., p. 153.
8 Hopkins, op. cit., p. 160.
9 West et al., op. cit., p. 140.
10 Hopkins, op. cit., p. 280.
11 Ibid., p. 206.
12 West et al., op. cit., p. 210.
13 Ibid., p. 187.
14 Mann, op. cit., p. 187.
15 Wendell Rawls, Jr., "Presley Associates Say Torment and Drugs Marked Final Months," *New York Times*, September 23, 1979, p. 20.
16 West et al., op. cit., p. 188.
17 Hopkins, op. cit., p. 293.

Sources

Hopkins, Jerry. *Elvis: A Biography*. New York: Warner Books, 1971.

Mann, May. *The Private Elvis* (or *Elvis and The Colonel*). New York: Pocket Books, 1977.

West, Red, Sonny West, and Dave Hebler (with Steve Dunlevy). *Elvis: What Happened?* New York: Ballantine Books, 1977.

ARTHUR RIMBAUD
1854-1891

The poet makes himself a *visionary* through a long, a prodigious and rational disordering of *all* the senses. Every form of love, of suffering, of madness; he searches himself, he consumes all the poisons in him, keeping only their quintessences. Ineffable torture in which he will need all his faith and superhuman strength, the great criminal, the great sickman, the accursed—and the Supreme Savant! For he arrives at the Unknown! [1]

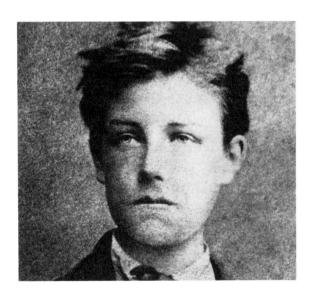

ARTHUR RIMBAUD. French poet and inspiration for the Symbolist movement. He endured for thirty-seven years. During five of those years, from the age of fifteen to nineteen, he created verse and prose poems that would have a profound influence on modern poetry. He dispensed with logic and traditional forms to probe the obscure and dreamlike world of his subconscious and his memories. Poetry was magic, and Rimbaud was an alchemist who played with words, transforming them into new materials. *Illuminations*, his prose poems, is generally considered the highest manifestation of his genius.

Rimbaud was a vagabond, trader, and gunrunner. He left the world the legacy of his life as well as his poetry. He continues to be read as the embodiment of a man in revolt, a hero of rebellion against society and self.

> For, I is someone else. If brass wakes up a trumpet, it isn't to blame. To me this is evident: I witness the birth of my thought: I look at it, I listen to it: I give a stroke of the bow: the symphony begins to stir in the depths or comes bursting onto the stage.[2]

Arthur Rimbaud was born on October 20, 1854, in Charleville,

France, a small provincial town on the Meuse River. He was the second child and second son of an army captain and Vitalie Cuif, the daughter of a farmer. Two sisters, Vitalie and Isabelle, would follow.

When Rimbaud was six, Captain Rimbaud deserted his wife and four children, never to be seen again. Vitalie, a cold, strict, obstinate woman, vented her bitterness at her abandonment by raising her sons without sparing the rod.

> And the Mother, closing the exercise book,
> Went off satisfied and very proud, without seeing,
> In the blue eyes and under his brow covered with bumps,
> The soul of her child given over to repugnance.[3]

Rimbaud showed great promise as a student at the Collège de Charleville, so much so that Vitalie hired a private tutor who encouraged the young boy to write poetry. George Izambard came to the school to teach in Rimbaud's last year. Rimbaud found a sympathetic ear in the young master who further encouraged his intellectual curiosity by offering him works like Hugo's *Les Misérables*, books his mother considered "dangerous." By the age of fifteen, Rimbaud was far more intellectually sophisticated than his contemporaries and hungry for more nourishment.

> To Théodore de Banville (poet):
> In two years, in one year perhaps, I will be in Paris. *Anch'io*, gentlemen of the press, I will be a Parnassian! I do not know what is inside me . . . that wants to come out. . . . I swear, *cher Maître*, I will always worship the two goddesses, the Muse and Liberty.[4]

In January, 1870, Rimbaud had a poem published in Latin in *La Revue Pour Tous*, and won first prize in the Concours Académique. That summer the Franco-Prussian war forced the closing of the schools and kept the Rimbaud family confined to Charleville. Rimbaud grew restless in the small, dull town.

> To George Izambard:
> I am at a loss, ill, mad, stupid, astounded; I had hopes

for sunbaths, long walks, rest, travel, adventure, bohemian
larks, in a word; especially I had hoped for newspapers and
books. . . . But there is nothing! The mail delivers nothing
to bookstores, Paris is coyly making fun of us: not a single
new book: everything is dead![5]

Rimbaud ran away from home twice during this period. The first
time he arrived in Paris by train without a ticket or money to pay for
one and was arrested and thrown in jail. He wrote a frantic letter
to Izambard, who bailed him out; Rimbaud spent three weeks with
him and his three elderly aunts before returning to his wrathful
mother. He bolted from home again almost immediately, wandering
through northern France and Belgium, a gangly adolescent, his white-
blue eyes recording the images of the countryside. Finally he arrived
back at the house of Izambard's aunts where he spent the days copying out the new poems he had written.

I went off, my fists in my torn pockets;
My coat too was becoming ideal;
I walked under the blue sky, Muse!
    and I was your vassal;
Oh! Oh! What brilliant loves I dreamed
    of![6]

In February, 1871, Rimbaud sold his watch and using the money
to buy a train ticket, made his way to Paris hoping to join the Com-
mune that was forming in revolt against the Prussian government.
The sixteen-year-old boy spent two weeks sleeping in doorways and
under bridges, begging and eating out of garbage pails. It is suspected
that Rimbaud suffered some kind of traumatic homosexual experience in Paris, one that had a permanent effect on him.

When they have used up their quid,
How will I act, O stolen heart?
There will be Bacchic hiccups,
When they have used up their quid:
I will have stomach retchings,
If my heart is degraded:

When they have used up their quid
How will I act, O stolen heart? [7]

When Rimbaud returned to Charleville he was changed. He let his hair grow unkempt and dirty, he refused to bathe, and he walked the streets of the town in grubby clothes, smoking a pipe with its bowl upside down. He hung around the cafés hustling free drinks and tobacco in exchange for volleys of blasphemous pronouncements against the Church, priests, and women.

> To George Izambard:
>   Now I'm going in for debauch. Why? I want to be a poet; and I'm working to make myself a *visionary*. . . . To arrive at the unknown through the disordering of *all the senses,* that's the point. [8]

Izambard was unsympathetic to Rimbaud's new state of mind and their friendship ended. His new mentor became Charles Bretagne, a customs official who introduced Rimbaud to magic and the occult. Rimbaud was formulating his theory of poetry and of the function of the poet as a voyant, a seer. He was writing "Le Bateau Ivre," and reading the poems of Baudelaire and a new poet, Paul Verlaine. At Bretagne's suggestion, Rimbaud sent Verlaine some poems accompanied by Bretagne's letter of introduction. Verlaine was intrigued by the poems and responded by inviting Rimbaud to his home in Paris and sending him money for the trip.

Verlaine, twenty-six, was living with his pregnant wife Mathilde in her parents' home. His marriage was not happy and Verlaine often drank too much. When Rimbaud arrived in September, 1871, Verlaine was astonished at his youth and, at the same time, enchanted by the young outspoken poet.

So then, the poet is truly a thief of fire. [9]

Rimbaud was ill-mannered, bratty, and insolent. The seventeen-year-old poet succeeded in alienating everyone around him with his obscene behavior, including the Paris literati. The single exception was Paul Verlaine, who had fallen under his spell. Mathilde's parents asked Rimbaud to leave their household, and he disappeared into the city.

He moved around Paris, often destitute, until Verlaine managed to find him. He brought him to Théodore de Banville, who put him up in the attic room of his house, until, once again, Rimbaud's behavior forced him to give up his lodgings. Verlaine paid for Rimbaud's next room with his own money and the two poets embarked on a sexual relationship that would become a scandal.

> I had, in truth, pledged myself to restore him to his primitive state of child of the Sun—and, nourished by the wine of caverns and the biscuit of the road, we wandered, I impatient to find the place and the formula.[10]

Verlaine's wife tried to retrieve her husband, first imploring and then threatening, but by September, 1872, Rimbaud and Verlaine were living together in Soho in London and openly flaunting their relationship. They wandered around the city, exploring the East End and the docks, drinking in pubs, smoking opium in Chinese dens. They learned English and, to earn money, they gave French lessons. Their friendship was volatile and they often quarreled.

In the spring of 1873, Rimbaud, exhausted and dissipated, returned alone to France, going to his mother's farm in Roche. Verlaine, who had been ill in London, had earlier decided to return to his wife and persuade her to call off the divorce proceedings, but instead he went to Belgium.

At home, Rimbaud began to struggle with the writing of *Une Saison en Enfer*. He kept to himself, wandering in the woods, staying up late into the night. His sister Isabelle "could hear him groaning as if he were struggling with some devil." [11]

> Paterne Berrichon (biographer):
> [Rimbaud's] complexion had become grey and livid and on his cheekbones stood out two red patches of color. His eyes . . . seemed now to have faded, and the pupils were constantly dilating and contracting so as almost to disappear, giving his eyes a vague and dying appearance. For hours he used to lie stretched on his bed with half-open eyes, not

saying a word. When the time for the meals came round his sisters used to call him to the table, but when he arrived he would refuse to eat. . . . all he asked was to be left in peace.[12]

At the end of May, Verlaine persuaded Rimbaud to return to London with him. Rimbaud treated him with such contempt and cruelty that Verlaine, threatening suicide, fled to Brussels. Rimbaud followed a few days later and found him very drunk. They quarreled, and when Rimbaud tried to leave, Verlaine shot him, wounding him in the wrist. Frightened, Rimbaud summoned the police, who arrested Verlaine. He was tried, found guilty of attempted murder, and sentenced to two years at hard labor.

Rimbaud returned to Roche and in August, 1873, completed *Une Saison En Enfer* at his mother's farm. He arranged to have the book printed, and copies sent to literary people he knew in Paris.

He followed the book to the city to see how it was being received. Both the book and the author were deliberately ignored, largely because of Verlaine's imprisonment for which Rimbaud was considered responsible. Disgusted and defeated, Rimbaud returned to Charleville on foot. Legend has it that he now burned all his manuscripts and papers. (Many copies of *Une Saison en Enfer* in fact were stored in Brussels and discovered after his death.) Rimbaud stopped writing for good.

> An exile here, I once had a stage on which to play all the masterpieces of literature. I would show you unheard-of riches, I note the story of the treasures you discovered. I see the outcome. My wisdom is scorned as chaos. What is my nothingness to the stupor that awaits you?[13]

In January, 1875, Rimbaud met one last time with Verlaine, who was fresh out of jail and had traced the young poet to Stuttgart where he was studying German. It is likely that Rimbaud gave Verlaine the manuscript of *Illuminations* at this meeting. After visiting several bars, the two, as usual, quarreled and fought. They went their separate ways and never saw each other again.

During the next three years Rimbaud wandered in Europe, always landing back home at Charleville, the victim of some stroke of bad luck, broke and often sick.

In November, 1878, he went to Cyprus where he worked as an interpreter in a quarry for six months until he was felled by typhoid fever and forced to return once more to Charleville.

> I! I who called myself angel or seer, exempt from all morality, I am returned to the soil with a duty to seek and rough reality to embrace! Peasant! [14]

Rimbaud left France for the last time in March, 1880, and traveled to Africa where he spent the last decade of his life trying to establish a place for himself in the world. In Aden, he worked in the office of a coffee merchant. His next stop was Harrar in Ethiopia where he was in charge of a trading post, and from there he ventured briefly into the interior where no white man had ever been. The poet had been irrevocably replaced by a man whose concerns were building a life, making money, succeeding in a job. Instead of poetry, Rimbaud was interested in technical books and wrote his mother discussing plans to write a book for the Geographic Society.

> To his family:
> Alas, what is the point of these trips back and forth, the fatigue and the adventures with unfamiliar races, and the languages we memorize, and the endless discomforts, if I cannot one day, after a few years, settle down in one fairly pleasant place, and found a family and at least have a son . . . whom I will see grow into a famous engineer, a man made powerful and rich by science? [15]

Meanwhile, in Paris, the name and work of Arthur Rimbaud were becoming known. In 1884, Verlaine wrote about him in *Les Poètes maudits,* and included a selection of his poems, which had been well received. In 1886, Verlaine published *Illuminations,* the prose poems Rimbaud had given him at their last meeting. The author was described as "the late Arthur Rimbaud," as Verlaine had not been able to contact him. The avant-garde poets made Rimbaud their idol.

And even if, half crazed, in the end, he loses the understanding of his visions, he has seen them! Let him be destroyed in his leap by those unnamable, unutterable and innumerable things.[16]

When the Moslems took over Harrar, Rimbaud returned to Aden with a girl from a local tribe with whom he lived for a year. He became involved in a gunrunning scheme and lost all his money. His health deteriorated. He was bored, isolated, and lonely.

On April 2, 1891, Rimbaud, suffering from a painful tumor in his right knee, went to Aden to seek medical treatment. A hospital stay did not improve his condition and he was forced to return to France. Arriving in Marseilles in May, he was admitted to the Hospital of the Immaculate Conception. His right leg was amputated and his illness diagnosed as cancer. His prognosis was grave.

True I have wept too much! Dawns are heartbreaking;
Cruel all moons and bitter the suns.
Drunk with love's acrid torpors.
O let my keel burst! Let me go to the sea![17]

In July, Rimbaud returned to the farm at Roche where he was devotedly cared for by his sister Isabelle. The disease continued to ravage his body and he grew progressively weaker. In August, in order to avoid the coming harsh weather of fall and winter in northern France, Isabelle took him to Marseilles. When they arrived, Rimbaud, nearly comatose from the strain of the journey, was taken back to the Hospital of the Immaculate Conception where he died on November 10, 1891. He was thirty-seven years old.

Seen enough. The vision was met with in every air.

Had enough. Sounds of cities, in the evening and in the sun and always.

Known enough. Life's halts—O Sounds and Visions!

Departure in new affection and new noise.[18]

Notes

1 Rimbaud, *Illuminations*, pp. xxx–xxxi.
2 Ibid., p. xxix.
3 Fowlie, *Rimbaud: Complete Works and Selected Letters*, p. 75.
4 Ibid., p. 297.
5 Ibid., p. 299.
6 Ibid., p. 63.
7 Ibid., p. 83.
8 Rimbaud, *Illuminations*, p. xxvii.
9 Ibid., p. xxxi.
10 Ibid., p. 67.
11 Starkie, *Arthur Rimbaud*, p. 265.
12 Ibid., p. 264.
13 Rimbaud, *Illuminations*, p. 29.
14 Rimbaud, *A Season in Hell*, p. 87.
15 Fowlie, op. cit., pp. 341–43.
16 Rimbaud, *Illuminations*, p. xxxi.
17 Rimbaud, *The Drunken Boat*, p. 101.
18 Rimbaud, *Illuminations*, p. 35.

Sources

Fowlie, Wallace, ed. and translator. *Rimbaud: Complete Works and Selected Letters*. Chicago: University of Chicago Press, 1966.
Rimbaud, Arthur. *A Season in Hell and The Drunken Boat*. Translated by Louise Varese. New York: New Directions, 1961.
———. *Illuminations*. Translated by Louise Varese. New York: New Directions, 1957.
Starkie, Enid. *Arthur Rimbaud*. New York: New Directions, 1968.

ANNE SEXTON
1928-1974

I say *Live, Live* because of the sun, the dream,
the excitable gift.[1]

ANNE SEXTON. American poet, Pulitzer Prize winner. A leading member of the "confessional" school. Her poetry is autobiographical, an intimate chronicle of her life, a relentlessly honest
examination of her nervous breakdown, melancholy, and depression.
She called herself "an imagist who deals with reality and its hard
fact." Her influences were Rilke, Rimbaud, Kafka, Neruda—as well
as her psychiatrists. Her poems are haunted by her love and fear of
death, her own above all. It was her subject, her obsession. She
considered it, tasted it, embraced it. It was her poetry.

> Not that it was beautiful,
> but that, in the end, there was
> a certain sense of order there;
> something worth learning
> in that narrow diary of my mind,
> in the commonplaces of the asylum
> where the cracked mirror
> or my own selfish death
> outstared me.[2]

Anne Gray Harvey was born on November 3, 1928, in Newton,

Massachusetts, to Mary Staples Harvey and Ralph Churchill Harvey, founder of a successful woolens firm in Boston. She was the last of three girls: "The last given/and the last taken—/. . . being the unwanted, the mistake." [3]

She grew up in the family's large house in Weston, Massachusetts, with summers spent in Squirrel Island, Maine. She attended Rogers Hall, a boarding school in Lowell, and the Garland School, a two-year college in Boston. Never a good student, Sexton was headstrong, and temperamental, impatient, rebellious. She demanded and got attention. At nineteen, dark-haired, tall and thin like a model, she appeared sophisticated and worldly beyond her years.

> The sky breaks.
> It sags and breathes upon my face.
> *in the presence of mine enemies, mine enemies*
> The world is full of enemies.
> There is no safe place.[4]

In August, 1948, she eloped with Alfred Muller Sexton II ("Kayo"), a Colgate freshman. He soon dropped out of college, and went to work in the wool business for her father. The couple moved into a house near her parents' in Newton Lower Falls. In 1953, their first child, Linda Gray Sexton, was born. Two years later Joyce Sexton arrived.

With motherhood came the first significant crisis in Anne Sexton's mental health: unable to cope with the demands of her babies, she attempted suicide more than once and was hospitalized. This marked the beginning of her intense involvement in psychoanalysis.

> A woman who writes feels too much,
> those trances and portents!
> As if cycles and children and islands
> weren't enough; as if mourners and gossips
> and vegetables were never enough.
> She thinks she can warn the stars.
> A writer is essentially a spy.
> Dear love, I am that girl.[5]

She came to her art at a late stage. "I wrote my first poem in 1957 or 1958. I was watching television, a program on the form of the sonnet, and I said, 'I can do that.' So I wrote a poem. It wasn't very good and I didn't offer it for publication." Sexton began to study poetry, attending seminars and writing workshops. She studied with poets W. D. Snodgrass (with whom she became a close friend) and Robert Lowell, in whose class at Boston University she met George Starbuck and Sylvia Plath. The three poets would attend class and then spend hours at the Ritz Carlton drinking martinis and talking. Sexton's poems began to appear regularly in poetry magazines and literary periodicals.

> My business is words. Words are like labels,
> or coins, or better, like swarming bees.
> I confess I am only broken by the sources of things;
> as if words were counted like dead bees in the attic,
> unbuckled from their yellow eyes and their dry wings.[6]

The year 1959 was filled with death for Sexton. She watched her mother die of cancer, and a few months later her father died suddenly of a heart attack. *To Bedlam and Part Way Back*, her first book of poems, was published by Houghton Mifflin in 1960. It is a record of her nervous breakdown and recovery, interlaced with images of death. *All My Pretty Ones* (1962) continued this theme. Nominated for the National Book Award, it was acclaimed by critics and helped to establish her as one of America's outstanding contemporary poets. Her work was ranked alongside that of Robert Lowell and Sylvia Plath.

In 1963, the American Academy of Arts and Letters awarded her a $6,500 traveling fellowship to spend a year abroad. With her husband's support and encouragement, she left for Europe in August accompanied by a friend. The trip was aborted when Sexton discovered she could not cope without therapy. She returned to the U. S. in October, disappointed and defeated.

> Oh starry starry night! This is how
> I want to die:
>
> into that rushing beast of the night,

sucked up by that great dragon, to split
from my life with no flag,
no belly,
no cry.[7]

Live or Die, for which she would win the Pulitzer Prize, was
published in 1966. She described the volume as "a fever chart
for a bad case of melancholy." The period preceding its publication had been difficult for Sexton, who was struggling to stay sane
as well as to write. In addition, she was fighting a new enemy—
acceptance, success, praise. She landed in Massachusetts General
Hospital and her doctor prescribed thorazine. The drug temporarily
stabilized her, but in July, 1966, she again attempted suicide, taking
an overdose of pills, and was back in the hospital, her stomach
pumped, strapped into bed.

Erica Jong (poet and friend):
Anne Sexton sometimes seemed like a woman without
skin. She felt everything so intensely, had so little capacity to
filter out pain that everyday events often seemed unbearable
to her. Paradoxically, it is also that skinlessness which makes
a good poet. One must have the gift of language, of course,
but even a great gift is useless without the other curse: the
eyes that see so sharply they often want to close.[8]

While battling with mental problems, Anne Sexton was becom-
ing both a popular and successful poet: she received fan mail, she
was requested for readings. In 1968, she was awarded an honorary
Phi Beta Kappa from Harvard; in 1969, she received a Guggenheim
Fellowship. Several universities bestowed honorary doctorates on her.
In 1969, Houghton Mifflin published *Love Poems*, and in 1971,
Transformations, a book of Grimm's fairy tales reworked for modern
times. This volume outsold all other Sexton books in hardcover. *The
Book of Folly* followed in 1972 as well as a play entitled *Mercy Street*.
Anne Sexton had, in a certain sense, become a star. All the while
she fought her depression with the help of therapy and thorazine,
upon which she had become dependent.

Anne, Anne,
flee on your donkey,
flee this sad hotel. . . .

In this place everyone talks to his own mouth.
That's what it means to be crazy.
Those I loved best died of it—
the fool's disease.[9]

Sexton began to teach poetry, first at Wayland High School, and then at McLean's, a private mental hospital. She ran a poetry workshop at home for Oberlin College students. In 1970, she was appointed Lecturer in English at Boston University where she conducted a workshop once a week. In 1972, she taught at Colgate University. She was a good teacher, unorthodox and exciting, who succeeded in inspiring her students.

But when it comes to my death let it be slow,
let it be pantomime, this last peep show,
so that I may squat at the edge trying on
my black necessary trousseau.[10]

In 1973, Anne Sexton asked her husband for a divorce. Despite his strong protests, she went through with the proceedings, cutting herself off from one of her vital mainstays. Soon after, her relationship with her current psychiatrist deteriorated. She was often hospitalized that year, and, when not in the hospital, she was drinking excessively.

Denise Levertov (poet):
Anne Sexton's struggle has its political dimensions too—but hers is the story of a victim—not a conscious participant. Anne Sexton, the well-to-do suburban housewife, Anne Sexton in Bedlam, Anne Sexton "halfway back," Anne Sexton the glamorous performer, Anne Sexton timid and insecure, Anne Sexton saying she had always hoped to publish a posthumous volume, Anne Sexton in her garage breathing in deadly fumes, was—whatever the clinical description of

*Sexton's last poetry reading, Sanders Theater, Harvard University,
March 7, 1974*

her depression—"caught in history's crossfire" . . . because she herself was unable to separate her depression and her obsession with death from poetry itself, and precisely because her most enthusiastic readers and critics encouraged that inability.[11]

On March 7, 1974, Sexton gave a standing-room-only reading at Harvard University to mark the publication in February of *The Death Notebooks*. The reviews were poor but this had been expected. Another book was in the works, *The Awful Rowing Toward God*.

On October 4, 1974, Anne Sexton was found dead, sitting in an idling car inside her garage. The medical examiner ruled her death a suicide by carbon-monoxide poisoning. Shortly before her death she had carefully corrected the galley proofs for her new book. Anne Sexton, forty-five years old, had finally achieved her desire to lie down with "Mr. Death."

Say the woman is forty-four.
Say she is five-seven-and-a-half.
Say her hair is stick color.
Say her eyes are chameleon.
Would you put her in a sack and bury her,
Suck her down into the dumb dirt?
Some would,
If not, time will.[11]

Notes

1 Sexton, "Live," *Live or Die*, p. 90.
2 Sexton, "For John, Who Begs Me Not to Enquire Further," *To Bedlam and Part Way Back*, p. 51.
3 Sexton, "Those Times . . ." *Live or Die*, p. 29.
4 Sexton, "Noon Walk on the Asylum Lawn," *To Bedlam and Part Way Back*, p. 39.
5 Sexton, "The Black Art," *All My Pretty Ones*, p. 65.
6 Sexton, "Said the Poet to the Analyst," *To Bedlam and Part Way Back*, p. 17.

7 Sexton, "The Starry Night," *All My Pretty Ones*, p. 9.
8 Erica Jong, "Remembering Anne Sexton," *New York Times*, October 27, 1974, Section 7, p. 63.
9 Sexton, "Flee on Your Donkey," *Live or Die*, p. 11.
10 Sexton, "For Mr. Death Who Stands With His Door Open," *The Death Notebooks*, p. 6.
11 Denise Levertov, "Anne Sexton: Light Up the Cave," *Ramparts*, December, 1974, p. 63.
12 Sexton, "Hurry Up Please It's Time," *The Death Notebooks*, p. 66.

Sources

Sexton, Anne. *All My Pretty Ones*. Boston: Houghton Mifflin Co., 1962.
———. *The Awful Rowing Toward God*. Boston: Houghton Mifflin Co., 1975.
———. *The Book of Folly*. Boston: Houghton Mifflin Co., 1972.
———. *The Death Notebooks*. Boston: Houghton Mifflin Co., 1974.
———. *45 Mercy Street*. Edited by Linda Gray Sexton. Boston: Houghton Mifflin Co., 1976.
———. *Live or Die*. Boston: Houghton Mifflin Co., 1966.
———. *Love Poems*. Boston: Houghton Mifflin Co., 1969.
———. *To Bedlam and Part Way Back*. Boston: Houghton Mifflin Co., 1960.
———. *Transformations*. Boston: Houghton Mifflin Co., 1971.

DYLAN THOMAS
1914-1953

The force that through the green fuse drives the flower
Drives my green age; that blasts the roots of trees
Is my destroyer.[1]

DYLAN THOMAS. Welsh lyric poet. Called the last of the Romantic poets, he followed the tradition of Shelley and Keats. He was a poet in love with words, not with their meaning but with their sound. An alchemist working magical transmutations, his themes were birth, copulation, and death. Above all, his own mortality whispered in his ear. He was plagued by his mortal flesh and bones. Thomas's legacy is a collection of approximately ninety poems written between 1934 and 1952, two small volumes of collected prose and fiction, and *Under Milk Wood*, a play for voices.

Dylan Thomas called himself "the drunkest man in the world," a man in search of "naked women in wet mackintoshes." This was his public persona which he eagerly fostered, "instant Dylan," the character who could be found hoisting one down in the pubs of London and the bars of America, and always ready to go one more round.

> In the beginning was the word, the word
> That from the solid bases of the light
> Abstracted all the letters of the void;
> And from the cloudy bases of the breath
> The word flowed up, translating to the heart
> First characters of birth and death.[2]

Dylan Marlais Thomas was born on October 27, 1914, in Swansea by the sea in southwest Wales. He was the second child and only son born to Florence Williams and D. J. Thomas; his sister Nancy was eight years old. D. J. Thomas was Senior English Master at Swansea Grammar School, a somewhat disappointed man occasionally given to drink, who had ambitions to be a poet. He encouraged similar ambitions in his son. His mother, Florence, the daughter of a farmer, was cheerful, optimistic, and loving.

> To Bert Trick (friend):
> My own eye, I know, squints inwards. When and if I look at the exterior world I see nothing or me; I should like very much to say that I see *everything* through the inner eye, but all I see is darkness, naked and not very nice.[3]

Small and fragile, his head haloed by a profusion of white-blond curls, he was a cherub given to both real and imaginary illnesses to which his mother responded with doting ministrations. His childhood was "too happy." His father read him Shakespeare from a volume in his splendid library; his mother fed him dollops of sugary milk-soaked bread. In short, he was indulged. Outside he made mischief with his friends, and always got away with it because of his disarmingly innocent appearance—an appearance that he began to remold when he broke his nose at a young age, and it healed into a less pleasing shape.

> Caitlin Thomas (wife):
> He was never his proper self until there was something wrong with him; and, if ever there was a danger of him becoming "whole," which was very remote, he would crack another of his chicken bones, without delay, and wander happily around in his sling.[4]

At the age of thirteen Thomas was writing poems for the school magazine. When the muse resisted, he stole a poem and put his name on it. By sixteen, Thomas was beginning to fill notebooks with poetry. He was, however, except in English, a poor student. Thomas failed his university exams, leaving school for good in July, 1931. He got a job on the *South Wales Daily Post*, starting off as proofreader and moving up to cub reporter. The job lasted eighteen months, and before he was fired served to introduce Thomas to serious drinking and the ecstasy of pub life. Living at home, and without a job, he worked free-lance when he could, and acted in productions given by the Swansea Little Theater, sometimes with his sister Nancy. His performances showed a natural acting talent.

> He'd be about seventeen or eighteen . . . and above medium height . . . for Wales, I mean, he's five foot six and a half. Thick blubber lips; snub nose; curly mouse-brown hair; one front tooth broken after playing a game called cats and dogs in the Mermaid Mumbles; speaks rather fancy; truculent; plausible; a bit of a shower-off . . . a bombastic adolescent provincial bohemian with a thick knotted artist's tie made out of his sister's scarf . . . and a cricket shirt dyed bottle-green; a gabbing, ambitious, mock-tough, pretentious young man; and mole-y, too.[5]

This was one of the richest and most creative periods of his life as poet. In what he called his "womb with a view" at home his note-books filled up. At least half the poems he would ever publish were basically written before he left Swansea. At the urging of his friend Bert Trick, also a poet, he began submitting poems for publication. His first published poem, "And death shall have no dominion," appeared in the *New English Weekly* in May, 1933. In June, "The Romantic Isle" was one of thirty poems chosen by the BBC to be read over the radio. In September, 1933, the *Sunday Referee* published "That Sanity Be Kept." As a result, he received a letter from another young poet and writer, Pamela Hansford Johnson. They began a correspondence that bloomed into Thomas's first serious love affair.

> I am a painstaking, conscientious, involved and devious crafts-man in words. . . . I use everything and anything to make my poems work and move in the directions I want them to: old tricks, new tricks, puns, portmanteau-words, paradox, al-lusion, paranomasia, paragram, catachresis, slang, assonatonal

rhymes, vowel rhymes, sprung rhythm. . . . Poets have got to enjoy themselves sometimes.[6]

During 1933 the sanctuary of his home was disturbed when his father, diagnosed as having cancer of the mouth, was given five years to live. D. J. Thomas stopped teaching to undergo radium treatments. Thomas's poems began to tell of this horror—as did his drinking, which became a more important part of his daily life, resulting in his dismissal from a lead part in a play at the Little Theater. This marked his last involvement with stage-acting.

> My throat knew thirst before the structure
> Of skin and vein around the well
> Where words and water make a mixture
> Unfailing till the blood runs foul;
> My heart knew love, my belly hunger;
> I smelt the maggot in my stool.[7]

In April, 1934, *The Referee* chose to sponsor the publication of a collection of Thomas's poems, eventually finding a publisher in bookstore-owner David Archer. Thomas had begun to make trips to London, a city that both attracted and frightened him. He was being treated like a young poet on the rise, and his poems appeared regularly now in newspapers and magazines. Marriage to Pamela Hansford Johnson was being seriously considered. However, their relationship eventually deteriorated, Thomas choosing "Comrade Bottle" instead of her.

> To Pamela Hansford Johnson:
> It gives me now a *physical* pain to write poetry. I feel all my muscles contract as I try to drag out, from the whirlpooling words around my everlasting ideas of the importance of death on the living, some connected words that will explain how the starry system of the dead is seen, ordered as in the grave's sky, along the orbit of a foot or flower. But when the words do come, I pick them so thoroughly of the *live* associations that only the *death* in the words remains.[8]

In November, 1934, Thomas moved to London where he shared an apartment with Fred Janes, a painter, who also shared his mad and chaotic life-style. His first book, 18 *Poems*, was published in December and by spring had been very favorably reviewed by the *Spectator, New Verse*, the *Times Literary Supplement*, among others. Dylan Thomas, barely twenty, was firmly launched as poet.

> I'm a freak user of words, not a poet. That's really the truth. No self-pity there. A freak *user* of words, not a poet. That's terribly true.[9]

Thomas's life took on a pattern over the next two years of retreating home to Swansea sick and exhausted, or being spirited away by watchful friends to some safe spot in the countryside to recuperate and to write, after a period of unchecked drunkenness in London. Thomas's second book, 25 *poems*, was published on September 10, 1936, by J. M. Dent. Although some critics pointed out an element of nonsense about some of the poems, Edith Sitwell, esteemed poet, lavishly praised the book in a review for the *Sunday Times* and it sold very well.

> John Pudney (friend):
> Meeting Dylan in a pub, he could get to be rather boring. He'd offer to bite the caps off bottles of beer with his teeth. . . . Or he'd say "Let's be dogs." That used to be one of his great things—he'd go behind the counter, biting people. Then he'd say "Let's go somewhere else," and he'd want to do the same thing there. The need for an audience, that was the boring part.[10]

On July 11, 1937, Thomas married Caitlin Macnamara, one year his senior, whom he had met on the arm of painter Augustus John in a London pub. Yellow-haired, blue-eyed, Caitlin was a spectacular-looking, untamed and unconventional daughter of Protestant Irish parents. A dancer, she had been living in London and working as a chorus girl at the Palladium. They were married in a registry office, and lived with Thomas's parents or Caitlin's mother until the spring of 1938 when they moved into Sea View, a three-story house in Laugharne, Wales. Caitlin was pregnant. There was no money but life, at least for a spell, was careless and happy.

> Caitlin Thomas:
> Dylan and dying, Dylan and dying, they don't go together; or is it that they were bound to go together; he said so often enough, but I did not heed him.[11]

In 1939 a son was born to the Thomases. In September the war against Germany commenced. Thomas managed to avoid the Army, but during the war it was difficult for a poet to make a living. His third book, *Map of Love*, published the previous September, had sold only a few hundred copies. Thomas did hack writing jobs when he could get them and, in 1941, he sold his Swansea notebooks to a manuscript dealer for forty pounds. He and Caitlin shifted around penniless much of the time except when a begging letter to agent, publisher, or loyal friend achieved its purpose.

> Caitlin Thomas:
> The valuable quality of moderation was totally lacking in both of us; in one was bad enough, but in both it was fatal.[12]

A script writing job for Strand Films in London managed to see Thomas and his growing family (a baby girl arrived in 1943) through to the end of the war. The job kept him away from poetry. It also kept him in the city and, for a period of time, away from Caitlin. He drank heavily in the pubs, gradually acquiring his " 'London look'— bloodshot and yellowed eyes, blotched complexion, inextricably tangled locks, an air of having slept in his bulky clothes for nights on end." [13]

In August, 1944, the family moved to a cottage in New Quay on the Cardigan Bay in Wales where Thomas enjoyed a year of poetic creativity, writing many of the poems that appeared in *Deaths and Entrances*, published in February, 1946. This volume established Thomas as a major poet—and it contained what were to be his last poems. By then, the family was housed in Oxford as the result of the patronage of Mrs. Margaret Taylor, a woman with some money to spend, who provided them with housing for the rest of Thomas's life.

> To Vernon Watkins:
> I have found increasingly, as time goes on, or around, or backwards, or stays quite still as the brain races, the heart absorbs and expels, and the arteries harden, that the problems of physical life, of social contact, of daily posture and armour, of the choice between dissipations, of the abhorred needs enforced by a reluctance to "miss anything," that old fear of death, are as insoluble to me as those of the spirit.[14]

Over the next few years Thomas worked for the BBC as a performer and continued to do free-lance script writing, earning enough money for the tax authorities to hound him. Despite this, he was far from secure financially. In 1949, the family moved to the Boat House in Laugharne, Wales, purchased for them by Mrs. Taylor. Complete with a shed where Thomas could write, it seemed to be the ideal home for them. But Thomas couldn't write. Poor health and accidents plagued him. Rather than a "womb with a view," the Boat House became a kind of jail for Thomas.

> Caitlin Thomas:
> The home was to Dylan . . . a private sanctum, where for once he was not compelled, by himself admittedly, to put on an act, to be amusing, to perpetuate the myth of the Enfant Terrible: one of the most damaging myths, and a curse to grow out of.[15]

An invitation to America came from John Malcolm Brinnin, poet and newly appointed Director of the Poetry Center at the Y. M. H. A. in New York City. Thomas would be paid $500 for reading there and if Thomas wished, Brinnin would act as his agent for other readings. Thomas accepted and flew to New York on February 20, 1950. He spent three and a half months in America, giving splendid readings at colleges and universities across the country. Offstage he amused and shocked his audiences and hosts with his drunken, clowning, fool-playing behavior. He earned $7,600 that trip, but when he arrived back in Laugharne, sick and worn out, the only money remaining was $800 secreted by Brinnin in a gift for Caitlin. The money on which he had planned to support Caitlin and his children for the next year had melted away.

> Caitlin Thomas:
> Jesus, he even kept saying he would die before me: would never reach forty: and I would be a flighty widow dancing on his grave. And I laughed, completely unmoved; for all the impression it made on me, he might as well have been talking to an elephant.[16]

In 1951, Thomas wrote his last complete poem, "Poem on His Birthday." In the shed at the Boat House he worked on a play for voices which he called *Llareggub* ("Bugger all" spelled backward). Thomas ventured a second trip to America, this time with Caitlin, from January 20, 1952, to May 16, 1952. It was more exhausting and less profitable than the first, although his reputation was growing and his readings were well attended. No matter how much he drank, Thomas was always able to pull himself together once he began to read.

> John Malcolm Brinnin:
> I knew as well as he that his unhappiness lay in the conviction that his creative powers were failing, that his great work was finished. He had moved from "darkness into some measure of light," a progress attended by the acclaim of the literate part of the English-speaking world; but now that he had arrived, he was without the creative resources to maintain and expand his position. As a consequence he saw his success as fraudulent and himself as an impostor.[17]

Collected Poems 1934–1952 was published by J. M. Dent on November 10, 1952. The volume contained all the poems that Thomas wished to preserve. The book was hailed as a major literary event; Thomas was proclaimed the greatest living poet.

On December 16, 1952, his father, blind and in pain, died. Four months later, with the unfinished script for *Llareggub*, now called *Under Milk Wood*, under his arm, Thomas escaped once again to America for six weeks. A successful reading performance of a tentative version of the play was given at the Poetry Center in New York in May.

Thomas returned to Laugharne in June with a broken arm and suffering from increasingly frequent attacks of gout. He was hopeful, however: Stravinsky had met with him while he was in New York to discuss plans for a new opera for which he wanted Thomas to write the libretto. The project excited Thomas. Its execution, however, rested on getting it commissioned. Back at the Boat House, he became unhappy once again.

> Charles Fisher (friend):
> Ah. Here is the green man at the height of his acclaim. He sits in a corner propped up by two walls, a smouldering soggy firework sending up stars of singular lucidity. His admirers surround him. What will he do next? they wonder. Will he burst or explode! [18]

Dylan Thomas made his final journey to America in October, 1953, arriving in New York for the first performance of *Under Milk Wood*, the opening event at the Poetry Center. In an obvious state of physical and mental deterioration, he was watched over by Liz Reitell, Brinnin's assistant. While he managed, despite his condition, to participate in the performance of *Under Milk Wood* on Sunday, October 25, it was to be his last. After several more days of drinking and parties, at which his behavior was often irrational, Thomas became physically ill, vomiting uncontrollably. Liz Reitell called in a doctor who, on his third visit, administered a dose of morphine sulphate. Several hours later Dylan Thomas lapsed into a coma from which he would not awaken. He died in Greenwich Village's St. Vincent's Hospital on November 9, 1953. He was thirty-nine years old.

> Dressed to die, the sensual strut begun,
> With my red veins full of money,
> In the final direction of the elementary town
> I advance for as long as forever is. [19]

Thomas in studio, Laugharne, Wales, 1953

Notes

1 Thomas, "The Force That Through the Green Fuse Drives the Flower," *Collected Poems (1934–1952)*, p. 10.
2 Thomas, "In the Beginning," *Collected Poems*, p. 27.
3 Fitzgibbon, *The Life of Dylan Thomas*, p. 170.
4 Caitlin Thomas, *Leftover Life to Kill*, p. 32.
5 Thomas, *Quite Early One Morning*, p. 45.
6 Sinclair, *Dylan Thomas: No Man More Magical*, pp. 231–32.
7 Thomas, "Before I Knocked," *Collected Poems*, p. 9.
8 Fitzgibbon, op. cit., p. 119.
9 Ibid., pp. 119–20.
10 Ferris, *Dylan Thomas*, p. 140.
11 Caitlin Thomas, op. cit., p. 6.
12 Ibid., p. 64.
13 Brinnin, *Dylan Thomas in America*, p. 179.
14 Ferris, op. cit., p. 195.
15 Caitlin Thomas, op. cit., p. 33.
16 Ibid.
17 Brinnin, op. cit., p. 175.
18 Fitzgibbon, op. cit., p. 279.
19 Thomas, "Twenty Four Years," *Collected Poems*, p. 110.

Sources

Brinnin, John Malcolm. *Dylan Thomas in America*. Boston: Atlantic-Little, Brown, 1955.
Ferris, Paul. *Dylan Thomas*. New York: The Dial Press, 1977.
Fitzgibbon, Constantine. *The Life of Dylan Thomas*. Boston: Atlantic-Little, Brown, 1965.
Sinclair, Andrew. *Dylan Thomas: No Man More Magical*. New York: Holt Rinehart & Winston, 1975.
Thomas, Caitlin. *Leftover Life to Kill*. Boston: Little, Brown & Co., 1957.
Thomas, Dylan. *Collected Poems (1934–1952)*. New York: New Directions, 1971.
———. *Quite Early One Morning*. New York: New Directions, 1960.

VINCENT VAN GOGH
1853-1890

How short life is, and how like smoke! [1]

VINCENT VAN GOGH. Dutch painter. Recognized as one of the seminal figures in the history of modern art, and today one of the most popular. He made the leap from the rigid classicism of the nineteenth century into the unexplored universe of modern art. His influence was profound: the Fauves, the Nabis, Postimpressionism, German Expressionism, all show the effects of his groundbreaking work. Yet during his lifetime he was unrecognized, virtually unknown, and among those few familiar with his work, the subject of ridicule.

Van Gogh's life has become an archetype of the "mad genius." For little more than a decade, from 1880 to 1890, Van Gogh drew and painted as if possessed, fanatic in his absolute devotion to his work, sacrificing all human comfort, often in isolated and lonely circumstances. The single sustaining comfort was his younger brother Theo, who literally supported and encouraged him, listened and responded to him. Theo was Van Gogh's other half, his complement, able to function in the world where Vincent could not.

> To Theo:
> I have a sure *faith* in art, a sure confidence that it is a powerful stream, which bears man to harbor, though he himself must do his bit too; and at all events I think it such a great

blessing, when a man has found his work, that I can't count myself among the unfortunate.[2]

Vincent Van Gogh was born on March 30, 1853, in the village of Groot-Zundert in the province of Brabant, the Netherlands. He was the first of six children born to Anna Carbentus and Theodorus Van Gogh, a Protestant minister whose brother was a partner in the prosperous Goupil and Company art galleries.

At the age of sixteen, Van Gogh, red-haired and broad-shouldered, was sent to work at the branch of Goupil and Company in The Hague, where he was the youngest employee. He was popular and performed his job well; it was a good start on the road to becoming an art dealer.

> To Theo:
> Now one of the reasons why I am out of employment now, why I have been out of employment for years, is simply that I have other ideas than the gentlemen who give the places to men who think like they do.[3]

Four years later Van Gogh was transferred to the London branch of the gallery. There he fell in love with Ursula Loyer, the young daughter of the widow with whom he boarded. When his love was unrequited, Van Gogh's personality underwent a radical transformation: he became withdrawn and disagreeable and obsessed with religion. His conversation was filled with references to God and quotes from the Scriptures. He lost all interest in art dealing and was finally dismissed from his job in 1876.

At home he was gloomy and silent, alienating even his siblings. His new ambition was to become an evangelist and devote his life to preaching the word of God. Although his father disapproved of this, he finally consented to let his son go to Amsterdam to study for the ministry. The course proved to be too rigorous for twenty-four-year-old Van Gogh, who dropped out after a year. In 1878, he entered the School of Evangelization in Brussels.

> To Theo:
> I am rather faithful in my unfaithfulness, and though changed, I am the same, and my only anxiety is: how can I

be of use in the world, cannot I serve some purpose and be of any good . . .[4]

As a result of his inability to conform to certain rules of behavior, Van Gogh failed to qualify for an appointment as an evangelist. The committee, however, agreed to allow him to go to the Borinage (a mining district in southern Belgium) at his own expense to preach the Gospel for a trial period.

His zeal knew no bounds. In his desire to immerse himself in the life of the miners, he gave up his lodging, his clothes, his money, and his meals. He lived in a hut in rags and filth and thus became indistinguishable from the miners. His behavior outraged the inspectors from the School of Evangelization and Van Gogh was dismissed. After a brief and awkward stay at home, he returned to the Borinage to drift without purpose.

To Theo:

One cannot always tell what it is that keeps us shut in, confines us, seems to bury us, but still one feels certain barriers, certain gates, certain walls. Is all this imagination, fantasy? I do not think so. And then one asks "My God! is it for long, is it for ever, is it for eternity?" Do you know what frees one from this captivity? It is very deep serious affection. Being friends, being brothers, love, that is what opens the prison by supreme power, by some magic force. But without this one remains in prison.[5]

Although in earlier letters to Theo he had mentioned sketching, Van Gogh had not pursued it seriously because he feared it would keep him from his "real work," preaching. Now, in the Borinage, Van Gogh took up his pencil and began to draw with a new consciousness of purpose. Living in a tiny room in a miner's house, he sketched the men going to and from the mines and during the day he copied the works of the French painter Millet. At twenty-seven, Van Gogh had begun his life's work. With financial contributions from Theo to sustain him, he began the methodical and painstaking learning of his craft.

To Theo:

I am in a rage of work. Do not fear me. If I can only continue, that will somehow or other set me right again. For the moment it does not give very brilliant results. But I hope these thorns will bear their white blossoms in due time, and that this apparently sterile struggle is no other than the labor of childbirth. First the pain, then the joy.[6]

Van Gogh spent the winter of 1881 in Brussels where he met other young artists, especially Rappard, a Dutch painter with whom he shared a studio and a rare close friendship. In April, to ease his financial burden, he went home to his parents, now living in Etten. That summer he suffered his second rejection in love when he pursued, without success, his cousin Kee Vos, a young widow.

To Theo:

Life has become very dear to me, and I am glad that I love. My life and my love are one. For the present I consider that "No, never, never" as a block of ice that I press to my heart to thaw it. Which will win, the coldness of that block of ice or the warmth of my heart?[7]

Van Gogh, brokenhearted, fled to The Hague where he rented a small studio close by Anton Mauve, a painter who encouraged and supported his work. He took in Sien, a sickly and pregnant prostitute whom he supported for over a year, depleting his meager finances and also bringing about his ostracism from the artistic community.

To Theo:

If for a moment I feel rising within me the desire for a life without care, for *prosperity*, each time I go fondly back to the trouble and the cares, to a *life full of hardship*, and think: it is better so, I learn more from it, it does not degrade me, this is not the road on which one perishes.[8]

He stubbornly persevered with his work and continued his relationship with Sien. Often unable to buy food for himself, he fasted for days at a time while spending his money on art supplies and on Sien. His health gradually deteriorated; he was plagued by insomnia, fever, weakness, and eventually hospitalized for several weeks of rest.

> To Theo:
> I promised myself to consider my illness, or rather the remains of it, as nonexistent. Art is jealous; she does not want us to choose illness in preference to her, so I do what she wishes. Enough time has been lost; my hands have become too white. People such as I are not allowed to be ill.[9]

Van Gogh sold twelve small drawings of The Hague that year to his uncle, C. M. Van Gogh, for 2.50 guilders apiece, the only profit he would ever reap from his work. Among the many other drawings he made, a pencil and ink drawing of Sien which he entitled *Sorrow* was one of his most successful. Explaining it to Theo, Van Gogh said: "I want to make drawings that *touch* some people." He considered himself a nobody, an eccentric and disagreeable man. Yet his art was propelled by an irresistible need to convey a "calm pure harmony and music." He saw drawings and pictures in "the poorest huts, in the dirtiest corners."

In 1882 Van Gogh began to paint. He discovered his instinct for color and was more convinced than ever that painting was in his bone and marrow.

> To Theo:
> How I paint it *I do not know myself*. I sit down with a white board before the spot that strikes me, I look at what it is before me, I say to myself that white board must become something; I come back dissatisfied—I put it away, and when I have rested a little, I go to look at it with a kind of fear. . . . But after all I find in my work an echo of what struck me. I see that nature has told me something, has spoken to me, and that I have put it down in shorthand.[10]

In September, 1883, Theo visited Van Gogh and convinced him

to give up Sien, who had given birth to a child. Van Gogh departed for Drenthe, an area of hamlets and heaths in northern Holland. The weather was turning cold and he was broke, ill, and alone.

> To Theo:
> I say loneliness, and not solitude; I mean the loneliness a painter has to bear who in some unfrequented region is regarded by everyone as a lunatic, a murderer, a tramp. This may be a slight misery, but it is a sorrow nonetheless—a feeling of being outcast, particularly strange and unpleasant, though the country be ever so stimulating and beautiful.[11]

In December, 1883, Van Gogh returned home once again, to his father's new vicarage in Nuenen in Brabant. There he was surrounded by subjects that fascinated him: the countryside, peasants, and weavers. He rented a nearby studio and remained for two years, painting. Once again, his involvement with a woman, a neighbor, resulted in an unpleasant incident when the woman attempted suicide.

In the spring of 1885, shortly after his father's death, Van Gogh completed *The Potato Eaters*, his first major work in oil. He had been having trouble in the community after one of his young models became pregnant and the local priest forbade the peasants to pose for him. Without models, Van Gogh could not work so he had to depart.

Van Gogh arrived in Antwerp in November. City life, especially the colorful types who haunted the back alleys and poorer sections of town, excited him. He spent his money paying for models and art supplies and neglected to eat. By spring he had reached a state of mental and physical exhaustion.

He went to Paris where he and Theo shared an apartment, complete with studio for Van Gogh, for the next two years. The art scene in Paris was stimulating. He met Paul Gauguin and John Russell; he painted the portrait of Tanguy, an art dealer who exhibited some of Van Gogh's work in his shop; he collected Japanese prints, something he had begun in Antwerp. More than the Parisian Impressionists and Neo-Impressionists, it was the Japanese who had an important and decided influence on his work.

Predictably, Van Gogh and his brother had a difficult time living together. Theo suffered as a result of his brother's disagreeable moods, especially during the winter when the painter was confined to working indoors. As soon as the weather began to warm up, Van Gogh departed for Arles in Provence.

The sun and mild weather restored his health and the beauty of the countryside excited him to work, even when the mistral blew and he had to hold his canvas down.

> To Theo:
>
> If I am alone—I can't help it; but I have less need of company than of headlong work, and that is why I go on boldly ordering canvas and paints. It's the only time I feel I am alive . . . alone, I count only on the exaltation that comes to me at certain moments.[12]

During this period he painted some of his most familiar works: *Night Café, The Postman Roulin, Sunflowers, The Artist's Bedroom.* His peasant paintings had been executed in dark earth tones; his new canvases were bright with color and rich new textures.

In September, 1888, he moved into the Yellow House at 2 Place Lamartine and prepared for the arrival of Paul Gauguin, whom he had persuaded to come live and work with him, and share living costs. At last, Van Gogh would have his longed-for comradeship with another painter. Gauguin arrived in October. The two painters, however, were not compatible and quarreled frequently and violently.

On December 23, shortly after hearing from Theo that he was planning to marry, Van Gogh experienced his first epileptic seizure. He slashed off part of his ear and tried to give it to a girl in a brothel. He was hospitalized; Gauguin returned to Paris.

> To Theo:
>
> The more I am spent, ill, the cracked pot, by so much more am I the artist—the creative artist.[13]

He spent two weeks in the hospital recovering from his wound and the aftereffects of the epileptic seizure. He was depressed and dazed. In February, 1889, he suffered two more attacks. After his neighbors signed a petition, Van Gogh was confined to the hospital in Arles.

To Theo:

Faced with the suffering of these attacks, I feel very frightened too—like someone who meant to commit suicide but, finding the water too cold, struggles to regain the bank.[14]

In May, 1889, Van Gogh was transferred from Arles to an asylum in St. Rémy where he remained for a year. He continued to paint although he suffered several more seizures that left him incapacitated for weeks at a time. One of his most moving paintings, *Starry Night*, was done at St. Rémy.

Van Gogh, The Starry Night, *1889. Oil on canvas, 29" x 36¼"*

To Theo:

To look at the stars always makes me dream as simply as I dream over the black dots of a map representing towns and villages. Why, I ask myself, should the shining dots of the sky not be as accessible as the black dots on the map of France? If we take a train to get to Tarascon or Rouen we take death to reach a star.[15]

Theo arranged for Van Gogh to move to Auvers in May, 1890, where he would be looked after by Dr. Gachet, a semiretired physician. During the last two months of his life, Van Gogh painted a remarkab!e quantity of works, *Crows in a Wheatfield* among them. Early in July, he visited Theo and his wife and new baby in Paris. The visit made clear to him the financial and emotional strain his brother was under with his new family responsibilities and he realized what a burden he had become. When Van Gogh returned to Auvers he felt threatened and "done for."

On July 27, a letter to Theo in his pocket, Vincent Van Gogh, thirty-seven years old, shot and mortally wounded himself. He died two days later, his brother—who would soon follow him—at his side.

Antonin Artaud:

Van Gogh did not die of a state of delirium properly speaking,

but of having been bodily the battlefield of a problem around which the evil spirit of humanity has been struggling from the beginning.

The problem of the predominance of flesh over spirit, or of body over flesh, or of spirit over both.

And where in this delirium is the place of the human self?

Van Gogh searched for his throughout his life, with a strange energy and determination,

And he did not commit suicide in a fit of madness, in dread of not succeeding,

on the contrary, he had just succeeded, and discovered what he was and who he was, when the collective consciousness of society, to punish him for escaping its clutches, suicided him.[16]

Notes

1 Stone, *Dear Theo: The Autobiography of Vincent Van Gogh*, p. 367.
2 Roskill, *The Letters of Vincent Van Gogh*, p. 188.
3 Ibid., pp. 120–21.
4 Ibid., p. 122.
5 Ibid. p. 126
6 Stone, op. cit., p. 49.
7 Ibid., p. 63.
8 Roskill, op. cit., p. 152.
9 Stone, op. cit., p. 139.
10 Roskill, op. cit., p. 167.
11 Stone, op. cit., p. 260.
12 Ibid., p. 359.
13 Ibid., p. 366.
14 Ibid., p. 447.
15 Ibid., p. 360.
16 Antonin Artaud, "Van Gogh, The Man Suicided by Society," *Selected Writings*, New York: Farrar Straus and Giroux, 1976, p. 487.

Sources

Roskill, Mark, ed. *The Letters of Vincent Van Gogh*. New York: Atheneum, 1977.
Stone, Irving. *Dear Theo: The Autobiography of Vincent Van Gogh*. New York: New American Library, 1969.
———. *Lust for Life*. New York: Pocket Books, 1946.

SIMONE WEIL
1907-1943

I never allowed myself to think of a future state,
but I always believed that the instant of death is
the center and object of life. I used to think
that, for those who live as they should, it is the
instant when, for an infinitesimal fraction of
time, pure truth, naked, certain, and eternal,
enters the soul.[1]

SIMONE WEIL. French social philosopher of the left wing, and mystic. Her writings, posthumously collected and published, are informal confessions, recordings of her experiences and ideas as she encountered them in her life: *Waiting for God*, an anthology of letters and essays; *Gravity and Grace*, a collection of writings from her notebooks; *The Need for Roots*, written during her employment at Free French headquarters, London, during the last year of her life.

Simone Weil has been called many things: T. S. Eliot proclaimed her a genius of the kind "akin to that of the saints"; Leslie Fiedler defined her as "Outsider as Saint in an age of alienation." Others not so kind have called her a fool, irresponsible, absurd, a fanatic in search of a mania. She came into the world with an unquenchable thirst for martyrdom—that much is certain. And she pursued her own death with an almost irritating persistence—like that of a pestering child. "Her life," said Fiedler, "is her chief work."

> We participate in the creation of the world by decreating ourselves.[2]

Simone Weil was born in Paris on February 3, 1909, four years after her brother André. Her parents were Jews, cultured, well off, and agnostic. Her father, Bernard Weil, was a doctor; her mother, Salomea, was from a musical family. She was a brilliant and sickly child, who was pampered and indulged by her parents. Her appetite was poor and she came to despise food and consider the act of eating a difficult, repulsive function. She was precocious and eccentric: at the age of five, she refused to eat sugar because it was not available to the French soldiers at the front. Later, noticing that poor children went barefooted, she refused to wear socks. Throughout her life she would deliberately deny herself the middle-class comforts and luxuries her family could afford.

During her teenage years, Weil suffered in the shadow of her brilliant older brother André, who was destined to become a world-renowned mathematician. He set a difficult example for her to follow. She felt she could not compete with him intellectually; nor could she fall back on beauty. Thick glasses hid her eyes. Her head was crowned with a crop of short frizzy hair. She was skinny, awkward, and clumsy —and she knew it. Instead of concealing her shortcomings, she emphasized them in her dress and manner.

> At fourteen I fell into one of those fits of bottomless despair that come with adolescence, and I seriously thought of dying because of the mediocrity of my natural faculties. . . . I did not mind having no visible successes, but what did grieve me was the idea of being excluded from that transcendent kingdom to which only the great have access and wherein truth abides.[3]

Weil earned the nickname "The Red Virgin" during her four years of study at L'Ecole Normale Supérieur because of her Marxist politics. She had begun to formulate her ideas for a revolution of the workers, along with an ambition to work in a factory. The migraine headaches that would torment her for the rest of her life, and often completely incapacitate her, began during this period.

Weil earned her philosophy degree in 1931 at the age of twenty-two, and was qualified to teach. Her first appointment was at a lycée for girls in Le Puy.

Simone Pétrement (biographer and friend):

Mme Weil secretly protected Simone and sometimes would deceive her a bit in order to protect her. When she came to Le Puy, she would often bring a skirt, stockings, or some other clothes and slip them on the sly among Simone's things. . . . When they first moved in, Mme Weil had brought a large supply of coal. . . . Believing that the unemployed could not afford coal for heating, she had decided not to heat her room. She slept with the window open and worked without a fire, swathed in shawls.[4]

At Le Puy she participated in demonstrations of unemployed workers and often appeared at the head of a protest group, presenting worker demands. The head of the lycée threatened to dismiss her for her activities and she challenged him to do so. Although he backed down, her relationship with the school board was strained. In her next two jobs she was usually at odds with the staff because of her outspoken politics.

I have the essential need, and I think I can say the vocation, to move among men of every class and complexion, mixing with them and sharing their life and outlook . . . merging into the crowd and disappearing among them, so that they show themselves as they are, putting off all disguises with me. It is because I long to know them so as to love them just as they are.[5]

In June, 1934, Weil requested a leave of absence from her teaching job in order to fulfill her ambition to work in a factory. After some difficulty, she was hired as a power-press operator. She was determined to live just as the other workers did on the wages earned at the factory. Weil rented a small room nearby and reported for work. The job was physically torturous and exhausted her completely. She ate very little and was plagued by headaches and fatigue. Weil confided to her friend, Simone Pétrement, that if she could not endure her job at the factory she was determined to kill herself.

Man placed himself outside the current of Obedience. God

chose as his punishments labor and death. Consequently, labor and death, if Man undergoes them in a spirit of willingness, constitute a transference back into the current of Supreme Good, which is obedience to God.[6]

Weil was reprieved from her first factory job as the result of an injury. She was fired from her second job after only a month, but found another job in a Renault plant where she was put to work on a milling machine. Weil suffered at this job for three months before being forced to quit, debilitated by blinding headaches and physical exhaustion. Her parents came to her aid, as they would time and time again, and took her to Portugal to recuperate.

> As I worked in the factory, indistinguishable to all eyes, including my own, from the anonymous mass, the affliction of others entered into my flesh and my soul. Nothing separated me from it, for I had really forgotten my past and I looked forward to no future, finding it difficult to imagine the possibility of surviving all the fatigue. . . . There I received forever the mark of a slave, like the branding of the red-hot iron the Romans put on the foreheads of their most despised slaves. Since then I have always regarded myself as a slave.[7]

Her difficult and defeating experience as a factory worker severely dampened Weil's hopes for bringing about a revolution of workers— in fact, she seemed to be profoundly and permanently discouraged from the dreams she hoped to realize through her political activities.

> It is great sorrow for me to fear that the thoughts that have descended into me should be condemned to death through the contagion of my inadequacy and wretchedness. I never read the story of the barren fig tree without trembling. I think that it is a portrait of me. In it also, nature was powerless, and yet it was not excused. Christ cursed it.[8]

In 1936, the Spanish Civil War beckoned. She managed to find her way to the front as a journalist, and joined up with an international commando group stationed on the Ebro River. Her clumsiness prevented her from participating in, or even witnessing, the battle, for she stepped into a pot of hot oil and was severely burned. A few days later, her parents, who had been following their daughter a few days behind, persuaded Weil to return with them to France, where she soon resumed teaching.

> Leslie Fiedler:
> She was always willing to take the step beyond the trivially silly; and the ridiculous pushed far enough, absurdity compounded, becomes something else—the Absurd as a religious category, the madness of the Holy Fool beside which the wisdom of this world is revealed as folly.[9]

By 1938, the severity of Weil's headaches had increased to the point where she was forced to ask for sick leave from her teaching post. Consultations with doctors and a variety of treatments all failed; the cause of her headaches remained a mystery. That spring she journeyed with her mother to the French village of Solesmes to hear the famous Gregorian chants at the Benedictine Abbey de Sainte-Pierre. This was the beginning of her mystical religious conversion.

> I was suffering from splitting headaches; each sound hurt me like a blow; by an extreme effort of concentration I was able to rise above this wretched flesh, to leave it to suffer by itself, heaped up in a corner, and to find a pure and perfect joy in the unimaginable beauty of the chanting and the words. . . . In the course of these services the thought of the Passion of Christ entered into my being once and for all.[10]

The onset of the Second World War found Simone Weil passionately desirous of becoming physically involved in a dangerous mission. She conceived a plan for organizing a group of nurses to be sent to the front lines to care for the wounded soldiers. The essence of the plan was that she would be one of the nurses. Although Weil presented the idea to several people who labeled it "mad," she persisted in her attempts to implement it over the next several years.

Weil with her students

In June, 1940, Paris was declared an open city; the arrival of the Germans became imminent. Although she did not want to run away, the Weils finally persuaded her to go with them to Marseilles where it would then be possible to leave the country if necessary. While living there, Weil inquired about finding work as a farm laborer. She was introduced to Father Perrin, a Dominican priest, with whom she began to have intense discussions about her spiritual state, baptism, and her reluctance to join the Catholic Church.

> I do not want to be adopted into a circle, to live among people who say "we" and to be part of an "us," to find I am "at home" in any human *milieu* whatever it may be. In saying I do not want this, I am expressing myself badly, for I should like it very much; I should find it all delightful. But I feel it is not permissible for me. I feel that it is necessary and ordained that I should be alone, a stranger and an exile in relation to every human circle without exception.[11]

Perrin was sympathetic to Weil's need for physical labor and persuaded Gustave Thibon, a Catholic writer, to put her to work on his farm. While at Thibon's she insisted upon living in a bare shack, and she ate very little. Thibon allowed her to perform simple labors, and during the harvest, she worked picking grapes in Saint-Julien. For the first time in her life, she prayed and took Communion although she would never allow herself to undergo baptism.

In the summer of 1942, she was persuaded by her parents to sail with them for the United States.

> To Father Perrin:
> You know that for me there is no question in this departure of an escape from suffering and danger. My anguish comes precisely from the fear that in spite of myself, and unwittingly, by going I shall be doing what I want above everything else not to do—that is to say running away.[12]

Upon their arrival in New York City, the Weils rented an apartment on Riverside Drive and installed their daughter in one of the rooms overlooking the Hudson River. When not visiting churches in

Harlem, Weil tried to find a way to go to England where she might be able to realize her plan for the front-line nurses.

> To Maurice Schumann (former classmate; member of the Free French in London):
> The suffering all over the world obsesses me and overwhelms me to the point of annihilating my faculties, and the only way I can revive them and release myself from the obsession is by getting for myself a larger share of danger and hardship. . . . I beseech for you to get for me, if you can, the amount of hardship and danger that can save me from being wasted by sterile grief. That is a necessary condition before I can exert my capacity for work. . . . It is not, I am certain, a question of character only, but of vocation.[13]

Weil finally succeeded in getting authorization to go to England, and sailed from New York in November, 1942, leaving her parents behind and unable to follow her this time. To her utter dismay, when she arrived in London she was not sent to the front but given an office job as writer of policy papers for the Free French fighting services. During her months in this post she wrote *The Need for Roots*.

> Death and labor are things of necessity and not of choice. The world only gives itself to Man in the form of food and warmth if Man gives himself to the world in the form of labor. But death and labor can be submitted to either in an attitude of revolt or in one of consent. They can be submitted to in their naked truth or else wrapped around with lies.[14]

She rented a small room in a boarding house in Notting Hill where she lived like a pauper and ate very little, refusing any foods that she felt were not also available to the French people. Her failure to get sent on a dangerous mission deeply frustrated and disappointed her.

On April 15, 1943, Weil was discovered unconscious in her room and taken to Middlesex Hospital where she was discovered to have tuberculosis. Her chances of recovery were judged good. Weil, however, was an uncooperative patient, eating very little or not at all, and eventually refusing medical treatment.

> T. S. Eliot:
> Simone Weil was one who might have become a saint. Like some who have achieved this state, she had greater obstacles to overcome, as well as greater strength for overcoming them than the rest of us. A potential saint can be a very difficult person: I suspect that Simone Weil could be at times unsupportable. One is struck, here and there, by a contrast between an almost superhuman humility and what appears to be an almost outrageous arrogance.[15]

In August, she was transferred to a sanitorium in Ashford in Kent, where, wasted and running a high fever, she lapsed into a coma. Simone Weil died on August 24 at the age of thirty-five. The coroner ruled her death a suicide.

> Consent to suffer death, when death is there and seen in all its nakedness, constitutes a final, sudden wrenching away from what each one calls "I."[16]

Notes

1 Weil, *Waiting for God*, p. 63.
2 Weil, *Gravity and Grace*, p. 29.
3 Ibid., p. 64.
4 Pétrement, *Simone Weil: A Life*, p. 81.
5 Weil, *Gravity and Grace*, p. 48.
6 Weil, *The Need for Roots*, p. 300.
7 Weil, *Waiting for God*, p. 66.
8 Ibid., p. 100.
9 Ibid., p. 19.
10 Ibid., p. 68.
11 Ibid., p. 54.
12 Ibid., p. 60.
13 Pétrement, op. cit., p. 482.
14 Weil, *The Need for Roots*, p. 301.

15 Ibid., p. vi.
16 Ibid., p. 301.

Sources

Pétrement, Simone. *Simone Weil: A Life.* Translated by Raymond Rosen-
    thal. New York: Pantheon Books, 1976.
Weil, Simone. *Gravity and Grace.* Translated by Emma Craufurd. Lon-
    don: Routledge and Paul, 1963.
————. *The Need for Roots.* Translated by Arthur Wills. New York:
    Harper & Row, 1971.
————. *Waiting for God.* Translated by Emma Craufurd. New York:
    Harper & Row, 1973.

EPILOGUE

THOMAS "TYLER" BOOTMAN
1940-1977

Meaning dances
in the Night
when the tired raise their heads
& look through the long Broken Promise
made dark by a Lamp gone out.[1]

THOMAS "TYLER" BOOTMAN was born on November 8, 1940, in Cumberland, Maryland. His father, Roy Bootman, from a working-class background, was a brilliant engineer. His mother, Mary, was a Southern beauty from a wealthy Baltimore family. The second of three children, Tom was their only son. Delivered by cesarean section, he would later give significance to the fact that he had not experienced the struggle of a normal birth; somehow this made him less well-prepared for life.

While he always got along with his mother, a warm, sympathetic woman who adored him, Tom's relationship with his father was uneasy; they were often at odds. One of his fantasies was that he had a different, unknown father.

> from a bastard son
> I bought a pound
> of fruit, and in its tasting
> were the foul seeds
> of upbringing: meat
> of the orange
> was sour, bananas
> all skin, and

the price of the whole shebang
is hardly worth
the cost of living.[2]

When Tom was nine or ten, his father was hired by Westinghouse and the family moved to Steubenville, Ohio, a mining town on the Ohio River. There, in a large, gray-shingled house, away from the smoke and soot of the mines, he grew up like many midwestern boys in the 1950s. He attended Steubenville High School where sports reigned supreme. Although he aspired to be a "jock" he was too tall and thin to play football. Instead, he became a member of the swimming team and ran track. He was co-sports editor of the school paper and wrote a column called "Athlete's Feat." A popular student, he had inherited his mother's good looks and was conscious of the effect of his appearance, especially on the opposite sex. He and the star quarterback had an ongoing rivalry for the prettiest girl in school.

> William Siegel (classmate):
> Tom was cool. He wanted to be cool. That was even better than being an athlete. Cool was being unperturbed. Nothing fazed you and you didn't have to work hard to get what you wanted. Tom was tall, wiry, and good-looking. He had the moves and the knack to create an image, a bit of a helpless image. He was the swimmer and he was the swain, the one who loves. He relished being different, being the loner, always on the outside looking in.[3]

Tom entered the University of Virginia in Charlottesville in 1959 and joined St. Anthony's fraternity, whose members were the epitome of Southern gentlemen: they owned polo ponies and expensive sports cars, wore ascots, and bought their girl friends diamonds in downtown Charlottesville. He distinguished himself as the black sheep of the fraternity, the perennial outsider. He wore blue jeans and his hair was long. He was either sneered at for being different, or idolized for being cool. Soon, he was living off campus on the top floor of one of the oldest houses in town with two roommates and a rabbit that drank beer.

Literature, art, music, and philosophy were Tom's subjects. He was a good student. His main interests: poetry and beautiful women. His friends were a small group of bohemian types whose passions were folk music, beer, and drugs where they could be had. His apartment was infamous enough to attract Bob Dylan for an afternoon of beer-drinking and music-making.

In June, 1962, Tom went to Europe for the summer with André Harvey, a college friend. He wrote his first poem. He also changed his name. He began to introduce himself to people as "Tyler" Bootman. The name Tom was too common for a poet.

> André Harvey:
> We were on the road, hitchhiking, living on nothing, sleeping under bridges and in cafés. We went to Pamplona for the running of the bulls because of Hemingway, and we searched for the places in Paris where Modigliani hung out. Everything was new and very exciting. We were on an adventure and we were having fun. Our motto was "live fast, love fast, die young, and have a beautiful corpse." (I think Hemingway said that.) Tom kept a notebook that summer. He was gathering experience and probably deciding what path he was going to take. He was becoming a poet.[4]

I entered his life upon his return from Europe. He met me in October, 1962, during the first few weeks of his senior year at the University of Virginia. I was a freshman at Hollins College in Roanoke, Virginia. He had seen my picture in a college publication, "Freshman Faces." He called the school and left a message for me: "I have something important to tell you. Please meet me at 7 P.M. Tom Bootman." The cryptic message was a successful ploy because I was waiting for him that evening, filled with curiosity, uncertainty, and a trace of annoyance. I was totally unprepared to be greeted by an extraordinarily handsome young man: tall and lean with thick curly brown hair, large blue eyes, and an intense, unsettling expression. He brimmed over with nervous energy. I remember him bowing slightly as he introduced himself. We spent four hours together in a local tavern drinking watery beer and talking about ourselves. He swept me away that night. When I returned to my room I told my roommate that I had fallen in love.

I began to take the train to Charlottesville to see him on weekends. At his apartment we listened to Beethoven and *Mahagonny* and *La Bohème;* we read the poems of Dylan Thomas. He toured me around the University and showed me the room where Poe had lived. We walked in the woods or took long drives in the mountains.

We were in love. We decided to spend our lives together, as lovers and as pals. We would never marry. We would operate outside all forms and conventions. Freedom was the code word. Freedom from the middle-class, nine-to-five life. Freedom from parents and family. Freedom to do what we wanted, to go where we wanted. Freedom and poetry and passion.

It was an exciting, heady relationship—except for one devastating problem. Tom's commitment to me did not include monogamy. He was a compulsive and stunningly successful womanizer. Every female was a body for him to conquer, a heart to be won, and he seldom failed in his quests.

I was shocked the first time I found out, several months after we had met. I waited for him on the porch of his house in Charlottesville while he was in bed with another woman. I felt betrayed, heartbroken. When I confronted him he explained that I would have to accept who he was. His affairs with other women were meaningless, he said. They didn't count.

> I've been sitting on the porch for two hours.
>   yesterday, your back flaunting me,
>   suitcase bruising your thigh.
> A woodpecker banged its head against the tree
> near the path; it was beautiful.
> I can smell black in the earth: spring
> rain soon coming.
>   chilly now
> Bells sound, wind shifts motion.
> (red car stopping) Someone
> is playing wretched music across the street.
>
> Maybe it was better that way.
>   can't catch the tune

Love goes stale.
(getting out, legs long and supple)
only pain endures:
                    (such green the eyes)
        cleaving the ear
        carving the mind
Girl, (new rhythm), I let you ride.[5]

In June, 1963, Tom graduated from the University of Virginia at the age of twenty-three. We drove to Cambridge, Massachusetts, in his new white Triumph convertible, where we parted for the summer. This was the first leg of his summer trip across the U. S. and down to Mexico. His plans were to return to Cambridge in the fall to live and work and pursue his career as a poet.

To K.M.

I'm sitting here in Aspen, Colorado, between three huge mountains missing the ocean. I'm living in a little place called the Studio for fifteen dollars a week with an artist from Kentucky, two mustachioed sculptors from New Jersey, and a "Mr. Peepers" from Milwaukee who writes the worst poetry I have ever read. I made friends with some people from the music school and as a result am getting two meals a day free at the music cafeteria.

Except for the music school, Aspen is full of arty beards and people who are writing the first page of never-get-to-the-second-page novels, painting the first stroke of never-finished paintings, not an atmosphere in which I want to stay.

Have gotten a little work done myself: three new poems, one of which is very good, I think, and one revision.

Write to me c/o General Delivery, Mexico City.

Haven't seen the girl who can match you.[6]

On July 27, exactly one year after he wrote his first poem, driving at night in a downpour, seventy-five miles north of Mexico City, Tom was involved in a head-on collision. His car was demolished. Tom suffered a punctured lung, multiple fractures of his ribs and feet, a shattered kneecap, and a badly damaged heel. His face and head had been spared. His life was saved by an emergency operation on his lung.

> Imagination, like a kettle drum
> stretches skin
> taut along the eyes: orchestras of pain
> tune the strings of bones. Harmonies
> squirt from knees in fugue,
> one over one, until they fill the shoes.
> Chest is mute. Shock conductors
> blur the score
> to Debussy or to Ravel: final cadence:
> —black—
> (a piano tuner picks me from the wreck) [7]

Because of a Mexican law, Tom was held responsible for the accident. He was placed under arrest, a guard stationed outside his hospital room. The U. S. Embassy was powerless to help. His parents, who had been summoned from their home in Miami, engaged several lawyers to gain his freedom: they took the Bootmans' money and disappeared.

Tom was in critical condition for many days, and in constant pain. The poor quality of the care he received resulted in infections and gangrene. To make matters worse, the police had confiscated all his poetry and books and he was afraid that he would never get them back.

> To K.M.:
> Just woke up—middle of the night—great pain—have rung for another injection. This is the time I've written you about —all alone, all pain—my heel feels like it is on fire. It must be about four in the morning. I'll be able to take anything after this. My knee is as big as this room. *I'm going to get well.* Tinka, I feel that you're with me now. [8]

In September, his parents hired a lawyer who finally got Tom freed on a $400 bond (the Mexican government had originally asked for $3,000). The guard was removed; his poetry and books were returned. On September 25 he was flown to Miami and admitted to North Miami Hospital. By then I had returned to Hollins for my sophomore year and was ready to go to him as soon as he was well enough.

I arranged with the college to leave for weeks at a time as well as to spend all my vacations with him at his parents' home in Miami. Although he was slowly recovering, he was unhappy and angry. He resented being confined to a wheelchair, unable to walk, and helpless. His broken body was a trap. That winter André Harvey visited him. They stayed up all night drinking and Tom talked about suicide. Shortly afterward, he swallowed a bottle of sleeping pills; his mother discovered him in time.

> How we hold on,
> (night of no morning), counting
> bed-sheets or watching clocks
> illuminating pain with ticks:
> second-hand, minutes pass
> like gypsies in a gypsy-truck,
> (red wagon): dragging
> meaning down like sheep.
>
> Morning sun
> and finally sleep, my arms
> spider-gripping
> you . . . all for nothing:
> involvement like a broken bone
> gangrenous, Sunday needles and alarm,
> anything to grab me back.
> Just a bad dream, you laugh.[9]

During his long months of recovery, late at night, after his family had gone to bed, he drank beer and wrote poetry until dawn. In the daytime, he swam laps in the pool to build up his wasted muscles and, slowly, he began to walk again. He had lost his right kneecap and as a result had only a small degree of bend in his right leg. He would always limp slightly. His feet, although mended, were misshapen and would always cause him pain, and properly fitting shoes were almost impossible to find. For the rest of his life Tom would be plagued by the wound in his heel which periodically opened up and would require a new skin graft.

By April, 1964, he was walking with a cane and was well enough to leave home. After spending a transitional month near me in a house across the street from Hollins, he returned to Cambridge alone and rented an apartment for the summer.

> Street
> lined by trees, (rain)
> how often I've been
> here: seen leaves
> clog the gutter,
> lanes from nowhere
> lead to pools.
>
> Now it stops, (sun)
> breaking cement
> to prism: I watch
> myself, my face
> cut in chips
> fragments of rock.
>
> I touch the stone,
> begin my walk.[10]

Cambridge was filled with students attending Harvard Summer School. It was a paradise for Tom. Somehow his attractiveness to women, already profound, had been enhanced by the accident. His cane, his slight limp, added a degree of intensity to his demeanor. He was the young poet back from the dead. When I went to see him on weekends (I had a summer job in New York) he made no secret of what he was up to—namely, meeting and conquering the most beautiful women he could find, which resulted in many an accidental encounter with his love-struck Cambridge girl friends. To me he said "Tighten your belt."

Tim Matson (K.M.'s brother):
Tom lived in a crazy apartment in Cambridge. It had an

incredible bohemian feeling. When I read Kerouac now I think about Tom. He was the closest link for me to that literary beer-drinking bohemia. He was definitely a poet, and an adventurer. He was a beautiful character and, for me, there was always something existentially glamorous about him.[11]

By now, Tom had accumulated enough poems to begin shaping them into the first draft of a book. He also began to submit individual poems to literary magazines. He worked on his book all summer, arranging and revising. He was a perfectionist, and deadly serious.

To K.M.:

Sitting here at 11 Dana Street listening to the Four Seasons on Bill's radio (9:30 A.M.). Went to a boring party last night, and ended up walking about five miles back home. I was so tired that I got cramps in both legs when I finally sat down. I think it was good for me though.

Finished revising and retyping the book; I found a great-looking cover for it and am pleased with its appearance. But most of all I think it's a damned good book, even better since revisions.

I dreamt that I loved you and woke up knowing that I do.[12]

Unable to find a job in Cambridge, Tom moved to New York City in September where I was living with my family, having transferred from Hollins to the New School. He rented a one-room apartment on Bank Street in Greenwich Village and began job-hunting. He had decided that the only reason to work was to earn money in order to travel. The concept of expatriate poet sat in his head in quotation marks. He found a job working for a credit investigation agency. Except for his living expenses, all his salary was stashed in the bank. Whenever we went out, whenever we did *anything* that cost money, we would split the bill fifty-fifty down to the penny. The idea of having no money at all, being flat broke, frightened him. One of his nightmare fantasies was that he would wind up as a bum on the Bowery.

Bobbie Harvey (André's wife):

Tom had an incredible magnetism and charm that I can't really explain. He seemed to hold people under a spell. When he'd come for dinner, if he just casually mentioned that it would be nice to have avocados, for example, even though we were broke I'd suddenly find myself going all the way to the store to get avocados for Tom! And he would never offer to share the cost, and I wouldn't think of asking him. Tom took care of Tom and so did everyone else.[13]

Tom pursued his interest in poetry with a passion and a compulsive single-mindedness that characterized the way he wrote. He scoured the bookstores for new books, especially by young poets. He stood for hours at magazine racks, reading the poetry magazines, scanning them for interesting poems; he read the newspapers for reviews. Tom studied the craft and he learned. He frequently attended poetry readings at the YMHA and later at St. Mark's in the Bowery on Second Avenue where the poets of the New York School read. He wanted to know who the poets were, what they looked like, how they read their poems. He was assessing the field, deciding which poets he should take seriously, and which poets he could dismiss. From the start, however, he remained apart from any community of writers who could have given him support and a context within which to simply *be* a poet. He would make it on his own merit because he was good, not because of whom he knew or hung around with. He stood outside, a cool observer, keeping his distance, always slightly mysterious.

Our relationship continued to be passionate and stormy. Always there was his carousing and my jealous outbursts. I would find ill-concealed notes of love and ecstasy from other women in his apartment. I would hear rumors of his other involvements. "I'm ruled by my cock. I need my mistresses," he would say, and then try to cajole and mollify me. The only time I would have his complete attention was if he felt threatened by the presence of a rival. As far as he was concerned, I could see other men, but not sleep with them. He had little to worry about on this account, but if I even hinted of interest in someone else he would be by my side in a flash and talking about monogamy.

Joan (friend of K.M.):

He was one of the most beautiful and seductive men I
have ever met. He was also very persuasive, and very per-
sistent. I rebuffed him once but he came back. I finally gave
in a little bit but something ultimately stopped me. He had a
strange fever shining in his eyes. I thought Tom Bootman was
crazy.[14]

In the spring of 1965 Tom and I went to Europe. We were trying to stretch our money so we hitchhiked when we could get rides
and slept in the cheapest hotels or pensions we could find. Sometimes
we slept in the back of a truck or in a railroad station. Sometimes we
didn't eat for days. In Arles we read the letters of Van Gogh; in Paris
we read Starkie's biography of Rimbaud. We lived on bread, cheese,
and wine. Tom wrote poems. We wandered: each night we would get
out our map and decide our next stop. The trip ended in London after
four months and I flew back to New York to return to school. Tom
returned shortly afterward, after having an affair with a sixteen-year-
old English school girl: he told her his name was André Harvey and
a few years later she came looking for Tom and showed up on André's
doorstep.

Tom rented an apartment on West Fourth Street. I had my own
place on Bank Street. After working for a year as a librarian for the
New-York Historical Society, he had his first book of poetry published
by October House, a small publisher that had also published works by
poets Yevtushenko and e. e. cummings. The title of his book was
Myself in the Street. He used the name Tyler Bootman. The cover
was a black-and-white photograph of Tom standing on a New York
street, wearing the trenchcoat that had become his uniform, and star-
ing intently into the camera.

May Swenson (poet):

The poems seem to come from walking, looking, and
thinking, from being concerned with self-awareness, and from
observing the effects of a city environment. His strong
point . . . is his ability to watch himself—his own processes
and reactions—his awareness of his singular self within a

scene. . . . [His poems] seem to be striving for emotional honesty and clear thought, for a kind of cool appraisal.[15]

Tom was his own publicity and promotion team. He had extra book jackets made up and stood on street corners passing them out to any pretty girl who would take one. He made the rounds of bookstores routinely to see if copies were in stock, and, if they were, placed them conspicuously on the shelves.

Tom was realistic and had prepared himself for the inevitable scenario for the publication of an unknown poet: nothing happened. No reviews. No attention. Few sales. Yet the fact that the book was published was a cause for celebration and optimism. The future held promise. He was twenty-six years old and just beginning.

In January, 1968, we embarked on a major trip, our ultimate destination being the Greek Islands. But first Tom wanted to explore North Africa while I lived in London and worked for a literary agency. After six months we were reunited in Spain. Tom was thinner than I had ever seen him. He had contracted a severe case of amoebic dysentery in Tangiers from which he had not yet recovered. Sunburned, his eyes bluer than I remembered, he melted my heart once more. We embraced in the train station. The Spaniards who had ogled me on the train from Madrid hung out the train windows and cheered.

After traveling around Europe together for four months Tom told me he wanted to separate for a while. He wanted to go off alone to explore Greece and begin work on his second book. It was his idea that I go to Malta for the winter to work on a novel I had been writing.

I did not want to leave Tom and when I arrived in Malta I was miserable. And for three weeks there was no word from him. I assumed he would write to me when he was ready. What I didn't know was that he was desperately trying to reach me but his several letters and telegrams had been misplaced by the post office in Malta.

To K.M.:

My heart is breaking. I don't know where you are. I want to be with you, here, you right beside me. *If anything has happened to you I think I'll go mad.* So please for both of us take care of your self, because I don't want us to die, do you? You said in France that you might not be able to come back to me again the way you did in Spain. I don't think you realize that everything I say or do is dependent on you. My life since we met has been six years of fighting against and accepting love. And you have been everything to me which must be the definition of love. And I do think you're beautiful. The most beautiful woman I've ever seen. And I know you don't believe it because I take it for granted.

Greece is for us, just the way we've imagined it, even as long ago as Charlottesville. You belong with me, you should know that even when I say good-bye. Your life is my life. Soon we'll be together. By New Year's if I can find you.[16]

In the meantime I had become involved with another man, a young Swiss tourist. We decided to take a trip together to the nearby island of Gozo. As we were leaving my apartment with our suitcases, Tom appeared. He understood the situation immediately, took me aside, and pleaded with me not to leave. Feeling sick and crazy, I said no to him. For the first time I was turning the tables. I gave him the keys to my apartment and told him that I would be back in a few days. He was composed and polite but underneath I could tell he was frantic. I spent two days on Gozo in total confusion. I knew what Tom was going through and before the end of the trip I told my friend that I wouldn't be able to see him again.

Tom was very shaky on my return. For the next few weeks he spent most of his time sitting in the garden getting drunk on red wine. Our relationship would never be the same again.

We lived together and traveled until January, 1970. By then I was exhausted. The endless traveling seemed so pointless. I flew back to New York. Tom went to Formentera, an island off Spain where there was an expatriate colony. While there he took acid for the first time and later told me he had seen death in the shape of a dog. Two weeks after my arrival in New York I received a telegram: *Arriving Wednesday. Can't make it without you. Tom.*

Back in town. Been away.
Just like the good old days
freaked between the buildings. Feel like
gambling cards

feel like a hustler working 42nd street
knowing how there ain't a hope
for a city going from indoors to indoors
indoors. Back in jail.[17]

Once again we tried. We found a cheap apartment on East
Tenth Street on Tompkins Square Park which we cleaned up,
plastered, and painted. Tom said it looked like a Dutch barn. It was
quickly apparent, however, that it wouldn't work. The confines of
our living together made him unhappy. So we hunted again and
found him a place on Prince Street in Little Italy. We cleaned up,
plastered, and painted that place too, and he moved in. To pay my
rent I found a job in the picture department of a sensational tabloid.
It was a weird outfit, but the job demanded little of me, which is
what I had to give.

In September, 1972, we took our America trip. We drove across
the country to the Pacific Ocean and down the coast to Mexico. Our
happiest moments were in the car, just driving and looking at the
scenery; I had Tom all to myself. I told him that. He laughed.

Since this was the first time he had been back in Mexico since
his accident nine years before, Tom wondered if he was still a wanted
man. The country was beautiful but inhospitable: our car was robbed
three times; Tom was arrested and briefly detained for no apparent
reasons. "They're just trying to scare me," he said. On the trip his
drinking took on a new recklessness and determination. Mescal, which
was cheap and had a powerful effect, began to get the better of him,
and he suffered wicked hangovers, "poison headaches," he called
them. When I drove across the border into Texas he was drunk.
He was searched by the Mexican customs officials from head to toe
because of his strange behavior. He gave the official the last few
swallows from his bottle. I felt relieved to be back in the U. S. and
heading home.

> We play the queen of hearts
> princess
> there are cards each leaves behind
> like a shark's tooth beneath the fin
> we drive through the countryside
> talk together tuning in the radio
> telling time by the sea
> rolling down all the windows
> while the highway
> stretches out fast under us
> making love all night in the hay
> sleeping at sunrise in the grass
> sweet musik on the highway
> everywhere we went.[18]

We would never take another trip together. Some candle that had been burning inside of me for Tom had gone out, used itself up. I slowly detached myself from him, and began to see him with some measure of objectivity. I sensed an element of self-destructiveness in him that began to show itself in his looks and appearance. Tom and I began to see less of each other. In 1973, I began to study acting and got a job working for a producer. My life was taking a direction of its own. Tom got a part-time job in a bookstore and was involved with a woman he had met there. I was seeing other men. We were trying to remain friends but this was sometimes difficult. Part of him still felt as if he owned me; part of me could not imagine life without him.

Tom pursued his interest in country music and astrology. In 1974 he finished his second book of poems, which he called *The New York City Fool*. Tom *was* the New York City Fool—troubador/poet with dulcimer under his arm and a grin, slightly askew, on his face. The poems express his vision of the fall of New York City, which represents America. They are filled with images of blood and violence, explosions in the streets, and the darkness of night. He labored on the book with an almost irrational compulsion: he was counting on it to be a breakthrough for him. He waged a campaign to find a publisher for the book but with no success. This failure was a crushing blow to Tom. He was thirty-three years old and suddenly his image of himself as poet had been exploded.

His life began to take on a bizarre quality. He was often drunk or spaced out on drugs. He couldn't sleep. He roamed the streets during the early-morning hours haunting seedy bars from the Bowery to City Island. He would call me at four in the morning, drunk and incoherent, shouting for oblivion: he wanted to die. It was as if the fates were pursuing him, or he was pursuing his fate. He was a man in torment.

Tom had always been gentle. Now he was becoming aggressive and violent. Even though he was with a new woman, he still insisted on being a dramatic presence in my life. Late one night he came to my apartment, drunk and armed with rocks to challenge a man I was seeing. He had to be led away by the police. On another night his face was cut up in a bar fight. His mental condition deteriorated; he committed himself to Bellevue but left after a few days.

By now I was trying unsuccessfully to completely end our connection, even to the point of getting an unlisted telephone number. Somehow he always could find me. I was relieved and hopeful when, in June, 1975, he told me that he was leaving New York with his new girl friend for a long trip.

K.M.'s journal: August, 1975:

Tom blasted in late last night out of the blue back from Mexico. He looked wild, his hair really long. Too thin. He said he had no place to stay. His girl had bailed out on him in Texas and he went to Mexico alone. He gave me a present—a bag full of silver earrings. He told me he held up a souvenir shop in Mexico with a gun and stole the earrings from an old woman. I don't know whether to believe him or not. He seemed to be bragging about it—also challenging me somehow. He told me that he had fallen off a porch in Mexico when he was drunk on tequila and practically broken his back. He was all alone and couldn't get up. Spent hours lying on the ground until someone found him. Every time he goes to Mexico he gets into trouble. He asked if he could sleep on my couch, but was up all night pacing the floor. He's in a frenzy. Seems out of control. I don't know what will happen to him.[19]

It was as if Tom and I were passing each other on escalators going in opposite directions. While he continued to deteriorate, my life had taken a positive direction. I had decided that acting was not for me and got a job with a successful literary agency. The work was creative, and the people interesting. Also I was in love. The relationship was serious and my commitment to this man was as total as it had ever been to Tom. For the first time in a long while I had a sense of place in the world. In March, 1976, I left East Tenth Street and moved to the West Seventies. It was a new beginning.

I saw Tom for the last time during the summer. It was an accidental meeting. I discovered him sitting on a bench in the park behind the Museum of Natural History. Although he was dressed in a familiar brown crew-neck sweater, a green shirt, and jeans, his clothes were filthy and his face and hands were grimy with dirt. He looked like he had been sleeping outside. His face was puffy and his eyes were glassy. He had an opened quart of beer by his side. I was stunned by his appearance. I sat down with him for a few minutes and we made small talk. He asked me how I was and said I looked wonderful. I think I said *"Why are you doing this?"* or *"What are you doing?"* I wanted to burst out crying, I wanted to take him by the shoulders and shake him hard and wake him up.

I couldn't rescue him this time. When I got up to leave he quietly said, "Don't go." "I have to," I said, and walked slowly away. I wanted to run. I didn't look back and this time he didn't chase after me.

> Gotham Town is falling down
> The sacred past has a sweet voice
> a Pink Streak of sorrow
> city, heartbreak
> ripped by the first White Light of shock
> shrieking thru each wreckage
> its promise in a thousand dying branches
> then comes the dynamite

"The New York City Fool"

an exploding Blood Street, the Red Light of death
this is the very last look at New York

Light of death, total Red

gone like wine.[20]

Soon after that meeting he was jailed for ten days for trespassing.
His sister bailed him out and put him on a plane for Florida where
his mother took him in.

I heard from him for the last time about six months later. He
wrote to me from Miami on St. Valentine's Day, 1977. He said
he missed me and remembered when I was his. He said he was
trying to eat well and cut his drinking down to weekends only. He
was thinking about writing a novel. He was thinking about design-
ing jewelry. He had met a young woman.

In August, Tom left Miami and headed across the country for
Washington, where a friend had promised to help him get a job.
His mother's last words to him were to warn him: "Don't go to
Mexico." Yet he could not resist returning there once more. While
traveling in Mexico, he developed an infected tooth. Instead of
going back to the U. S. for treatment, he went to a local clinic. On
September 28 he was given a shot of antibiotics. Suddenly and
unexplainedly he became violently ill and fell into a coma. Several
hours later, Tom Bootman, poet, died. He was thirty-six years old.
His body was cremated in Mexico.

in New York City the mayor names a fool
to cruise the dirty town in cap & bells
kicking salt from his shoes going home
so I'm dreaming I ride my days
moment by moment in search of some peace
an outlaw in the eyes of America.[21]

Notes

1 Bootman, "Manhattan Trilogy," *The New York City Fool*, p. 73.
2 Bootman, "Foodstuff Poems," *Myself in the Street*, p. 4.

3   Conversation with William Siegel, September, 1979.
4   Conversation with André Harvey, September, 1979.
5   Bootman, "Day of Reckoning," *Myself in the Street*, p. 28.
6   Bootman, letter to Katinka Matson, June, 1963.
7   Bootman, "Collision," *Myself in the Street*, p. 50.
8   Bootman, letter to Matson, August, 1963.
9   Bootman, "Collision," *Myself in the Street*, p. 50.
10 Bootman, "Myself in the Street—Finale," *Myself in the Street*, p. 58.
11 Conversation with Tim Matson, September, 1979.
12 Bootman, letter to Matson, July, 1964.
13 Conversation with Bobbie Harvey, September, 1979.
14 Conversation with Joan, September, 1979.
15 May Swenson, jacket copy for *Myself in the Street*.
16 Bootman, letter to Matson, December, 1968.
17 Bootman, "New York Blues," *The New York City Fool*, p. 60.
18 Bootman, "Four Sonnets," *The New York City Fool*, p. 25.
19 K. Matson's journal, August, 1975.
20 Bootman, "Red Dynamite," *The New York City Fool*, p. 13.
21 Ibid., p. 39.

Sources

Bootman, Tyler. *Myself in the Street*. New York: October House, 1966.
———. *The New York City Fool*. Unpublished ms., 1974.

PHOTO CREDITS

The author would like to thank the following for permission to reproduce photographs:

Ardis Publishers, p. 111, p. 123, © 1976 by Ardis Publishers; from *Esenin, A Life* by Gordon McVay; Cynthia Benjamins/Black Star: p. 347; Columbia University Libraries: p. 65, p. 75; Joe Covello/Black Star: p. 149; The Dance Collection, The New York Public Library at Lincoln Center: p. 119, p. 275, p. 281; Jay Good/Black Star: p. 165; The Granger Collection, New York: p. 79, p. 125, p. 145, p. 249, p. 263, p. 271, p. 301, p. 309, p. 317, p. 331; The Solomon R. Guggenheim Museum: p. 259; André Harvey: p. 407; The Jack London Estate: p. 199, p. 207; Margerie Lowry: p. 219; Fred W. McDarrah: p. 185, © 1979 by Fred W. McDarrah; Rollie McKenna: p. 297, p. 341, p. 361, © Rollie McKenna; p. 351, Photo by Nora Summers, Courtesy of Rollie McKenna; Morris Library, Southern Illinois University: p. 91, p. 97; Museum of Modern Art/Film Stills Archives: p. 13, p. 21; Collection, The Museum of Modern Art, New York. Acquired through the Lillie P. Bliss Bequest: p. 371; Aurelia Schober Plath: p. 289; Cervin Robinson: p. 389; Scala Editorial Photo Color Archives: p. 363; Snark/Editorial Photo Color Archives: p. 375, p. 381; Dennis Stock/Magnum Photos, Inc.: p. 39, p. 101; United Press International: p. 29, p. 63, p. 153, p. 171, p. 177, p. 195, p. 241, p. 243, p. 327; Wide World Photos: p. 53, p. 87, p. 107, p. 133, p. 139, p. 161, p. 189, p. 211, p. 235, p. 285.

ABOUT THE AUTHOR

Katinka Matson is a New York literary agent, a former actress, and the author of two previous books: *The Working Actor* (Viking, 1976; Penguin, 1978) and *The Psychology Today Omnibook of Personal Development* (Morrow, 1977).